T0285641

ICONS & INSTINCTS

ICONS & INSTINCTS

Choreographing and Directing Entertainment's Biggest Stars

by Vincent Paterson and Amy Tofte

RARE BIRD
LOS ANGELES, CALIF.

THIS IS A GENUINE RARE BIRD BOOK

Rare Bird Books
6044 North Figueroa Street
Los Angeles, CA 90042
rarebirdbooks.com

For more information, address:
Rare Bird Books Subsidiary Rights Department
6044 North Figueroa Street
Los Angeles, CA 90042

Set in Dante
Printed in the United States

*Cover photographs by Herb Ritts, Kim Kaufman,
Antony Payne, Zentropa, and Sam Emerson*

Author photograph © 2022 Sethaffoumado.com

10 9 8 7 6 5 4 3 2 1

Library of Congress Cataloging-in-Publication Data

Names: Paterson, Vincent, author. | Tofte, Amy, author.
Title: Icons and instincts : dancing, divas & directing and choreographing
entertainment's biggest stars / by Vincent Paterson and Amy Tofte.
Description: Los Angeles : Rare Bird Books, 2022.
Identifiers: LCCN 2022000483 | ISBN 9781644282632 (hardcover)
Subjects: LCSH: Patterson, Vincent. | Dance in motion pictures, television,
etc. | Choreographers—United States—Biography.
Classification: LCC GV1785.P2854 A3 2022 | DDC 792.8/2092
[B]--dc23/eng/20220201

LC record available at https://lccn.loc.gov/2022000483

For my three angels:
Dorothy Caruso, Leslie Kaeufer, Rene Lamontagne.
—Vincent Paterson

For all the kids from the small towns who dream of something bigger.
—Amy Tofte

Contents

Introduction

"HEY, VINCENT," MADONNA ONCE said to me, "you know what your problem is? You don't know how interesting you are."

I've never cared about being interesting; I've cared about creating good work. But I sure hope I'm interesting because I just wrote this book.

You might not recognize my name, but billions of people have seen my work. That's not a typo...billions. Some of my creations might be on your list of ten favorite moments in film or music video history. You might have practiced some of my iconic dance moves in front of your mirror at home.

I've worked with innumerable pop, rock, theater, film, and sports stars from 1980 to the present as a dancer, actor, director, and choreographer. Some of those relationships, at times, felt closer than family. I interacted with some celebrities and pop stars in ways I never imagined I would. As a choreographer and director, my role is usually behind the scenes, making the stars shine brighter. I saw behind the veneer of their fame and witnessed their artistic process. I'm grateful for every moment.

This book is a collection of stories from my career as I remember them, anecdotes I've been sharing with my closest friends over the years. It's not always chronological, but sometimes memory jumps around to tell the best stories. Making it in Hollywood is tough, but every success and every failure has a story behind it. Those of us in this business wouldn't trade it for anything—even at its worst—because there's nothing like it.

My wish is that these recollections might offer insight into what it means to be a working artist in this volatile industry. My career even provides a bit of a time capsule for American pop culture from the 1980s to today. I encourage you to have fun and Google things as you go, so much of my creative life is archived on fan pages and YouTube links, even some of the obscure performances from the late 1970s.

Mostly, I hope my stories entertain you, maybe even inspire you to follow your own passion, a reminder of how we each choreograph the steps to our individual dances in life.

And you might learn, as I have, that we can all take a few life lessons from a diva.

Or two.

1.

Having No Talent and Too Old to Dance

The winding road to "Beat It"

M Y FATHER, ALSO NAMED Vincent Paterson, was tall, handsome, and danced better than anyone around. He was well-known in the area for teaching social dance at Dupont Country Club, and his students loved his infectious charm. But he was different at home where he ruled over us with an iron fist at all times. "In this house," he'd boom, "I'm God! You do as I say! You don't ask questions!"

This was Brookhaven, Pennsylvania (1950 population: 1,042), a blue-collar town along the Delaware River, eighteen miles outside Philadelphia. My mother, Dorothy Caruso, was a petite beauty with dark hair and porcelain skin. They met at an Italian social hall where they fell in love dancing to a fifteen-piece band. They married in 1948, just after my mother graduated high school. I was born two years later.

I grew up the eldest of three brothers—Bill, Kent, and Kerry— and a sister, Leslie. We cherished our often shy, reserved mother; however, because of Dad, our home was a regular battleground of ferocious words, overturned Thanksgiving dinners, and yanked-down Christmas trees. Dad had believed he was destined for earth-shattering fame, not the crowded life we lived in a tiny two-bedroom house with only one bathroom. If he felt in any way disrespected, my brothers and I were brutally beaten with metal cooking utensils and thick leather belts.

Dad taught dance classes late into the night, often returning home drenched in perfume. My mother's usual calm would erupt into raging fury, "I know you're having an affair with your dance partner, Mr. Big Shit!" From the top of the stairs, we'd witness deafening arguments that always came to blows. "Shut the fuck up, woman, or I swear to Christ I'll have to hit you! Do you hear me?" I can still hear his voice.

We'd clasp our toy guns in the shadows and whisper, "Let's kill him!" He regularly punched my mother in the face, ripped her handmade dresses, or threw her out into the snow. If we ran down the stairs to let her back in the house, we'd be flung against the walls. From the upstairs window, we'd look down at Mom in her robe, shivering in the snowy darkness, all of us crying together.

We were forever being picked up by a family member and driven to my nan's house in the middle of the night, but we'd always return to the combat zone at 217 Morris Avenue. Divorce wasn't customary in the 1950s, but as we got older we begged Mom to get one. They finally did when I was fourteen, and we all breathed lighter air.

After that, Dad dropped in on occasion to give Mom child support, but even if the outright physical abuse had stopped, his emotional claws found their way into us throughout the rest of his life. As a kid, I had learned all the social dances he taught. During the eighties (and once I started having a dance career in Hollywood), I developed a more civil relationship with him, although his pompousness remained constant. When I visited Pennsylvania, Dad would treat me to lunch at a local diner. He'd loudly say to a waitress, "Miss. Miss. Do you recognize him?" as he pointed to me.

"Um, no…should I?"

"Have you seen 'Beat It'? He's the white gang leader in Michael Jackson's 'Beat It' video. The knife fight guy. Did you know that?"

"Uh…no."

I would nod, politely, embarrassed, then urge him not to do it anymore. "But everyone should know who you are," he would say, as if it were about me. It was always about him.

My father died from cirrhosis at seventy-nine, alcoholism. He had danced and taught through bouts of cancer and diabetes. I am grateful to have inherited his dancing DNA. But I never understood his violence.

After the divorce, I discovered acting at Brookhaven Junior High and then Sun Valley High School. From my James Dean role in *Rebel Without a Cause* to a lawyer in *The Night of January 16th*, inhabiting characters and investing in lives far from my own rescued me. I became addicted to the magic of theater.

I also became the father figure of our house. It was tough to be a disciplinarian and still a friend to my younger siblings. By sixteen, I was working at the Dairy Queen and used some of the money I earned to take acting classes at the nearby Hedgerow Theater. I made the four-mile walk from my house once a week during my seventeenth summer. My eighty-year-old acting teacher, Jasper Deeter, best known for his role in *The Blob*, was thin as a skeleton and the creaky, old theater felt like a haunted house.

In 1968, I prepared to attend Dickinson College, a small liberal arts college in Pennsylvania. My father told me he could only afford to give me one thousand dollars toward tuition for all four years. So I applied for scholarships and financial aid. One scholarship I received was from the local Lions Club that gave one hundred dollars to one male student from the graduating senior class who needed financial support for continuing education. In the late sixties, this was a lot of money because annual tuition at Dickinson would have been around $3,500. I was invited to attend a Lions Club luncheon to receive their award and was asked to bring my father.

After lunch, the Lions Club president rose and said, "We want to give this award to Vincent Paterson because..." I stood up, graciously accepted the check, thanking the club members as I explained how this would really help because I needed the financial assistance. Just as I took my seat…*Ding, ding, ding, ding, ding.*

My father stood up, clinking his glass with his spoon. All eyes turned to him. "Hello, gentlemen. I'm Vincent Paterson *Senior.*" With a sweeping gesture, he pulled out his checkbook from inside his suit-jacket and announced with bravura, "Right here, right now, I am writing the Lions Club a one hundred dollar check so you can make some father next year as happy as you've made me." There was confused applause. I sat still, my face burning with embarrassment.

I attended Dickinson to become a trial lawyer, believing I could make excellent money winning every case with my theatrical prowess. And I might have, had I not joined the school's acting company, the Mermaid Players. David Brubaker, the head of the theater department, cast me in plays during my freshman year, a year earlier than usually permitted—classical dramas, comedies, and Shakespeare. David was the first adult male in my life who was wise and showed me some attention. He was like a guiding parent, encouraging me to become an artist. "Mr. B" was the first professional to believe in me, and his generous love and support provided the initial steps for me to believe in myself.

Early in my sophomore year, Marcel Marceau performed at Dickinson and I was exposed to mime. I began a friendship with Mr. Marceau, and we became artistic pen pals, his lengthy letters filled with doodles on both edges. I began to experiment with mime and movement and worked on a project inspired by Marceau.

David Brubaker offered, "Why don't you think about putting together your own theater company? Use the theater when it's available." Wow. I assembled an eclectic twelve-member company who created pieces that were physical, political, intelligent, and edgy. We were straight-A students and hippies who loved exploring our creativity, often by using drugs. We would sometimes drop LSD and go into the theater late at night to create.

One of our performances included constructing a glow-in-the-dark, oversized cat's cradle and another concluded with rolling an imaginary, ten-foot-long marijuana joint, miming lighting it, and then each of us inhaling a monstrous hit. At the edge of the stage, we exhaled imaginary smoke toward the audience as the lights slowly faded to black.

I directed an avant-garde version of the play *Woyzeck*, the tragic tale of a military barber who murders his beloved common-law wife, Marie, played by the stellar actress Frances Conroy. (Yes, *that* Frances Conroy...*Six Feet Under, American Horror Story*, etc.) I staged it in the concourse of the chemistry building with puppets and masks. I began to experiment with dance, dialogue, and song in my pieces while directing Jean Claude van Itallie's *The Serpent*, which draws on iconic references from the Garden of Eden to the Kennedy assassination. On Good Friday, 1971, our company of actors gathered in front of the dining hall in tattered-looking Biblical costumes we had pulled from the wardrobe department. We had built a life-sized wooden cross and a crown of "thorns." Just before noon, we began a procession through the campus, reenacting Christ's last walk. With my hippie hair and blue eyes, who else to play Christ but me! We proceeded to a mid-campus grassy knoll where I was "nailed" to the cross and suspended in the middle of the green for three hours. Students passed by as the other actors stood at the bottom of the cross. At three in the afternoon, my fellow actors took me down, wrapped me in a sheet, and carried me away.

By my junior year I had to select a major course of study. David Brubaker urged me to audition for NYU because Dickinson had no drama major. I auditioned and was accepted but wasn't offered any financial help. Mr. B informed Dickinson that I was considering leaving, and I was not only awarded a generous scholarship to stay at Dickinson, but I was also invited to create the first theater major at the school, a Bachelor of Arts in Theater Arts and Dramatic Literature. That's exactly what I did.

My time at Dickinson was a boon to both my creativity and my discipline. I had no idea then how much it was preparing me for my future. All I knew was that I was thriving. I could have coined the phrase "side hustle" back then with my eclectic résumé of jobs. By the time I was twenty-two, I had been a babysitter, a door-to-door magazine sales boy, an ice cream dipper at the Dairy Queen, and a tour guide of historical Philadelphia. I had dressed in a full rubber suit and cleaned massive oil tanks in the summer heat at Sun Oil Refinery. I was a minimum wage earner in the ninety-degree, hundred-percent humidity fabric-drying room at the Robert Bruce sweater factory in Philadelphia. I was even once a waiter in an Italian restaurant wearing a cheap Liza Minnelli-style wig—because I had hair almost to my waist and was not about to cut it. At one point, I drove a hundred-passenger high school bus, was on the landscaping crew at Swarthmore College, and worked as a roofer.

After graduating from college, I had the lead role in *The Screens* by Jean Genet at Society Hill Playhouse in Philadelphia. Though fair-haired and blue-eyed, I played Said, an Arab. (The Liza Minnelli wig came in handy!) When the play closed in January 1973, I decided I'd had enough of cold weather and called a high school friend, Karen Barner.

"Karen, I know you hate it here as much as I do. Why don't we load up your car and drive until we find someplace warm?"

We drove through the South, eventually stopping in Tucson, Arizona, where January's eighty-degree heat and the mystery of the desert enticed me to stay. Karen moved on to Colorado. It was tough finding work in Tucson, even the 7-Eleven made you take a lie detector test to find out if you had ever smoked marijuana. As luck would have it, there was an opening as a ballroom dance instructor for beginner-level students at Arthur Murray Dance Studio. My early social dancing knowledge came in handy. I spent hours partnering sweet, wealthy, elderly ladies in need of companionship and glamour across the glossy dance floor. Those were hot afternoons of much too much face powder, perfume, and turquoise jewelry. One day, the Mormon couple who ran the studio called the instructors into the office.

"We feel like you're our family, and we want to share with you that the world's about to end. We want to pay you in wheat, corn, and rice, rather than write you a check." I declined the offer, telling them, "If the world's about to end, I don't want to be the only one on my block with the food!" I opted for a paycheck and promptly quit.

A girlfriend took me to my first dance concert in Tucson, and I was intrigued. I contacted one of the dancers and asked where I might take classes, thinking a little exercise would do me good. He recommended Stephanie Stiger's Ballet Academy, which I passed every day on my way to work. Stephanie was a petite former ballerina in her mid-thirties. She had long blonde hair as thick as a horse's mane, a muscular little body, and the tenacity of a pit bull.

"Have you ever had class before? Well, I suggest you begin by taking beginning ballet barre with the ten- to fourteen-year-old girls." I was twenty-three. I loved it. I approached those dance classes the only way I knew how, as an actor stepping into a character. I went to the library, checked out books on the famous Russian ballet dancers Vaslav Nijinsky and Rudolf Nureyev, and tried to "be" Nureyev in class. I wasn't Vincent Paterson, I was Rudolf Nureyev performing in *Les Sylphides* or *Don Quixote*.

My body in no way resembled a dancer or an athlete. I had been a theater mole for years. When I bent over, I could only touch my knees, my shoulders hunched hideously forward, and I had no stretch in second position when I sat on the floor. So, I walked everywhere with a broomstick behind my back and wedged under my arms to straighten my posture. I carried a phone book in my backpack so when I sat on the floor, the added height allowed gravity to assist in stretching my legs to a wider second position. I carried a plastic Pepsi bottle filled with sand that I would roll under my feet to develop a higher arch in my foot. It was a painful process to deconstruct and then reconstruct my body. But the flow of endorphins while dancing created a sense of euphoria I had only experienced while smoking pot. When dancing, I felt the power of my three-dimensional self moving through space. I was hooked.

After six months, I ventured into a basic adult class in another studio taught by Patrick Frantz, a respected ballet instructor. After executing a few preliminary exercises at the barre, Mr. Frantz came over to me. "How old are you?"

"Twenty-four," I replied, humble but proud of my progress.

"Don't come back to my class," he continued. "You're too old. You have no talent, and you'll never do anything with dance. You're wasting my time." With my dance bag between my legs, I returned to Stephanie, who took me back with open arms.

There were a plethora of small dance companies in Tucson at that time, and they were all hurting for male dancers. Because of my stage presence, several companies recruited me to join them for an inconsequential salary and free classes. I danced with a company called City Dance Theater where I created my first piece of choreography to Elvis Presley's "Blue Suede Shoes." I immediately liked this choreography thing.

A friend had an early version of a videotape recorder and player. I recorded Michael Kidd's choreography for "Dancing in the Dark" from the movie *The Bandwagon* with Fred Astaire and Cyd Charisse. In the garage, I set up the video deck and a small monitor and dissected Fred and Cyd's beautiful pas de deux in the park. I discovered how one could choreograph to a string line or a flute, a saxophone or cello melody. I learned that it wasn't obligatory to choreograph steps to just the drumbeat. My friend Olivia Rassenti and I spent hours in that garage, learning that dance. Years later, I would befriend Michael Kidd as well as have the privilege of escorting Ms. Charisse to a dinner at the Monaco Dance Forum, cheerfully relating this story to each of them.

The Tucson Cultural Exchange Council invited Stephanie Stigers to be part of a company to tour five colonial cities in Mexico with an eleven-piece chamber orchestra. Stephanie choreographed a mini-ballet for Urvin Cox, herself, and me. In her ballet, inspired by Dante's *Inferno* and titled "Francesca and Paolo," a married man

(Urvin) goes off to war and his wife (Stephanie) takes a lover (me). When the husband returns, he and the lover duel with swords and the lover is killed. The husband kills his wife, and the dead lovers are forced to spend eternity spinning in the wind that circles the earth.

All went smoothly as we toured opera house after opera house in Mexico's breathtaking colonial towns, until we made our final stop in Guanajuato, a former silver-mining town known for its collection of mummies. The Teatro Juárez Opera House hinted at past days of glory but was now decrepit with broken wooden benches and a few exposed, hanging light bulbs over the stage. When we entered to block our dances, an old woman was throwing handfuls of bleach throughout the seating areas. The three of us looked at each other, "Well, we're grateful we're getting paid!"

That night there was a full house, even the balconies were packed. The enthusiastic applause before the show boded well. Act One belonged to the chamber orchestra who performed atonal compositions by Webern and Varese. As the discordant music wore on, the audience's enthusiasm morphed into heated mumblings, stomping feet, cries of "boo," and finally shouts of "Gordo! Gordo!" directed at an overweight cellist. Pieces of overripe fruit and vegetables were hurled onto the stage. The musicians ran into the dressing room. "Oh, my God, they're throwing fruit at us!" It didn't look good for Act Two and the melodramatic lovers of Dante's *Inferno*. I had to think fast.

Stephanie was a modest ballerina and our costumes covered up nearly all our skin. Only hands, necks, and faces were bare. "I have an idea," I said. "Who has scissors?"

"What are you going to do?" Stephanie asked nervously.

"Trust me." I grabbed the scissors and hacked off Stephanie's long dress to above her knees and sliced slits up both sides of her dress to her hips. I chopped off her long sleeves as well as those on Urvin's leotard. I cut his top into a deep V neckline to expose his strong pectorals. I clipped my long tunic to my waist and also cut off the sleeves.

"Take down your hair," I yelled to Stephanie as I snipped my way through the dressing room. I stood back to observe my handiwork. "There," I was sweating but content. "Now let's give them a show!"

When we stepped onstage there were a few remarks in Spanish. As we began to dance, they subsided. A hush fell over the audience. I knew they were engrossed in the narrative when they began to yell, "*Puta! Puta!*" (Whore! Whore!) as Stephanie and my character began to make dancing love once Urvin went off to war. When he returned and discovered his wife's deceit, our duel began. The audience began to scream for blood. As I lay mortally wounded and breathing my last breath, the audience erupted in enthusiastic applause, whistles, and stomping. We were a hit.

Back in Tucson, I continued to train and perform, while making short trips to Los Angeles (driving eight hours one way) to study with wonderful mentors there. Joe Tremaine was the reigning king of jazz dance classes, always packed with jubilant, sweaty bodies. Joe was all about fun energy, technique, and lots of head rolls.

The teachers Bill and Jacqui Landrum eventually became my family. They were a unique couple. They came from a background of Vegas and European cabarets combined with early TV shows like *Hollywood a Go-Go*. They had exquisite bodies, and their energy was infectious. The Landrum style was a new synthesis of jazz, ballet, modern, funk, and Vegas—a genre now labeled "contemporary." Class with them was a mind-blowing experience. Jacqui with her bee-stung lips and pouty bangs flawlessly demonstrated the movement we were to follow, while Bill properly aligned our bodies with his knowledgeable touch. Joe Tremaine and the Landrums were masters with whom I longed to study on a permanent basis.

By this time, I knew I had to make dance my profession, but I didn't see how that was going to happen in Tucson. Also, I was in my first romantic relationship with a man and my life was pretty near perfect, so I couldn't imagine leaving him. Richard Johnson was a few years older than I. He flew small commercial planes and traded in real estate. We had lived together for three years in Richard's sprawling, ranch-style home in the Tucson desert. But in 1976, fate intervened when our paradise in the desert was shattered.

I came home one night after a dance performance, and Richard wasn't there. There was no message on the machine, no note. He just wasn't there. This was unlike Richard. The night went on, and he didn't show up. His absence made me nervous, and I couldn't sleep. I first called his pager over and over, and then the police and nearby hospitals. Nothing. I frantically vacuumed the rugs—unknowingly sweeping up potential clues to what I later found out had been a home invasion. When daylight broke, I began weeding the cactus garden. While on my knees, a cold chill passed through my body, and I looked up. Richard was standing in front of me in his jeans, Frye boots, and white T-shirt.

"Richard," I whispered.

He replied, "Honey, I'm dead."

And then he vanished.

Immediately, the phone rang and I ran inside the house. It was a call from a friend's father, "Vincent, please, sit down. I just came over to my son's house. Burglars broke in while Richard was here feeding the horses. They tied him to a chair and strangled him. I'm sorry, Vincent, he's gone. I'm going to call the police."

Richard was twenty-nine. I was twenty-six. It was one of the darkest moments of my life. I was taken to the police station and questioned as a possible suspect. When the police realized that I was innocent, and devastated, I was released.

The police thought the killers had brought Richard from his friend's house to our home to rob it, then took him back to his friend's house to kill him. In the weeks following, my nights would be broken with 3:00 a.m. calls that hung up when I picked up the receiver. I began sleeping with a rifle under the bed. Our home wasn't safe anymore. I couldn't live alone in the dark, mysterious desert fearing for my safety. I was now seriously considering a move to Hollywood where I could hopefully become a professional dancer, but I only had fifty-four dollars to my name.

My friend Olivia took me to a small psychic church in the desert. During the service, the clairvoyant minister stood behind the pulpit and gave readings to members of the congregation. Olivia and I were sitting in the back row holding hands. Suddenly a jolt surged through my body to the tips of my fingers. Olivia felt it and looked at me. At that precise moment, the minister focused on me. "I have something for the young man in the back row. You are surrounded by a being, newly spirited. He wants you to know you will be fine. You have an incredible amount of positive energy around you. You are going to move to one of the coasts, and you will struggle very hard for about nine months. Then your career will begin to take off."

I began having dreams in which Richard showed me his three murderers—a blonde woman and two dark-haired men. I phoned the police and gave them descriptions of the three people I had seen in my dreams. They invited me to convene with a psychic whom they had brought in from the Midwest to help them solve the case.

The psychic was a slightly heavy woman in her mid-forties with red hair and bright blue eyes. When we met, she told me she had a message for an animal, not a person. I told her Richard jokingly called me "Cat-Boy" because I was constantly stretching in our home. Immediately, she let me know that Richard had left no written will but was telling her that he had left something for me to find in our home "in or around something large and rectangular."

When I got home, I was frantic. I took the back panel off the TV set that Richard had built from scratch. Nothing. Then I pulled the new refrigerator away from the wall in the kitchen. Nothing. I sat, perplexed, on the living room couch. I meditated to calm myself down. When I finished, I felt a need to walk down the hallway. There were four bedrooms. I'd enter a bedroom, and it would either feel warm or cold.

The first three bedrooms felt cold. I opened the final bedroom. Warm. I felt the warmth pulling me toward a large box I had cut in half and filled with old clothes and books to be given away. I moved to it. It felt more than warm; it felt hot. I began to take objects out of the box and my hands actually felt a burning sensation when I picked up Richard's pilot log. I thumbed through the book and out fell some money—two $1,000 bills and two $1 bills. Now, I could move to Los Angeles.

In the middle of January 1977, I packed all I owned into one duffle bag and left Arizona in my beige VW, a gift from Richard for my twenty-sixth birthday. Richard's friend Roy White invited me to stay with him in a tiny apartment in the middle of Hollywood. Roy was a Vietnam vet, a larger-than-life, screaming queen with the blackest skin I had ever seen and the most golden heart I could ever imagine. He shared a one-bedroom apartment with a girl who worked as an escort and her two French poodles. I can never repay their generosity. I was homeless. They gave me a corner of the bedroom floor for nine months and never asked for rent.

I had my car, duffle bag, sleeping bag, the money from Richard, and a hell of a lot of determination. I vowed to myself that if I couldn't make my living as a dancer, I would quit. I would not become someone who called himself a dancer but was really a waiter. So, I took classes, sometimes dancing for ten hours a day, six days a week. I auditioned for every possible gig I heard about—fast food and beer commercials for Mexico and Japan, as a back-up dancer for Mitzi Gaynor, for a role in the chorus in summer stock theaters, for industrial shows to demonstrate new products, even for a few suspicious modeling gigs.

I don't remember the show I was auditioning for, but I remember the time I embarrassed myself in front of Bob Fosse, not with my dancing but with my singing. I was a newbie. No one told me an audition to dance in a Broadway show for Fosse included a singing audition. I made the final cut of dancers but began to sweat bullets as the other guys pulled sheet music out of their dance bags. The remaining male candidates performed songs from famous musicals.

I was totally lost. When my turn arrived, I asked the pianist if he knew "Swing Low, Sweet Chariot."

"What key?"

"Uhhh…any key," I stalled. "You just try something, and I'll see if I can hit it." He began in a very low key, and I started singing in a tone that sounded like a bad imitation of Paul Robeson's "Ol' Man River." As the pianist crept up the scale, taking the keys higher and higher, I was possessed by the spirit of Lucille Ball in one of her auditions for her husband Ricky's Copacabana with my face all crinkled and my voice screeching like a dying chicken. "He just keeps rollin' along!" I have no recollection of how I got out of the room, but I do recall the looks on some faces that I hoped I would never see again in my life.

For months I continued to audition but got nothing. Thirty-five dollars was all that remained of the $2,002 that Richard had left for me. I hadn't eaten in two days and a friend offered to take me to Cafe Figaro for lunch. While eating, a sign on the wall kept staring at me: WAITERS WANTED.

After telling the cashier I had serving experience, I was asked to return after 5:00 p.m. to meet the manager. I decided to take my last dance class with the Landrums at Coronet Studios on La Cienega Boulevard. At the studio, I began the warm-up with a heavy heart. I savored every exercise as if it were my last meal. Halfway through class, the studio owner stuck his head in the room, "Is there a Vincent Paterson in here? You have a phone call." My heart stopped. I imagined something must have happened to someone in my family. I hurried to the phone.

"Hello, this is Vincent Paterson."

"Hey, this is Joe Bennett. I'm choreographing a TV special, and I need one more guy. The choreographer Lester Wilson gave me your name. Can I come over and watch you in class?"

"Please, Joe. That would be incredible. Thanks so much." Joe came and, after watching for about fifteen minutes, called me out of the room and gave me my first job dancing as a clown alongside Dick

Van Dyke. I even got my photo in *TV Guide!* Though there weren't a lot of dance jobs to be had, I slowly began to make a living doing what I loved.

My first touring dance gig was in 1978 as one of four dancers to perform with Shirley MacLaine. Months on the road with Shirley enabled me to finally afford my own apartment. At twenty-eight, I had some money in my pocket for the first time in my life, and it felt good. Working in LA, I became close friends with Michael Peters, having danced together in numerous gigs. Michael taught classes at Roland Dupree Dance Academy on Third Street, and I began assisting him. Michael wanted to experiment with choreography.

"Michael, I have some money from Shirley's tour," I said. "Why don't I rent some space here late at night? Let's each pick four dancers, and you can work out choreography."

Thus began an insane season of Michael Peters working our group of dancers to the bone as we followed his stunning choreography at the speed of light, sometimes moving from the floor to midair in a single breath. We would come out of those sessions beaten, bruised, and euphoric. Through these late-night madness sessions, Michael Peters began to find his voice as a choreographer, and we solidified our place as some of the hottest dancers in LA.

Around this same time, Michael Jackson was embarking on his solo career, having been the front man of The Jackson 5 since he was five years old. His solo music video, "Billie Jean," had great success. Bob Giraldi, who directed the commercial for the Broadway show *Dreamgirls*, was hired to direct Michael Jackson's second musical short film, "Beat It." (Mike never referred to his cinematic creations as "music videos," he always called them "short films.")

Michael Peters had co-choreographed *Dreamgirls*, which led to Bob hiring him to choreograph "Beat It." Peters met with Bob and Michael Jackson, then came by to tell me his sensational news. He was on cloud nine.

"It's going to be about gangs. Michael told Bob he wants LA's rival gangs, the Crips and the Bloods, to be in it," Peters came at me a mile a minute. "Michael Jackson wants this to be like a short film. I want you in it, Lenny." (He always called me Lenny.) "But Michael Jackson wants to OK the dancers, so you'll have to audition. He'll love you, doll."

I *had* to get this gig. The audition was held at Debbie Reynolds Dance Studio in North Hollywood. There were approximately 250 dancers auditioning for about eighteen parts. Knowing the video was about rival gangs, instead of wearing dancer drag to the audition, I wore jeans, a tight T-shirt, and an earring. I grew my beard for a few days so I had some stubble. All of the other dancers were wearing the typical audition uniform of a tank top, stretch jazz pants, leg warmers, and black jazz shoes. In my day-to-day life, I looked like an All-American college student—athletic, cultured, clean-cut—the day I auditioned, I could pass as a punk off the street.

When we entered the room, Michael Jackson was in the front of the studio speaking quietly with Michael Peters and Giraldi. He was unassuming in his street clothes, thin and bashful. He kept watching me. I was certainly conspicuous enough. Peters proceeded to give the audition combination, and I was able to throw back his choreography almost as fast as he presented it. I danced my ass off with technique amplified by a street attitude, and I could sense Michael Jackson's eyes on me throughout the audition. No one was immediately chosen, and we all left the studio.

A few hours later, Michael Peters called me. He clearly had news but wouldn't reveal it over the phone. I rushed to his apartment. He was sitting in his kitchen with a smirky grin on his face. "Well?" I asked, slightly terrified. "Well? Just tell me!"

"Well, doll, you worked it, baby," Michael Peters grinned even more. "You got the gig! And I'm going to be in the video, too, uh-huh, and you and I are going to be rival gang leaders!"

We jumped around the apartment screaming like six-year-olds. It was the beginning of my journey with Michael Jackson.

2.

The Boy Most Like Jesus Comes to Hollywood

M Y FATHER WAS A nonpracticing Catholic and my mother was a nonpracticing Methodist. In the fifties, the Catholic Church made the non-Catholic spouse sign a contract that the children would be raised Catholic, so my siblings and I attended elementary school at Our Lady of Charity. When I achieved the highest grade point average at the end of the school year, I received a plaster statue of the Virgin Mary of Christ exposing his Sacred Heart. By the age of fourteen, the nuns didn't care for me because I constantly challenged the tenets of Catholicism.

"Yes, Vincent, what is it now?"

"Sister, why would God let a baby stay in Purgatory forever rather than go to Heaven if it died before it was baptized? That seems like a cruel God."

"Paterson, come up here and hold out your hand." Smack with the ruler!

But the nuns were helpless when my male classmates voted me "The Sacred Heart Boy" for the eighth grade May Procession. This role traditionally belonged to the boy who was "most like Jesus." I was thin, had slicked-back, gelled hair, and a single flirty curl down the center of my forehead. Along with the mandatory long-sleeved, white shirt and green tie with the gold OLC logo, I wore pointed-toe, black suede, Cuban-heeled shoes and skin-tight pants.

What began as an innocent act of rebellion evolved into my first taste of celebrity. I *became* the boy most like Jesus, taking on my role with the fervor of Daniel Day-Lewis. I wore rope belts under my shirt to chafe my skin. I made collections for the poor children in Africa. When May Procession day finally came, I reverently walked in the long line of young students from the school to the church flanked by two first graders. Rather than recite the traditional prayer in front of the congregation, I wrote and orated my own prayer:

> *Oh, Sacred Heart of Jesus,*
> *We place our trust in Thee*
> *And pray that in thy loving arms,*
> *We may always be.*
> *Take our souls, our pliant minds*
> *Our hearts with which we share*
> *The love we feel for you, dear Lord*
> *Please, hold us in thy care.*

I had one disappointment that day because my own silent request to God wasn't answered. I had spent weeks begging Him to actually levitate me just a few inches above the church pew kneeler at that Sunday event. "Just a few inches," I had prayed. But kneeling at the altar, in front of the entire school, nothing happened. Nothing. After all the work I had put into fulfilling my role, it didn't seem like that big a request.

All joking aside, I always took acting roles seriously and the savior of mankind was no different. I think I was intrigued by the idea of anyone being so fundamentally good without the prospect of gaining anything in return. Someone who possessed fortitude, had a gentle voice, a magnanimous heart.

What I came to learn was that Michael Jackson had many of these characteristics. He was compassionate toward children, the needy, and the sick. I never heard him raise his voice in anger or speak ill of someone behind his or her back. He never bemoaned someone else's capabilities, their creativity, or lack thereof. In fact, he was always supportive of other artists. I found this rare in most celebrities, especially the musical ones.

The beginning of Mike's solo career was the perfect time for me to be introduced to the future King of Pop. Being in the right place at the right time—there's a lot to that old cliché. But I would also say that, because of Michael Peters and all the creative work I'd done leading up to that audition…I was also *prepared.*

Beat It

"BEAT IT" WAS THE beginning of my nearly two-decade creative relationship with Mike. It was the dawn of MTV, and pop musicians suddenly had a platform to present their music with visuals. And here I was in the middle of it all and with a featured role.

Rehearsals for "Beat It" took place at the Debbie Reynolds Dance Studio. Michael Peters, with Frances Morgan and me as his two assistant choreographers, worked for one day as Peters created the one dance sequence in "Beat It" when Mike unites both gangs in a sensual but masculine peace dance.

The next day, Mike joined us. He had been successful as the front man of The Jackson 5 since he was a kid, but he entered the rehearsal space without a shred of pretentious attitude. He complimented Peters on the choreography, and I was surprised how self-conscious he was as the four of us began to dance together. We three were used to laughing a lot in rehearsals and that loosened Mike up quickly.

Mike didn't say much, but after getting a good sense of the choreography Peters had created, he said, "I think I want to create my own moves for the rest of the song. For all the parts that I dance by myself." That was how Mike's collaboration began with Peters and how it would eventually continue with me.

The next day, Peters, Francis, and I worked with the seventeen other male dancers. We were excited for Mike's arrival at the studio, and the energy level rose dramatically when he joined us. He must have gone home after the rehearsal the day before and practiced nonstop because he danced every step perfectly. And when he began to move with the group, it was as though he was possessed by an alien energy that transformed him from a demure, gentle man to lightning in a bottle—harnessed, yet inexplicably powerful.

I will always remember that first feeling of dancing next to Michael Jackson in the rehearsal room when he let himself go. It felt like actual sparks were emanating from his body.

In early March 1983, we filmed "Beat It" over the course of two nights in downtown Los Angeles near Skid Row. Among the two gangs of dancers were real live members of LA's famous rival gangs, the Crips and the Bloods. Mike had little interaction with them on set but knew adding them to the mix would make the short film feel gritty and authentic. It was interesting to see the gang members interacting on set when in real life they were mortal enemies. As the clock ticked into the night, the gang members—unaccustomed to a lengthy shooting schedule—became restless. They thought they'd just show up, be in the video quickly, have a meal and a paycheck, and call it a day. They didn't realize that the same action would have to be repeated again and again until director Bob Giraldi decided he had the shot he needed. There was concern that the gang members might walk away before the shoot had completed, but it didn't happen.

During the two-night shoot when the cameras weren't rolling, Mike and I would hang together. At one point, we stood on the sidewalk next to one of the taller buildings along the street. Mike was wearing his red jacket from the video, and I saw something dripping onto his shoulder.

"Mike," I said. "What's this? Something's dripping on you." I touched it. "Oh, my God, I think it's blood." We looked up and saw a man crawling out of a window high above and onto the fire escape.

He disappeared inside another window, leaving a trail of blood on Mike's jacket. Though shooting a fantasy about violence, we were really in the middle of one of the roughest parts of LA.

This was the first music video most of us had ever created, and it felt like making a feature film. I got to dance beside Michael Jackson and I got to act, as most of my scenes were acting moments until the dance section at the end. Though there are only a few bars of repeated movement in the video, those steps that Michael Peters created have since been danced by millions around the world. My costume was nearly what I wore to the audition. Michael Peters wore baggy white pants and a white Kansai jacket. The red leather jacket Mike wore that night later became an international fashion statement. Michael Jackson was a natural in front of the camera. It was obvious from the first shots that he was extremely comfortable performing on film and that his energy could reach through the TV screen and touch an audience.

"Beat It" first aired on MTV in late March 1983, just a few weeks after we shot it. Michael Peters had a party at his apartment in the Hollywood Hills, and we huddled around his TV where our usually boisterous crowd was silent until the last image faded from the screen. Then the room erupted with screams, laughter, hugs, and congratulations. The video received accolades from the American Music Awards, the Black Gold Awards, the *Billboard* Video Awards and, eventually, was inducted into the Music Video Producer's Hall of Fame. Many of our lives changed after "Beat It" aired. None of us had any idea it would establish Michael Jackson as an international pop icon, but Mike's star became a comet blazing through the stratosphere. Michael Peters became the most acclaimed choreographer in pop music. I was offered leading roles in videos with Diana Ross and Olivia Newton-John. It was astounding.

A few months after the video premiered, I was walking through the dusty streets of Cabo San Lucas when it was still a quiet pueblo. We passed a ramshackle bar and "Beat It" was on the TV. We walked in for a beer and the bartender and his family recognized me. They were shocked as they pointed from my face to the TV screen. I'll never forget thinking, "Wow. If someone in a tiny Mexican town recognizes *me*, the world will never be the same for Michael Jackson."

—

As a choreographer, Michael Peters was inspiring. He was wiry and thin, countered with a flamboyant, larger-than-life personality. We had a lot of laughs while creating. Peters could also be a taskmaster. He was among the last of an old-school lineage of choreographers who believed they were beyond reproach. You did whatever you were told or felt the sting of a verbal whip. His choreography constantly challenged your technique and energy. While inspiring dancers to attain new heights, he sometimes pushed dancers too far. I once had a confrontation with him while rehearsing at Moro-Landis Studio into the early hours of the morning. After dancing for hours with every ounce of energy in our bodies, he wanted us to do the number "full out" before we went home. I put my foot down.

"Michael, we're tired, and we're not going to dance it full out," I said. "The lifts are dangerous and someone can get hurt. We're too tired."

"Don't tell me what you'll do or not do," he snapped. "You're going to dance it *full out*."

The dancers and I stood as a united front and went home. Safety over ego. To me, his hard-edged temperament was the only drawback to his otherwise incredible skill as a choreographer.

Michael Peters also had a fantastically wry sense of humor. In 1984, I was his assistant in creating a complicated routine to "Maniac" for a group of sensational female dancers for the Academy Awards. He had the women running, turning, and jumping in four-inch platform heels. Throughout rehearsal, the dancers were complaining.

"Michael, this is too difficult. This is impossible. We can't do this in these heels!"

That night Peters dragged me to a shoe store on Fairfax Avenue in West Hollywood, bought me a pair of women's four-inch heels, and made me learn the girls' dance before rehearsal the next morning. When the ladies arrived to rehearse, the complaining began. Peters clapped his hands like a schoolmarm drunk on sass…

"Okay, Miss Things!" he turned to me. "Lenny, go get those shoes on." I wedged my size-eleven feet into those white pumps and proceeded to demonstrate how the choreography could, in fact, be done in four-inch heels.

Thriller

BY THE TIME WE made "Thriller," Michael Jackson had become the King of Pop. Michael Peters had become the king of music video choreography. John Landis, who had directed *An American Werewolf in London*, had been chosen to direct "Thriller." I was Peters's sole assistant choreographer on "Thriller" and landed a role as a dancing zombie. We were the team. Peters and I spent a few days at Debbie Reynolds Dance Studio laying the groundwork for the choreography. Mike eventually joined us. Mike had gained a lot of confidence with the success of "Beat It," and upon entering the studio, told us, "I really want to be sure that the dance doesn't make the zombies come off as comical. I want them to be scary." We showed him what Peters had created, and Mike started jumping around the room. "That's what I'm talking about! Yeah! That's it!"

Though Peters created almost all of the movement, Mike slowly became more assertive in contributing choreography. He always wore his black Florsheim loafers, white socks, black pants, and a long-sleeve shirt with a white T-shirt. Sometimes he would say, "Ewwww, this move feels so good here, ewwwww, yeah, on this beat, because you have to feeeel it." Or, "That's too much like ballet." At one point he said, "Let's make monster faces in the mirror. Let's be scaaary." And the three of us made "monster" faces in the mirror, laughing like lunatics. On the second day of rehearsal, Mike wore monster makeup. He loved being in character and believed it enhanced the movement.

Peters and I held an audition after we went through the list of our favorite, outstanding dancers in Hollywood and invited them to the zombie party. With so much talent in one room, rehearsals were glorious. As an assistant choreographer, my primary responsibility was to make all of the choreography clean, making certain that everyone's bodylines were identical and that everyone was following the exact same rhythms. Often, I would pull Mike aside to see if he needed anything, if he was comfortable, or if he had questions. There was no doubt that Peters's choreography in "Beat It" elevated Mike's dancing prowess to a higher level. He was a prodigy student with Peters as his master teacher. As a member of the zombie cast, Mike was now dancing intricate choreography alongside the best dancers in Hollywood and not only holding his own but inspiring us to greater levels of performance so as not to be left in his wake. After our final rehearsal, we all applauded Mike. He applauded us back and bashfully said, "Thank you, everybody, for being in this short film. We're gonna make some history."

We shot the "Thriller" zombie dance sequence late at night at the junction of Union Pacific Avenue and South Calzona Street in East LA. It was mid-October 1983. Our costumes were made specifically for each of us. We had the privilege of having Oscar-winning makeup artist Rick Baker create original makeup for each of us, too. This was a unique experience for group dancers. We had dental plates made for us while precast prosthetics were used on our faces. Sitting in the makeup chair, watching myself age, die, and then become a zombie was as terrifying as it was fascinating. Though told not to, I snatched my zombie teeth as a souvenir, and I still have them. Bad, Zombie! Bad, bad, Zombie!

The cold, late night urban streets were hosed down with water to create a moodier atmosphere. John Landis was relentless, making us dance take after take on the hard, wet street. But, having to pee or not, dancers are accustomed to doing what we are told and though we were dog-tired and exhausted, every time we heard "action" we performed as if it were the first camera take of the night. Mike was flawless. He never complained, and he never missed a beat.

The "Thriller" short film aired on MTV on December 3, 1983. The choreography has become a part of global pop culture, danced everywhere from wedding receptions to Filipino prisons. With the creation of the short films "Beat It" and "Thriller," dance exploded in Hollywood. Adding break-dancers, gang members, and now dancing zombies to his videos, Michael Jackson, as well as Michael Peters's choreography, opened the door for men to become accepted as dancers without the stigma of sexual preference. Boys began to hone their street-dancing skills on the corners of cities all over the world. Formal dance classes in Los Angeles saw a rise in male attendance. The dancing in a music video was becoming just as important as the music.

Smooth Criminal

ONE NIGHT IN EARLY 1987, I was sitting in my apartment on Franklin Avenue in Hollywood and the telephone rang. When I answered, a high-pitched voice said, "Hi, is Vincent there?" I sensed a ridiculous prank coming on.

"Who's calling?" I replied skeptically.

"It's Michael Jackson," the voice whispered.

"This is not Michael Jackson."

"Yes, it is. It's Michael Jackson."

"This is not Michael Jackson. Who the fuck is this?"

Giggles from the other end then, "No, really, Vincent, it's me."

"Listen, if you don't tell me who the fuck this is, I'm hanging up right now!"

"This is me, it's really Michael!" Oh, shit. It was him.

"Oh, my God, Michael," I said. "Excuse me for my language, man. I'm so sorry!"

He laughed, then, "Are you busy right now?"

Mike was at the Sound Factory, a recording studio on Selma Avenue in Hollywood five minutes away, and he invited me to come over. When I arrived, I was led into the engineering room by an assistant. "I wanted to play this new song for you," Mike said. "I haven't finished any lyrics yet, but it's called 'Smooth Criminal.'"

I sat beside him as the engineer played the song. Loud. Really loud, just how Mike liked it. Mike would sing at a specific part each time, "*You've been hit by a Smooth Criminal*." When it finished, he asked me, "What do you think?" Though confused about why he was asking my opinion, I replied enthusiastically that I thought the song was powerful, had a really fresh sound, and would be incredible to dance to. We moved to the lounge.

I'll never forget that night. We shared our first intimate conversation as if we had been longtime friends. Mike turned to me with a childlike grin on his face, "Can I ask you a personal question?"

"Sure, Mike," I responded.

"Did you ever masturbate?" It was like we were twelve and having clandestine confessions under the school bleachers.

"Uh…yeah," I laughed, a little surprised. "Everybody does, though I have to tell you I was a late bloomer. My best friends in senior high school all thought I was a little weird because I didn't start until maybe eleventh grade."

"I don't," he said.

"Oh, Michael, come on, you do so," I teased him. "Everybody does!"

"Well," he giggled, "Okay, I do, but only in the shower."

"Well, whatever," I said.

"What do you call it?" he asked, a mischievousness creeping into his voice.

"What do you mean 'what do I call it?' I don't call 'it' anything!" I was laughing now.

"I call it Ocean Spray," he said, still giggling.

"Ocean Spray? You're so nuts," I poked at him. "You're crazy."

Then he said, "Can I ask you something else?"

"Of course, you crazy person!"

"Are you...gay?"

"Yeah," I said. "And I have a boyfriend."

"Is it true that some guys like to do it...*up there*?"

"Yeah," I said, "*some* guys do!"

He covered his mouth with his hand and emitted this half-surprised, half-embarrassed, "Oooooo! Oooooo!" We had become adolescent boys discussing something verboten. And I felt even closer to him as a friend. Michael Jackson wanted to discover and ask questions the way young boys do. He had been surrounded and protected by family his entire life. The more famous he became, the more difficult it was to step into the real world. His life was evolving more and more into a fantasy. He was becoming one of the most recognizable people on the planet. There was nowhere he could go where he could just be Michael. His closest friends were Hollywood celebrities like Elizabeth Taylor, Diana Ross, and Jimmy Stewart—people who could relate to Mike's superstardom life—and a few inner-circle friends like his driver and closest bodyguards.

That evening in the recording studio cemented a friendship between us. I never took his questions about my lifestyle as Michael being gay, and I never thought he was. I was privileged that Michael was comfortable sharing his personal life with me and wanted to know about mine.

This was just a small piece of the complicated enigma that was Michael Jackson. He created great work under the guidance of some formidable managers over the years—Sandy Gallin, Freddy DeMann, Frank DiLeo—without losing control of his own career. Mike called the shots and was highly knowledgeable about film, art, and the entertainment business. But in some ways, he was still a twelve-year-old boy with a limited social life beyond the confines of his immediate family.

Mike and I returned to the recording studio and listened to the "Smooth Criminal" music track a few more times. Then he handed me a cassette of the song to take home. "I want you to take it, and I want you to let the music talk to you," he said. "Let the music tell you what it wants to be."

"I don't understand," I said. "Are you making a short film? Are you asking me to dance in it?"

"No," he said. "I want you to come up with the idea for it, choreograph it, and direct it."

I was reeling, numb. I had no major credits to support Mike asking me to create a short film for him. "I was thinking," he continued. "Maybe it should be something like ten men in a swanky dinner club with long tuxedos and top hats on. But," he repeated, "let the music tell you what it wants to be."

I've read that Mike originally suggested "Smooth Criminal" have a Western theme, but he never mentioned it to me. I only heard of the Western idea from Mike much later, during a conversation we had at the Universal Sheraton Hotel in 2001. I took the track from Mike, said "thank you," and fumbled my way out of there, ecstatic and terrified.

While driving home on cloud nine, I was hit by a painful thought: what was my good friend Michael Peters going to say? Mike hadn't asked Peters to choreograph anything since their work together on a 1984 Pepsi commercial that left Mike severely injured. Fire from a pyrotechnic explosion had ignited Mike's hair, and he was rushed to the hospital with third degree scalp burns. The incident made international headlines and, if the rumors were true, many believe this was the beginning of Mike's addiction to painkillers. Mike used other choreographers after that, but I began to feel guilty that I had been asked to choreograph and direct the piece at all.

When I got home, I called Michael Peters and told him that Mike had asked me to create a new video for him. Silence. Dead silence. For a long time.

"I have no idea why he asked me, Michael. I feel so weird that he didn't ask you. Honestly, I didn't ask him to ask me. He just did."

Peters accused me of taking his job. He then accused me of undercutting his pay rate to do the job, but money had not been discussed. "Well, Lenny, if that's the way it's going to be, I guess that's the way it's going to be, doll. I'll talk to YOU later." He hung up on me.

I was crushed. Michael Peters was one of my mentors and closest friends. But I knew I was going to do "Smooth Criminal." I had to.

For the next several days, I did exactly what Mike suggested: I listened to the music over and over again. And over and over and over again. I got back to him, "Hey, Mike. I've listened to the music over and over. I've let it sink into my bones, and I did what you told me to do. I let it talk to me. I think 'Smooth Criminal' should be set in an underground club in the 1930s in Chicago. But with a few off-the-wall things happening." He embraced the idea wholeheartedly.

In Hollywood, cash is always king. Time equals money and budgets are finite. The schedules can be brutal on everyone; however, this was not the case for "Smooth Criminal." The time and resources set aside to create it were unprecedented for a music video and unlike anything I've ever witnessed. Because he was finishing his *BAD* album, Mike put his trust in me, giving me time, space, and the financial freedom to develop my ideas.

I held an audition at Debbie Reynolds Dance Studio to assemble the most competent and visually interesting collection of dancers. A group of ten became my initial skeleton dance crew. Mike arranged for me to have a sound stage at Culver Studios in Culver City where we would eventually shoot the short film. The production crew set up our seedy underground Chicago club in half of the huge soundstage. The other half became our rehearsal space complete with mirrors, a top-of-the-line Meyer sound system, and a sprung wooden dance floor to keep the dancer's bodies free from injury. He provided me with an Ikegami video camera so I could record the work as it progressed and share it with him. I started work with the skeleton crew, as well as my assistant choreographer, Joe Malone. Mike added Jeffrey Daniel from the singing group Shalamar to the mix, to choreograph some street movement. I had everything I needed to create at my fingertips. Rehearsals began in early 1987, without Mike. We had approximately one month of rehearsals and, later, several weeks of shooting.

A typical rehearsal day would start on the sound stage, where I led the dancers in a warm-up. Then I would teach the choreography I had created. After rehearsing, we would move over to the set to work in the actual performance space, keeping in mind where Mike would be at various points in the story and leaving gaps for his solo moments. Mike and I decided that I would create the story and the principal choreography and leave pockets where he could feature his own movement. Jeffrey would create two sections for the street dancers. I recorded the dancers on video then met with Mike at night in his family's compound on Hayvenhurst Avenue in the San Fernando Valley. We watched the footage together.

Mike was jubilant with the direction the piece was taking. "This is great. The fans are going to love this because it's coming from the heart. I can feel it. But don't you think we need more dancers?"

"Sure, Mike," I said. And I'd hire more dancers. That kept happening until we had a small army of dancers. Things continued with class, rehearsal, creating choreography, and then sharing the footage with Mike at night. He eventually asked, "Vince, do you think the set should be a little bigger? I think we could use a second floor, like a balcony. Don't you?"

"Sure, Mike," I said. I suggested a staircase on which he could be lowered down to the first floor. Before I knew it, a second floor had been built.

We worked together on the music, too. I would share a section of choreography with him and Mike would ask, "Do you want more bars of music here? So you can add more choreography?" Mike had done this on "Thriller" when he added the extended dance break for the zombie dance, but such luxury was still unheard of in the time-sensitive world of pop music. "Sure, Mike," I said and so he extended the musical breaks in "Smooth," adding over five minutes of music to the final version of the short film.

One night, after going over the day's rehearsal footage with him, Mike invited me to hang at the Jackson home so we could watch *The Third Man* in his private screening room. He thought the film had a similar sensibility to what we were creating. He had mountains of popcorn made but as we settled in to watch the movie, Bubbles, Mike's pet chimp, joined the party. Bubbles kept making noise and getting in the way of the screen. Mike and I threw popcorn at him, laughing.

"Get out of the way, Bubbles!" Mike took off one of his loafers and flung it at the chimp. Bubbles dodged, convinced we were playing a game. "Oh, Vince," Mike laughed, "if the ASPCA saw me now they'd have me arrested!"

Mike was accustomed to working in private sessions before joining the other dancers in rehearsal. We loved exploring rhythms, experimenting with different moves on different beats, or changing up the timing of a sequence. "You have to feeeel it," he would always say while making cool beatbox sounds with his voice.

We worked hard in those sessions and had a great time. With the section of movement I created that repeats itself throughout "Smooth," Mike spent over three hours in front of a mirror, repeating it again and again, until it was as natural to him as breathing. That was Michael—intense focus and a desire to gain perfection. Mike's commitment not only to dancing the choreography, but also to fully embodying a dance with his entire "emotional" being, made working with him extraordinary.

We were both fans of creating characters when we danced. Mike showed up for our private rehearsals in his all-white suit and hat while, in rehearsals with the dancers, I had already been wearing a long black coat and black hat to give me my own sense of character. I remember saying to him, "Hey, Mike, you look great in all white."

"Uh-huh," he said with a little attitude, the subtext being that he was referring to Michael Peters in "Beat It." He had shared with me that he had been upset that Michael Peters chose to wear all white for the "Beat It" video. Mike acknowledged it as a smart but inconsiderate move by Peters to steal focus.

With "Smooth Criminal," I had my first opportunity to develop dancers into actors. I had each dancer write a brief autobiography incorporating why they came to this club and what their relationship was to each other. I had them create names for their characters. Everyone had to enter and exit the set by the green door that was the entrance to the club. When they were on the set, they could only address each other by their character names. Everyone got into it, even Mike when he joined rehearsal, though his name never changed. These acting exercises allowed every dancer's face to be captured on film with a depth of history written on it. It shows in the final cut.

Inspired by Mike's desire to always be original, I had Mike flip a coin from across the room into the jukebox to begin the music. Then I created "the lean." Years earlier, I had seen the Momix Dance Company perform a piece in giant snow skis, tilting their bodies forward as they seemed to defy gravity. I decided to create that same illusion but with wires and pulleys.

Each dancer wore a harness under his suit with wires attached to small clips that extended out the left and right sides of his suit jacket. The wires reached to the ceiling of the soundstage, traveled over a pulley, and across the ceiling to the far side of the room, over another pulley, and then into the hands of stagehands below. Each dancer was controlled by two stagehands with the wires. When the stagehands released the tension on the wires, the dancers would angle into the antigravity lean. When the stagehands pulled the wires taut, the dancers were brought back to a standing position.

It was incredibly effective. Mike loved it. He eventually patented special shoes for a stage version of the lean so that he could replicate the move without the use of wires. The image of Mike in "the lean," one of his most-loved, iconic visual moments, has been recreated in sculptures, toys, videos, advertisements, and paintings.

One day, the South African a cappella group Ladysmith Black Mambazo showed up to visit while everyone was off to lunch. I said, "It is so nice to meet you. I have an idea. I want to surprise Mike if you want to play along." They agreed.

When Mike and the dancers returned, I had hidden Ladysmith behind a wall of the set. I gave my improvisation warm-up instructions that everyone should writhe like a seething mass of bodies moving in slow motion. Mike and the dancers started moving in silence. I went behind the wall and signaled Ladysmith to start singing one of their haunting chants. Rather than stop at the sound of the music, the dancers and Mike continued, driven by the sounds of Ladysmith. Some of the dancers began randomly crying out "Annie, are you okay? Are you okay, Annie?" Michael began to yell, "Ooooo," stomping his foot like he was at a Southern Baptist church revival. The movements and sounds built into a frenzied climax.

I brought the Ladysmith singers out from behind the wall and everyone cheered. We were all buzzing excitedly when Mike said above it all, "We're shooting that! The world has never seen anything like that, and we're shooting it tomorrow!" This moment in the film is a unique and haunting image inspired by that single moment of happenstance during our creative madness.

Elizabeth Taylor, Gregory Peck, and Jimmy Stewart were among the celebrities who visited the set. Liz was friendly and had that infectious idiosyncratic laugh and those electric purple eyes. Hermes Pan showed up one day. Hermes had collaborated with Fred Astaire as a choreographer on seventeen musical films and was considered Astaire's "idea man." I stood beside him at the camera monitor, my heart beating wildly, while we watched some of the dance being filmed. Mike came over to meet him, and Hermes told us excitedly, "Fred would have loved this!" We were over the moon with his approval.

On some days, Mike invited a terminally ill child from the Make-A-Wish Foundation to the set. I recall a conversation between my assistant choreographer, Joe, and Mike. Joe asked Mike how he could take the heartbreak of having these children near him so often. Mike replied, "Well, maybe you're seeing how little time they have left. I'm looking at how much joy they have right now."

Mike was shy, and I encouraged the dancers to talk to him during rehearsals and the filming. A few had danced in "Beat It" and "Thriller." I knew we had made progress on the treat-Mike-like-one-of-us front when Smith Wordes came up to me in her tight red dress. Mike had never danced with a female partner in a short film and maybe never in his life. I had paired Smith with Mike in a small section.

"Oh, Vincent…" she smiled, "guess who was looking down my dress?"

"Well, more power to him," I replied. From the corner of the soundstage came Mike's now familiar, boyish exclamation, "Ooooooo, oooooo!" He was covering his mouth and giggling. I had forgotten I was wearing a body mic for the ever-present documentary crew, and he heard our entire exchange.

I had never worked on a project where dancers were invited to watch dailies—the viewing of the footage that had been shot the day before. These sessions are usually exclusive to the creative team and the producers. But including the dancers is exactly what Mike did. Our shooting days consisted of filming in the morning, breaking for lunch, and all of us watching yesterday's dailies with Mike. The screening room became a party with whoops and yells and revival-tent-like testimonies being hurled through the air. The room resounded with constant applause as everyone, including Mike, supported everyone else's performances. Then, flying on that high, we'd all return to the set and shoot some more.

When "Smooth" became part of the feature film *Moonwalker*, we went with the flow. The plot with the trio of children who watch from the street and the arrival of the storm troopers were added. And Mike now had a machine gun to fire—which he loved!

I never got to direct my creation. *Moonwalker* was a union film so Colin Chilvers, a member of the Director's Guild of America, was brought in. I was credited only as the co-choreographer with Mike and Jeffrey. I had shot video of every passage throughout the club and handed that over to Colin when he came on board. Colin respected what I had already conceived and involved me in setting up the shots for the camera. He did a brilliant job and the final "Smooth Criminal" short was exactly as Mike and I had envisioned it.

"Smooth Criminal" did not have the immediate acclaim that "Thriller" had received. Mike and I were nominated for an MTV award for Best Choreography for a Music Video. I wanted it badly. I had put my heart and soul into this project, was proud of the work, and believed that I deserved the recognition. I lost the MTV award to Paula Abdul who won for "Straight Up." I admire and respect Paula. She looked gorgeous in that video and her tap dancing sizzled. But we were all heartbroken, considering the intricately detailed choreography in "Smooth," compared with "Straight Up."

Recognition by your peers for good work is always encouraging but, more importantly, the "Smooth Criminal" experience and Michael Jackson's trust allowed me to recognize that I really was a choreographer.

3.

M(adonna) is for Muse

MADONNA IS THE ONLY artist I have worked with who haunts my dreams. In my dreams, we laugh, we argue, we make out, we party, we fly together. I have a huge amount of respect for her, and, in my own way, I really love her. But it didn't begin that way.

The Pepsi Commercial

FOR THOSE WHO DON'T remember the pop music scene in the eighties, there were several female stars who were on the cusp of breaking out as the clear leader of the pack: Janet Jackson, Sade, Paula Abdul, Cyndi Lauper, Annie Lennox, Pat Benatar…and Madonna.

In February of 1989, I got a call from Joe Pytka, commercial director extraordinaire, asking me to meet him at Culver Studios. We had previously worked together on a few commercials.

"Hey, Vince, thanks for coming down," Joe said. Joe, six foot seven with his long mane of white hair, gave me a big bear hug. He explained he was shooting a two-minute commercial for Pepsi with Madonna using her new song "Like A Prayer." "She's been fucking adamant that she isn't going to dance and she isn't going to sing," he said, "but I want you here just to hang around and let's see what the fuck happens."

Just as he finished, Madonna came sweeping out of the sound-stage with her entourage, headed toward her trailer. Joe introduced me, "Madonna, I want you to meet Vincent Paterson. He's Michael Jackson's choreographer and—"

She didn't even glance at me. "I don't need a fucking choreographer," she said, and kept walking. Wow. Okay. My heart dropped; my face plummeted to the ground. Madonna could cut you down faster than anyone. After chasing my face around the studio backlot calling, "Here, face; here, face," I finally collected myself. Joe enticed me to stay.

Shooting began and I walked inside the soundstage. I hung out in the shadows and watched them work. Joe was attempting to get a solo shot of Madonna. He was using the camera on a crane, beginning at a position below stage level. The direction was for the camera to be at eye level to catch Madonna at the precise moment she finished a turn and faced the camera. It wasn't working. If Madonna was on, the camera was off, or vice versa. Her patience was wearing thin, and she was letting everyone know it.

"I think I can fix this," I whispered to Joe.

"Then go the fuck over and talk to her."

"Madonna," I said. "Hi, I'm Vincent. I'm not *choreographing* anything but if I put this on counts for you and the crane operator, Joe can get the shot and you can get out of here."

"Well, do it, then."

I asked Madonna and the crane operator to move on my counts so they would both hit the right spot at the same time. It worked. Joe got the shot in one take and everyone breathed a huge sigh of relief. On her way off the soundstage after the shot, Madonna passed by and smiled at me. Being smiled at by Madonna felt good. Really good. Joe looked at me for a moment with his wry smile and said, "Can you come back tomorrow?"

"Anything for you, Joe."

I came back. But the word from Madonna was still clear: No dancing! No singing! The story of the commercial began with

Madonna watching home movies of herself at her eighth birthday party. The child actress version of Madonna and adult Madonna crossed over between the two worlds. At one point in the commercial, Joe wanted some dancers to dance down a street and enter a soda fountain where Madonna would be hanging out.

I started putting together some choreography and teaching it to the dancers. They were learning the movement, until, one by one, everyone stopped paying attention to me and started staring over my shoulder. I turned around, and there was Madonna. She had come out of her makeup trailer in her big robe and slippers.

"What are you doing?" she asked.

"Oh, it's nothing for you," I replied nervously. "It's just something Joe wants in the background."

"Well, let me change my clothes and show me." Madonna was now curious.

I showed her. She liked it. From that moment on, Madonna was tuned in to me. She didn't dance very much in the commercial, but I focused on giving her suggestions for her movement. I created body language that looked natural on her. Madonna was happy; Joe was happy; I was happy. The final product was sexy and cool with just the right amount of physical narrative. I really hoped she would remember me.

It was 1989. When the commercial was released, it only aired once during an ad break for *The Cosby Show*, but it was viewed by 250 million people in forty countries. It was pulled by the networks almost immediately. Right-wing Christian groups were scandalized by the music video for "Like A Prayer," in which burning crosses fill the set and Madonna kisses a Black man who plays a Catholic saint. Because the same music track was used for the commercial, Pepsi was boycotted. But Madonna had already made her mark and emerged with a great song, a controversial commercial, and plenty of rebellious freedom-of-expression to start inching past her female competition.

Express Yourself

NOT LONG AFTER THE commercial, I was asked by Madonna and director David Fincher to choreograph the music video for "Express Yourself." Madonna had performed mostly freestyle dancing in all her previous videos, yet she called herself a dancer, having trained both in college and New York City. I wanted to exploit that. I sensed her hunger as well as her bravery. She was ballsy and beautiful, and no one was going to stop her.

First, I created calisthenics choreography for a group of male dancers in the video. Madonna's choreography included sensual movement performed in a boudoir while she's standing in front of a mirror in tight lingerie. Though we had rehearsed it, when the cameras rolled, she started changing a lot of my movement.

"Madonna," I told her, "if you don't need me, that's fine."

"No, I just want to look good."

"You can trust me," I said. "I know how to make a woman look good."

And I did. I had learned from my mentors Michael Peters and Lester Wilson, who had worked with sexy female stars like Ann-Margret, Lola Falana, Diana Ross, and the cast of *Dreamgirls*. Madonna danced my choreography on the rest of the takes, and she looked fantastic.

Throughout "Express Yourself," Fincher and Madonna realized that, as a choreographer, I created more than dance steps. I staged Madonna on even the smallest movements, showing her how to sit elegantly in a chair with a cigarette holder, how to walk across a room with slinky style, how to sensuously crawl across the floor and drink milk from a cat's bowl, how to sit half naked in a bed with just the right touch of eroticism. During that bed scene, Madonna made a huge fuss about clearing the set because she was naked under her white satin robe and bedding. The assistant director firmly shouted, "Clear the set! Everyone who doesn't have to be here, get out!" The irony, and I loved this about her, was that as soon as we all started working, Madonna had absolutely no problem exposing her breasts to anyone who wanted to gawk.

I could see the transformation as the shoot continued, and so could she. Madonna soaked everything up like a sponge, as clichéd as it sounds. She reminded me of Michael Jackson in that she wouldn't settle for anything less than perfection. We got to the scene in "Express Yourself" where she was dancing atop a gigantic staircase in a man's suit, and she had to strike a final pose for the shot.

"Hey, Vincent. What should I do with my left hand?" she called to me from the top of the staircase.

I called back, "Why don't you grab your balls? You've got bigger balls than anyone else here!"

So the female version of the crotch grab found its way into homes across the world through the magic of MTV, the brazenness of Madonna, and an off-handed joke.

The Blond Ambition Tour

"With the Blond Ambition Tour, Satan has been rereleased into the world."
—Pope John Paul II

DURING "EXPRESS YOURSELF," MADONNA told me she wanted me to work on her upcoming tour. We had been in sync in both of our previous collaborations, and I shared her work ethic.

A month went by and I heard through the grapevine that Madonna was holding auditions for dancers for her new tour. I was surprised and disappointed. My agents called her manager, Freddy DeMann, inquiring if she was still interested in my participation. The answer was firm, "No, Madonna has decided to go a different way and is going to work with someone else."

In her quest to be on the cutting edge, Madonna made the decision to hire Karole Armitage, a modern-ballet choreographer with a dance company in New York. After seeing about a thousand candidates, Madonna and Karole hired several Vogue street dancers from New York, a hip-hop dancer, and some ballet and jazz dancers from Los Angeles. I decided to let it go.

Several weeks later, I got a phone call from Madonna.

"Hi, Vincent. It's Madonna," she said. "How are you?"

She had never called my house before. She hemmed and hawed a bit, then blurted out that she had made a mistake because Karole didn't understand the pop world. After weeks of rehearsals, not one song had been staged. And to make matters worse, the dancers didn't respect Karole in the rehearsal room. It had reached a point, I heard, where some of the dancers were flicking lit cigarette butts at her. Tour dates had been set but the show was stalled, and Madonna sounded desperate. She asked me to come in and take over.

"You know how to work with me, how to talk to me," she said. "You have a sense of command and the dancers will respect you. You're the right person. Can you do this? Please."

I knew I was the right person, too, and I was dying to work with her again. It's especially exciting to create with a hugely talented performer early in their career, to contribute to an artist's image. At that early stage, they are hungry and they still listen. Madonna, like Michael Jackson, was ambitious, and she wanted to break every rule she could. She was calling this show the Blond Ambition Tour. Talking about it with her got me excited for the possibilities. Instead of simply presenting hit songs, she wanted to synthesize fashion, Broadway theater elements, and performance art. Together, we were going to reinvent the entire pop concert experience.

"Madonna, I'd love to do it. I have to get my agent involved because right now I'm choreographing the movie *Havana* for Sydney Pollack. But let's see what he can do with the schedule. And, Madonna, I want to direct it or codirect it with you. I don't want to be just the choreographer."

At that time, performers like Mike and Madonna took directing credits for their live tours, as did most performers before them. That's simply the way it was done. I wanted credit for choreographing *and* directing. I had worked on several projects without getting credit for my work or vision as a director, which was clearly what was going to happen here.

"Okay," she said. Her agents sent my agent an offer. Money had been spent on the first choreographer and her team wanted to pay me a smaller fee to help recoup some expenses. My agent came back to them with a figure that was not extravagant, considering the amount of work I was about to undertake. I had a month to create an entire two-hour show. The contract as a "work-for-hire" gave Madonna the rights and complete ownership to everything I would create. In retrospect, that was a mistake, but it was standard practice. Madonna's people refused our counteroffer. I had to weigh the pros and cons of working on the tour and decided that my offer was fair. I stood my ground. My agent picked up the phone a couple days later, and Madonna was on the line. She was furious. "What do you think I am," she fumed, "a bank?"

"No, Madonna," my agent replied, "you're not a bank, you're an institution." She refused to budge. So, on the day I was supposed to begin work, rather than be depressed about losing this incredible gig, I decided to go to the movies and shake off the sadness. When I got home later that afternoon, there were five messages on my machine from my agent. (This was pre-cell phone days.)

"Vincent, where are you?!"

With the clock ticking and the opening date looming, Madonna finally agreed to the deal. I rushed to Alley Kat Studio in Hollywood where Madonna and her company were rehearsing. When I walked in the room, the performers looked up with elated faces. Madonna was formal and cold, begrudging me my "win" in the negotiations, but I knew her attitude would soften. We had to get to work.

I asked everyone to show me what had been created. All that existed was a partially completed opening song, "Express Yourself," and the choreography was just a riff on what I had created for the music video. Maintaining the style from the video, I completed the entire piece with a section for the seven male dancers including

Kevin Stea, Carlton Wilborn, Gabriel Trupin, Oliver Crumes, Salim Gauwloos, another for Madonna, Niki Harris, and Donna DeLory (her two backup singers), and a third that included the entire company. The next day, they would film the video for "Vogue," directed by David Fincher. Luis Camacho and Jose Gutierrez, the two Vogue dancers from New York who completed the cast, had created fascinating movement. Madonna asked me if I would take a look and clean it, so I did. I had a feeling about this song.

That was the afternoon of day one. I would have twenty-three days to complete seventeen more songs for the tour. The one thing that saved me from feeling overwhelmed was the talent in that room. I knew those performers would execute anything I could devise with technical perfection and electric star power.

The first thing Madonna and I did together was revise the order of the song list for the Blond Ambition Tour. "Vogue" was originally placed in the center of the show, but I wanted to move it to the end of the concert as her finale. "Really?" she said to me. "You think it will be big?"

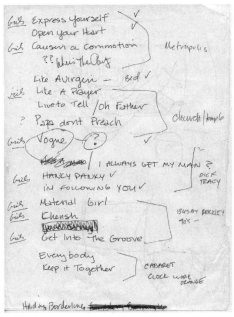

"I think it's gonna be huge," I said. My next suggestion was to put "Keep It Together" as her closing encore. Madonna planned on opening this song with an excerpt from "Family Affair" by Sly and the Family Stone, and I suggested she use the performance to say "goodbye" to her family of performers onstage as well as to the audience. From that point, we launched our twenty-three-day sprint in the rehearsal studio. There was no time to even contemplate the insanity of such a schedule.

This was my strategy: at night I would decide which song I would choreograph the next day. I recorded a cassette with that song repeated about fifty times. Just before sleep, I put the tape recorder by my bed, put the earphones on, and listened to the full tape as I fell asleep. In my dreams, I would visualize the concept and actual segments of choreography. In the morning, I'd wake up with a sketch in my head. I would meet with my assistants, Smith Wordes and Kevin Stea, at the rehearsal studio in the morning before anyone else arrived and we'd physically work out the piece. Around noon, we would teach the dancers and singers the choreography, and then Madonna would join us to learn her part. She spent every morning working out and rehearsing with the band prior to coming to me. That was the routine we committed to for three unbelievably intense weeks.

Madonna was now riding a wave of pop chart success. Tickets were selling. She was totally aware that the tour had to deliver fantastic reviews and sell-out crowds. Failure on any front was not an option. To say it was stressful for all of us would be an understatement, but we devoted ourselves to the challenge and the sweating, as the rehearsal room resounded with hard work and laughter.

Madonna granted me carte blanche to create whatever my imagination produced as I stuck my finger into the electric socket of creative energy. For "Like A Virgin," Madonna played me the song she and the band had put together. It was a raw, heavy, dark rock version with a Patti Smith feel. I had something a little different in mind.

I had recently befriended a Yemenite singer named Ofra Haza who had meshed her native Yemenite sound with club music. Ofra had given me her song "Im Nin'alu," which was topping charts all over Europe. It had a hot Middle-Eastern sound that was cutting edge in world music. I took it to Madonna. "This is a friend of mine. I want you to listen to this because it's fantastic, and I have an idea for 'Like a Virgin' using this style of arrangement." She took it home with her that night.

She loved the sensual and exotic style. I shared my vision about her on a giant bed with two of the male dancers at the top of the bed like bed posts with giant tree limbs strapped to their arms. I knew the two Voguers would give me the opportunity to do incredible movements with their flexibility and double-jointed bodies. When she came into rehearsal the following day, she had a sly smile on her face.

"Look wha-at I found," she almost sang. From out of a bag, she pulled an insane velvet cone bra that Jean Paul Gaultier had made for her but she had never used. I flipped. "Fabulous," I said. "Forget the tree arms. It's going to be all about these cone bras."

I couldn't have been happier than having both men dancing in cone bras. Madonna had Gaultier design a version of the cone bra for her costume. Throughout the song, the "eunuchs" fondled their bras as well as caressed Madonna's body and the piece ended with Madonna simulating masturbation as she thrashed around on the bed. It was sexy and humorous, totally innovative, and fucking outrageous.

The tour was faced with legal action more than once over the "Like A Virgin" performance. In several cities, including Toronto, the police came to the concert and threatened to physically stop the show if she performed the song. But Madonna, as I noted earlier, had big balls and loved to flaunt them. After the show caused major controversy in Italy, Madonna made a press statement:

"I am proud to be an American… It is the country that gave me the opportunity to be who I am today. And a country that believes in freedom of beliefs and artistic expression. My show is not a conventional pop show, but a theatrical presentation of my music, and, like theater, it asks questions, provokes thought, and takes you on an emotional journey. Portraying good and bad, light and dark, joy and sorrow…I do not endorse a way of life but describe one. And the audience is left to make its own decisions and judgments. This is what I consider freedom of speech, freedom of expression, and freedom of thought."

In hindsight, I realized that the time pressure in rehearsals worked to my advantage because there wasn't time for Madonna to question anything I created. Well, almost. When we worked on the "religious" section of the show that included "Like a Prayer," I wanted the guys to raise her above their heads in a lift. "I don't want to be lifted like some girl," Madonna declared decisively.

"No, Madonna, it's not like a girl," I said. "It's like a QUEEN."

"Okay, boys," she said. "Lift me!" We all broke into laughter.

Fast thinking was one of the keys to collaborating with Madonna. You had to be as quick as she was. When she pushes back, you damn well better be ready with an answer or a direction. She kept you on your toes every single moment. I was crazy about her.

After completing the work at Alley Kat, we moved to the Disney Studios to assemble the show on our stage. It was a major push to the very end. We had only a few weeks to piece everything together and complete the technical rehearsals. Madonna was dating Warren Beatty at the time, and he came by one day to watch the show, specifically the *Dick Tracy* section. She wanted Warren to give us notes.

After the run-through, Warren and I sat on the couch in Madonna's trailer waiting for her to change into comfortable clothes. She came out to greet us completely naked. "Madonna," I said. "Go put some clothes on."

"What's wrong?" she said playfully. "Can'cha handle it?"

"Oh, I can handle it," I said, "but we're going to have a serious conversation so, please, put some clothes on." Warren gave us a suggestion to put Madonna on the piano for "Sooner or Later," which I did.

The tour opened in Japan on April 13, 1990. It poured rain and was dangerous as hell as the dancers slipped and slid all over the stage. But we knew we had something very special and were dying to take it back to the States. The official US world tour kick-off was in Houston, Texas, on May 4, 1990. It was my fortieth birthday. My mom and her husband Hank came to the show, and it was glorious to share it with them. At the after-party, Madonna wheeled in a huge birthday cake and sang "Happy Birthday" to me. I felt like JFK being sung to by Marilyn Monroe.

The show catapulted Madonna beyond the stratosphere, leaving her female pop rivals in her wake. The controversial elements in Blond Ambition caused an additional stir and everyone from rabid fans to God-fearing detractors were talking about Madonna. Pope John Paul II condemned the show and called for Christians everywhere to boycott performances. He released a public statement through the Vatican calling the show an "abomination" and, yes, his most famous quote, "Satan has been rereleased into the world."

"Oh, my God," I thought with joy. "I did THAT?!?"

—

PHOTOS OF MADONNA IN her pale pink bustier and bleached blonde ponytail headlined newspapers and magazines. Video clips of segments of the show were broadcast around the world. *Rolling Stone* magazine named it "The Best Tour of 1990."

I didn't travel with the tour, except to fly to Stockholm to put the show in tip-top shape for the filming in Paris for the *Truth or Dare* documentary. When I saw it, after it being on tour, I was elated and proud but for one thing. By the time I got to Sweden, she had added nearly fifty "fucks" to her onstage banter to shock the audience. I mentioned to her that the show already had enough "shocking" moments, but with a smile she told me to "fuck off!" That was Madonna.

Madonna could also be sweet, adorable, and generous. She gave gifts, she took everyone to dinners at fantastic restaurants, and she invited the cast to go clubbing with her. She was gorgeous with her exquisite, porcelain skin and her wicked intellect. You can say anything you want about Madonna, but of any celebrity I've ever met, she knows how to *live*. She charges after everything she wants, usually gets it, and flourishes in the experience of living her life.

Critics and fans still talk about the Blond Ambition Tour as their favorite Madonna tour of all time. It was revolutionary. Madonna's intimate performance style influenced female pop stars including Lady Gaga, Britney Spears, and Beyoncé. More importantly, Madonna and I changed the face of pop tours from simple concerts to theatrical spectacles with themes, dazzling costumes, and extravagant production numbers.

In August 2016, twenty-six years after its premiere, *Madonna: Truth or Dare* (the documentary of the Blond Ambition Tour) was shown at MOMA in NYC. Madonna showed up for the screening in support of the film's director, Alek Keshishian. Guests were flabbergasted as Madonna sat through the movie with an entourage, including her exotically stunning daughter, Lourdes. As the final credits rolled, Madonna and her company began to leave the theater. I was standing in the back and, as she walked past me, I said, "Hi, Madonna."

"Vince," she said, grabbing my hand and kissing my cheek. Motioning toward the film screen, she said, "You did great work."

Vogue—Marie Antoinette

IT WAS 1990. THE Blond Ambition Tour had ended, and the MTV awards were about to happen. Madonna had decided to perform "Vogue" with the cast from the tour. She called to ask me if I could create yet another version of the song. After helping with the video and then conceiving a new interpretation for the tour, I wasn't sure I could find inspiration for yet another angle for "Vogue."

"I was thinking of putting the men in skirts and Donna, Niki, and me in men's suits," she said.

"But you've already done that," I replied. "Look, I'll go into a studio and if I feel I can create something new, I'll call you. And if I can't, you can find someone else."

In my closet, I had a collection of large fans leftover from a Diana Ross project that never happened. On a whim, I grabbed them. As I worked with the fans, I realized vogue-ing could be related to the gesturing of the mid-eighteenth-century men of the royal courts. I envisioned Madonna as Marie Antoinette as I played with the fans to the song. I called her, adrenalized.

"Madonna, I have an incredible idea. I have these large, lace fans, and I can create something with you as Marie Antoinette and everyone else as members of your court."

"That sounds like shit," said Madonna with a tang of humor in her voice.

She came to Alley Kat Studio to see what I had done. There was an earthquake just as she walked into the room. I remember pulling her into a doorway where we huddled together for some seconds of shaking. Then I showed her the piece.

As you may know, Madonna embraced the Marie Antoinette version of "Vogue" and opened the 1990 MTV music awards with it. It was stunning. She was dazzling. The performance became iconic, becoming viral before we knew what viral meant.

At the same time, I was directing an AIDS benefit in Los Angeles called Commitment To Life, starring Rod Stewart, Sarah Brightman, and Melissa Etheridge among others. It was happening the night immediately following the MTV awards. While running through the dance for the cameras in the afternoon of the MTV performance, I asked Madonna if she would be willing to open the Commitment To Life show with our Marie Antoinette "Vogue"...and not tell a soul it was going to happen. Of course, Madonna, who was a fervent activist at the front of the international AIDS crisis, jumped right on it.

The following evening, we opened the curtains in the intimate Wiltern Theater to Madonna, now the biggest female pop star in the world, and her incredible company. The packed house was treated to a live encore of her now buzzed-about Marie Antoinette "Vogue" and gave her and the dancers a seven-minute standing ovation.

The Academy Awards

MADONNA HAD RECORDED THE song "Sooner or Later" for the film *Dick Tracy*. It was written by Stephen Sondheim and nominated for an Academy Award. Madonna was asked to appear at the 1991 Oscars to perform the song. She called me.

"Hey, Vince. I'm gonna do Sondheim's song for the Oscars. Wanna have some fun?"

"I'd love to do it," I told her. "Why don't we push the Marilyn envelope and let's give the world a version of you they'll never forget."

We decided on four elements for the dance: a strapless beaded gown, a white mink stole, a stand-up microphone, and a hot pink Austrian-draped curtain. We rehearsed on Vine Street in Hollywood with a drummer and a pianist. It was just the four of us at the rehearsals and the ideas flowed easily between two creative friends. For her Oscar performance, I wanted a "gasp" moment at the top of the number, rising from beneath the floor in front of the pink Austrian drape. Madonna, in her strapless gown, sang the entire first verse with her back to the audience. After facing the audience, she sulked and oozed her way through the song in a terrific, titillating voice. A real chanteuse. Toward the finale, she smacked the floor with that white mink stole like a high-paid stripper, then, placing the microphone back in the stand, finished the song and slunk off the stage.

After the show, I drove home drunk on happiness. Sometimes things just go right. I listened to congratulatory phone messages from friends and family, then turned on the TV and watched the recorded segment. I grinned as I saw my name roll by on the screen with an entire single-card credit.

"Sooner or Later"
Choreography by Vincent Paterson

Things don't get better than this, I thought. The phone rang. It was about midnight. It was my father. "Hi, Hon. I just can't believe it," he was crying and drunk. "I watched the Academy Awards, and I still can't believe it!"

"What, Dad?"

"It's incredible. Did you know they said a BILLION people watched that program?"

"I think it was more like fifty thousand, Dad. But isn't that amazing?" I was still reeling, especially from the rare occurrence of having my name in the credits.

"Do you know what that means?" he asked.

"What, Dad?"

"That means A BILLION people saw my name up there!" Dear old Dad.

—

PEOPLE CAN LOVE HER or hate her, but Madonna's legacy is forever. After Blond Ambition, "Express Yourself," "Vogue," and her Oscar appearance, no one could touch her. And she wasn't done yet. Not with the world and not with me.

4.
Let's Get Physical
Dancing Through the '80s in La-La Land

I DIDN'T ARRIVE IN Hollywood and jump on the overnight-success train. Before I met Michael Jackson or Madonna, I made a lot of stops along the way, dancing in smaller jobs that kept me alive in between high-profile gigs. I want to paint a picture of the dance world in Hollywood in the eighties.

Being a successful working dancer in 1980s Los Angeles required a constant balance of on-going training while pursuing paid work however you could. I was able to enter the network of professional dancers and actually dance for a living after being hired by different choreographers.

Back then, there were no agencies representing dancers. Julie McDonald was a dancer who phoned me one day in the late eighties. "You don't know me, but everyone says I should ask your opinion. Do you think it would be a good idea to open a talent agency that represents dancers?"

"Absolutely," I replied.

Julie and her partner, Tony Selznick, (McDonald Selznick Associates) were the first of what are now many agencies throughout the country that represent dancers, directors, and choreographers. The dance agencies have changed the game for professional dancers outside Broadway. They have attempted to establish minimum wages, get credit for choreographers, make the environments safer, and make the work hours less backbreaking.

Before the existence of dance agencies, you got a dance gig in one of several ways: an audition through word of mouth, seeing a sign posted at a dance studio, or by receiving a direct phone call from a choreographer. When you got the gig, you kept your mouth shut during the rehearsals and did the work without complaining— no matter what the pay, the hours, the concrete floors, or lack of cleanliness in your workplace. You were getting paid to dance and fortunate to have the opportunity.

It wasn't as competitive in the late seventies and early eighties as it is today. Back then, I'd compete with three hundred other guys at an audition. Today, three thousand dancers might show up for a few available positions. I took classes in ballet, Graham, jazz, contemporary, and an acting class to keep me at the top of my game.

Each Hollywood choreographer had a distinctive style and had particular dancers with whom they tended to work. I was a dancer who moved among these dancing families. The major choreographers at the time were Alan Johnson, Scott Salmon, Lester Wilson, Michael Peters, Joe Bennett, Walter Painter, Tony Charmoli, Rob Iscove, Tony Stevens, Jacqui and Bill Landrum, Claude Thompson, Ron Field, Joanne DeVito, and Don Crichton. I had the pleasure of dancing for all of them.

—

TELEVISION SPECIALS INCLUDED THE Oscars, Emmys, Grammys, and variety shows created for celebrities like Cheryl Ladd, Lynda Carter, The Carpenters, David Copperfield, The Muppets, Dick Van Dyke, Danny Kaye, and The Osmonds. For those watching me on TV, I became an "almost" celebrity, one degree of separation from a real star. For these shows, there would be about a week of rehearsals before the taping. Bob Mackie often designed our wardrobe. The dancers only received group credits as the Scott Salmon Dancers, the Walter Painter Dancers, and the Alan Johnson Dancers.

In 1978, one of my first professional gigs was for choreographer Scott Salmon on the Grammys, dancing alongside the one-hit wonder Alicia Bridges for her song "I Love the Nightlife." It was the disco era, and we were squeezed into skin-tight, neon-colored stretch pants and tank tops.

I danced on one of Karen Carpenter's last television specials before her death. In one medley, each of the four male dancers individually performed a move with Karen then passed her off to the next dancer. My choreography was to hold her in my arms in a cradle lift. When I picked her up, the sick girl, suffering from anorexia nervosa, felt like she weighed sixty pounds. It was heartbreaking. She was incredibly gentle but seemed disoriented and couldn't hold her focus, as if a breath of wind might send her flying away.

In 1979, I danced on *A Christmas Together* with John Denver and The Muppets, choreographed by Tony Charmoli. I was a toy soldier with red painted cheeks dancing on a set with fake snow-covered pine trees, fake snowmen, and fake icicles—the perfectly fake Hollywood version of home. I met the kindly John Denver and Kermit on that gig, but the bonus was being kissed by Miss Piggy! A big, sloppy, wet kiss, and I have the photo to prove it.

At the 1980 Academy Awards, I had my second and final encounter with Bob Fosse while performing with Donald O'Connor for choreographer Walter Painter. Rehearsals were going beautifully until the producers decided they wanted a tap section for the opening number. Tap was one of the few genres I never studied. But I was still a dancer, and, well, a dancer dances! I sweated my ass off learning the new tap routine, practicing on every break and in my apartment. I must have done a reasonable job of faking a lot of air taps in rehearsal because I was put in the front line for the show. On stage at the Dorothy Chandler Pavilion in Downtown Los Angeles, the opening tap number began. There I was in the front line, nervous as hell, hoping to not be exposed as the tapping fraud I was. When I looked into the audience, Bob Fosse was sitting directly in front of me in the first row. I knew he'd been a hoofer since age nine, and he was staring straight at my feet. My only choice was to dance my heart out, smiling so hard that my cheeks hurt, trying desperately to lure Mr. Fosse's attention upward to my face, far, far away from my feet. The three-minute number felt like it dragged on for a year, and I was praying he wouldn't remember the identical toothy grin from my nightmare audition a few years prior singing "Swing Low, Sweet Chariot."

In the early eighties, I had an especially memorable time on the TV special *CBS: On the Air*. I was one of several dozen male dancers who wore pink coattails and pink top hats in a glamorous number featuring Bea Arthur and Lucille Ball, who wore formal evening gowns. A pie would be thrown in the faces of the two stars at the conclusion of the number as a comedic button to the serious routine. I was chosen to throw the pie in Lucy's face. It was a whipped-cream pie, which weighed practically nothing, and the pie had to be hurled from off-camera to get the laugh the writers intended. Throughout the rehearsal week, I had daily practice throwing pie after pie at a circle on a wall ten feet away. I got pretty good.

On the day of the shoot, there was a lot of tension on the set as other performances were late being filmed and overtime dollars were cha-chinging in everyone's mental calculator—happily for us, not too happily for the producers. Finally, we reached the pink hat and tails number. My fellow pie-throwing dancer and I were pulled aside by the choreographer and the producers.

"Guys, this is the twilight shot," he said. (Meaning the last shot of the day.) "We're running waaay overtime. Please, please, hit the ladies with the pies on the first throw. If you only partially hit them, they'll have to have their hair and makeup completely redone. We don't want this to happen, do we, guys?"

Not nervous. No pressure. Hell, no!

"Action!"

I started dancing far upstage from the camera and slowly danced my way forward. I hurried off-camera to grab the pie and positioned myself for the big moment. The ladies stepped into their final poses. With pie in hand and fierce determination in my heart, I hurled the crème missile! My partner hit Bea square in the center of her face. My pie only skimmed the side of Lucy's head.

A huge groan was heard throughout the soundstage. I was mortified. "Okay! Everybody, take a break! Ladies, we'll take you back to hair and makeup."

It was a deadly silent break. The other dancers looked at me with pity on their faces. Nobody spoke to me. Half an hour later, the ladies were back, and we began filming once again. We picked up the action where my partner and I danced off to get the pies. The ladies danced into their final positions. I prayed to any God that was listening, "Please let me nail Lucy."

With savage determination, I hurled that pie with the focus and precision of a major league pitcher in a World Series playoff, and my pie smacked Ms. Ball right between the eyes. Her head recoiled like a bobblehead on the dash of a '57 Chevy. Maybe it was a little too hard, but I nailed it. "That's a wrap!"

Leaving the CBS studios that night, I stepped into the elevator and Lucille Ball was standing there. "Ms. Ball," I said humbly, "my name is Vincent, and I was the one who threw the pie at you. I'm so sorry that I missed the first time."

She looked at me and in her deep-throated, gravelly voice from years of smoking Chesterfields said, "Honey, I don't know what the hell they were thinking. It's really hard to throw a whipped-cream pie from off-camera and hit your mark. But you know what's harder than that? Throwing a pie at Lucy!" As if I needed one more reason to love her.

I worked on a TV special that honored hair and makeup artists. I was chosen to accompany Bette Davis to and from the stage for every rehearsal and the show. Ms. Davis campaigned for years to create an Oscar category for hair and makeup. She felt they were the quintessential creative magicians on a film set yet were not acknowledged by the Academy of Motion Picture Arts and Sciences. I sat with her in her backstage dressing room while she smoked cigarette after cigarette, filling the room with a thick haze.

"Tell me 'bout chaself," she instructed. I gave her a brief history of my life in Hollywood. She really listened. "You're a nice kid," she said, in a way only Bette Davis could.

Television series such as *The Carol Burnett Show, The Redd Foxx Show,* and *The Osmonds* had their regular stable of dancers, but choreographers could bring in extra dancers for larger production numbers. I danced on all three of those shows. I never got to dance on *Solid Gold* but would have loved to.

Jacqui and Bill Landrum were asked by director Stanley Donen to choreograph a piece called "Big Man on Mulberry Street" for Bruce Willis and Cybill Shepherd on an episode of their TV series *Moonlighting.* I danced in the Landrums' Emmy-nominated, seven-minute piece, as did a slew of others who have now become names in the dance world: Jerry Mitchell, who directs and choreographs for Broadway; Sandahl Bergman, who was one of Bob Fosse's muses; Bonnie Story, who won an Emmy for her choreography of Disney's *High School Musical*; and Suzi Lonergan, one of the wisest and most popular pilates teachers in Los Angeles. I was also a member of Landrum Dance Theater in which I danced and choreographed my first company work.

I became a regular on the television series *Barbara Mandrell and the Mandrell Sisters* with Barbara, Louise, and Irlene Mandrell in the early eighties. Working with Barbara was like having your favorite sibling as your boss. Her support and kindness toward everyone working on the show made us all feel like family. The series ran for two seasons on NBC, from 1980 to 1982. Musical numbers and special guest performers were interspersed with family-friendly comedy sketches and seasonal spoofs.

Scott Salmon, on whose mantel should live a lifetime Mr. Congeniality award, choreographed the show. In the beginning of the first season, Barbara nervously told Scott, "Now, Scott, I have some concern about offending my country fans by having Hollywood dancers on the show." I was the first dancer hired. I appeared as a tuxedo-clad mannequin in a store window. In rehearsals, Barbara and Dolly Parton passed by the storefront and I was allowed to make one simple shift of my body. Barbara considered this for days before giving it the go-ahead. That was the first episode. But Barbara quickly fell in love with dance, with Scott, and with the dancers Scott brought in.

The second year, I was cast as Barbara's permanent partner and given a season contract. We began a new show every Monday. Scott would create on the three male dancers first, including Charles Ward (who was later replaced by Joe Malone), Ken Grant, and me. Eventually the Mandrells' would join us. Barbara learned quickly and with such ease, though I have a series of hysterical photos that show her clinging to me like a baby chimpanzee on its mother's back. We did everything from screwball sketches to an elaborate dance incorporating an array of dance styles. Barbara and I both prize a photo of us looking like John Travolta and Karen Lynn Gorney in an homage to *Saturday Night Fever*. In a Halloween spoof, dressed as Frankenstein in twelve-inch-high platform shoes, I partnered tiny Barbara, my Bride of Frankenstein. I often felt like Fred Astaire with Ginger Rogers in his arms.

Working on that show created a treasured bond. Deadlines could make things tense and the sisters had a lot to learn, but, damn, we had a good time. There is a blooper reel from the show on YouTube, and you can see how much fun the show was and how quick Barbara was to laugh at herself. And every week, Barbara introduced the three lead male dancers to her television audience. That recognition meant a lot to us.

Other country performers I've worked with include Dolly Parton, LeAnn Rimes, Minnie Pearl, Roy Rogers and Dale Evans, Wynonna Judd, John Denver, and Andraé Crouch. They all seemed to have a healthy perspective on fame. Maybe it's religion, maybe it's a family consciousness, but a different kind of happiness appeared to guide them, rather than stardom ruling their lives.

—

COMMERCIALS WERE THE GOLD mines every dancer hoped to claim. If you booked a commercial under a Screen Actors Guild contract, the biggest union for performers, you could earn a huge salary and be assured health insurance for a year. I once danced in a Maybelline commercial behind Lynda Carter. I had one day of rehearsal and a one-day shoot executing a pirouette and running through the background with a cheesy smile on my face. It resulted in about four seconds of screen time, and I made about $50,000 in residual payments because of the SAG contract. Had it been a nonunion job I would have walked away with only a day rate of a couple hundred dollars. I also choreographed my first big commercial with Lionel Richie directed by Bob Giraldi. I got to use all my dancing friends and appear in the commercial as well.

Every dancer wanted to be in a commercial directed by Joe Pytka, the King of Commercials. It was an assurance that the commercial would air so you would get residuals, and you knew you would be treated like royalty on the set because Joe loves dancers. His sets were gorgeous, the costumes easy to dance in, overtime aplenty, and his catered craft-services table was the best in town.

After meeting Joe through Michael Jackson, I became his choreographer for hundreds of commercials. He trusted me, handing me the storyboards, allowing me to cast the dancers, rehearsing the work, and bringing him a final product ready to film. Remember the Ray Charles "Uh-Huh, Diet Pepsi" spots? Joe called me one day. "Pepsi wants three girls to back-up Ray Charles," he said. "They want Naomi Campbell, Christie Brinkley, and somebody else. I think we can do it with dancers. Can you find three gorgeous girls who look and dance great? We'll do a screen test with some choreography and costumes."

We did, and we sold the idea to the Pepsi executives, launching over fifty commercials starring the "Uh-Huh" Girls—Darlene Dillinger, Gretchen Palmer, and Meilani Paul. Joe and I collaborated on commercials for almost three decades with so many luminaries— Ray Charles, Ringo Starr, Faith Hill, Tracey Ullman, Charles Barkley, Shakira, Bo Jackson, Carl Reiner, and Kathy Griffin, among others. Many of our commercials won Cleos (the Oscar for commercials) for Joe. But no awards for choreographers. I love choreographing commercials, and it thrills me to give commercial gigs to dancers. I get to work with the best directors in the world while challenging myself to design the most appropriate physical dialogue for a short amount of airtime.

There were several feature film gigs for dancers during the eighties. Some breakout films left indelible dance moments branded in our brains and became cultural phenomena all their own, like *Fame, Flashdance, Staying Alive, Breakin' 2: Electric Boogaloo*, and *Dirty Dancing*. I danced in the original *Footloose* with Kevin Bacon. If you look hard you can find me in the borderline-hysterical, over-jubilant, closing dance scene at the warehouse prom. I am wearing, once again, a pink tuxedo! I also choreographed my first feature film, *Mannequin*, with Andrew McCarthy and Kim Cattrall. Choreographing *Hook* for Steven Spielberg and *Havana* for Sydney Pollack also gave me more opportunities to put dancers of all ages into the mix.

I had a fantastic time being featured in several music videos. I played a dancing wolf-man in Diana Ross's "Pieces of Ice," capturing Miss Ross from her sequin-studded solitude on a deserted island. I played a rock musician with a mullet in Lionel Richie's "Dancing on the Ceiling" and a grease-covered, dancing garage mechanic with Billy Joel in "Uptown Girl," all of us pining to get near the breathtaking Christie Brinkley. I was the answer to Olivia Newton-John's need to be "Totally Hot" in that video, shot by Vilmos Zsigmond. The funniest video in which I ever danced was Mel Brooks's "To Be Or Not To Be" in 1983. Mel Brooks played a "rapping" Hitler and choreographer Alan Johnson had me play a shirtless Nazi soldier strapped to a pillar like Saint Sebastian, "tortured" by three gorgeous female dancers: Diane Day Crump-Richmond, Jamilah Halvorson, Sara Miles de Levita. There were a lot of laughs on that set. I was the only performer from the "Beat It" video who reprised his role in Weird Al Yankovic's parody video, "Eat It." Rather than have my hand tied to my rival gang leader for the knife fight, I suggested holding onto a rubber chicken.

My presence in the music video world also gave me opportunities to choreograph. I had David Lee Roth dancing in "California Girls" and staged Paul McCartney and his band in "Stranglehold." I created the moves for Van Halen in "Hot For Teacher." If you watch the video, you may see the early seeds of the crotch grab during the refrain: *"Got it bad, got it bad, got it bad..."* Al Gore's wife, Tipper, presented this video to a Senate panel as an example of how MTV was destroying the morality of American youth. I never saw myself as some kind of iconoclast, we were having fun.

Choreographing videos for artists like George Harrison, Sheena Easton, Jermaine Jackson, Buster Poindexter, Joni Mitchell, Julie Brown, the Divinyls, Brenda Russell, Hall & Oates, and Donna Summers allowed me to use some fantastic Los Angeles dancers.

Dancers were also employed in industrials, which are live shows produced by major corporations to present and demonstrate a new product. Cruise ship gigs saved some dancers' lives by providing steady pay. The shows on cruise ships these days have become spectacular forms of entertainment. Celebrities also played showrooms in Las Vegas and Tahoe casinos and always had dancers to back them up. I danced for The Osmonds, Barbara Mandrell, and Shirley MacLaine in Vegas.

Toward the end of the eighties, after the success of Michael Jackson's *BAD* Tour and Madonna's Blond Ambition Tour, pop artists hired dancers for their tours as the essential ingredient to make the show scintillate. But the pop tour experience can be a double-edged sword. Plucked from obscurity, dancers spend a year with a major recording star on stage as well as at clubs, restaurants, award events, and parties, amassing social media fans by the millions. The dancers appear on TV, in magazines, and, in some cases, marry the star, like Britney Spears and K. Fed. After one year of living a jet-setter's life, the tour ends. After tasting fame, generous paychecks, and traveling in limos and private jets, they return to their apartment in Hollywood or the San Fernando Valley with three roommates and have to begin job hunting.

Dancing on a pop tour can be a life-altering experience for the dancer, but it can be traumatic if not managed wisely. Particularly when their celebrity "best friend" has moved on to the next group of talented dancers for the next tour and they get left behind. But if you're an artist, if you have to dance to live, you'll survive. You'll find a way. Hell, you may even make it big.

Think it. Speak it. Ink it.

Then put it on your fridge.

5.
Shirley, Diana, and Hal...Oh, My!

MORE THAN ONCE DURING my career, I've found myself in challenging situations. There were three specific encounters with three of my artistic heroes that challenged my desire to remain in the entertainment industry. These encounters not only taught me who I wanted to be as an artist, but also about behavior I never wanted to emulate. Creative life lessons courtesy of Shirley MacLaine, Miss Diana Ross, and Hal Prince.

Shirley MacLaine

IN THE LATE SEVENTIES, Alan Johnson, one of the most respected choreographers on both coasts, was revamping Shirley MacLaine's wildly successful touring act. It included a male and female Caucasian couple and a male and female African-American couple. Shirley was replacing the white male dancer and black female dancer. Alan had won several Emmys. His choreography was extremely technical, and his rhythms were intricate. I had worked for him several times and he offered me the job. I was beside myself.

Shirley MacLaine could do no wrong, as far as I was concerned. I had read her books and seen her movies. As a performer, she was absolute perfection, and I followed her new-age guru-ism with a passion. Dancing for her tour would be the first long-term dance gig I'd had, as prior dance jobs lasted a week or less. I'd also be assured a steady paycheck. This was the dream.

The tour was open-ended, with the contracts stating no final dates. It was to begin in Reno, Tahoe, and Vegas, travel to Sydney, Melbourne, and Toronto, and then return to Vegas, ad infinitum. In Vegas, Reno, and Tahoe, each of the dancers' names would be on the marquee with Shirley's. With much smaller letters, of course, but my name in lights next to Shirley MacLaine!!! Mind. Blown.

There were a few realities that became evident early on in rehearsals: Larry Vickers, the dance captain, was very tight with Shirley. He had her ear. He could be sexually suggestive in a humorous way, and it all worked for Shirley. She preferred the Black dancers to the white dancers, seeming to feel extra hip when Larry and Jamilah Halvorson joked with her.

Shirley was a damn hard worker, and she demanded the same of everyone else. I loved that. She could be very "gypsy" friendly. ("Gypsies" is the moniker given to singers and dancers, usually in musical theater, because they travel from show to show.) I had not yet worked intimately with enough celebrities to realize that most celebrities never fully descend from the world of stardom no matter how chummy they appear to be with the dancers, the extras, or pretty much everyone else on the crew. Larry and Claire Culhane had been with Shirley for a while and knew how to work with her. I believed that if I tried hard enough, I could become a part of that well-oiled machine.

I was in great physical form. I have always been a freak about technique and that, combined with my insecurity at having started dancing at twenty-three and the fear of not being good enough, kept me in class. If I wasn't working a gig, I was in class. When I came into Shirley's world, I was all about the dancing. Even though Jamilah and I were both new, Larry seemed to put the emphasis on my being perfect in the rehearsals. He often corrected me in front of Shirley, but I felt it was his role, and I appreciated the opportunity to improve.

It wasn't long into performing the shows in Tahoe and Reno, that I began to have an inkling of tension in the atmosphere. Before every show, I would go to the stage and give myself a full class. It was my preparation and my meditation. My ritual began to instigate comments from Larry like, "You know, you don't need to work that hard. You already know the show."

During each performance, I stood in the wings mesmerized, watching Shirley deliver her monologues and "patter" to the audience. In every show, she hit the exact same beats, the exact same punch lines, the exact same pauses, making the audience think that she was lost in a memory or trying to collect just the right word to finish her already superbly written and completely memorized script. What seemed like a spontaneous comment or gesture from her was always a carefully sculpted piece of her act. I was repeatedly in awe of how she delivered 100 percent night after night, no matter what had happened to her personally during the day. Shirley was dedicated to precision, and I wanted to be the same.

The other dancers began to kid me about how I was in love with Shirley. Soon after, and I admit it could have been my imagination, I sensed subtle innuendos coming from Shirley—little looks and touches. I didn't know if it was all in my head. Shirley had no partner at the time. If she was open to something happening between us, she was letting me know it in such a subtle way that if it happened and went sour, she could easily claim she never brought it on. Not a single word about it was ever spoken aloud by either of us.

Sensing some sort of unspoken pressure from Shirley, I began to feel more and more isolated and alone within the tour. I felt distressed that my reverence for Shirley was beginning to crumble. There was no one on the tour that I could turn to. And then it got worse.

We went to Australia. I met a guy after one of the shows, and we began dating. He was a MacLaine fan and I took him backstage to meet Shirley, which was not uncommon because she would always sign autographs and take pictures with fans. I'll never forget the look on Shirley's face as I introduced my date, as if I had overstepped a boundary and completely offended her. She looked at him, then me, then with an off-the-cuff laugh, turned to someone else in the dressing room and ignored us.

Not long after this backstage incident, Shirley made an extravagant production of buying gifts for the dancers. She staged an event, having us open our gifts in front of everyone. I can't recall the exact gifts that the girls and Larry received. I can tell you that they were generous and beautiful, perhaps scarves, perhaps a leather coat. Shirley had exquisite taste. My turn. I opened the box from Shirley and pulled out…a woman's brown leather handbag with a thin shoulder strap. Not a man-purse, not a European satchel. *It was obviously a woman's purse.* A long, awkward silence fell over everyone as I held it up, completely flummoxed about what to say.

"Thank you, Shirley," I think I said. She shot me a smile as enigmatic as the Mona Lisa's. Claire, my dance partner, later acknowledged how awkward and uncomfortable that whole moment was. It gave me some consolation to know someone else caught on to the strangeness. I was learning more than I had ever wanted to know about Shirley.

The tour proceeded to Toronto and things settled into a pattern that I simply learned to navigate. It was in Toronto that I met Carl Dias, who would eventually become an important long-term relationship in my life. I brought Carl backstage to meet Shirley. It was no different from what had happened in Australia. It was embarrassing, and I apologized to Carl for Shirley's rudeness. My intuition was telling me that something was seriously wrong between us. No one on the team would confirm that I was being singled out with her harshness. Everyone seemed frightened of Shirley. I loved the ideal vision of my job, but this was becoming more than unpleasant. My insecurity mounted. And still…it got worse.

The highlight of the show was a production number set to "Sweet Georgia Brown" for which Alan had created dance segments incorporating several dance styles. We'd demonstrate Bob Fosse's style with precise hand and head movements, then Michael Kidd's style with cowboy gymnastics and the cancan. It was fun and a crowd-pleaser.

We had minor costume changes to augment the specific dance styles—white gloves and black Bowler hats for Fosse, cowboy hats and white neckerchiefs for Michael Kidd. During the musical vamp to each new section, Shirley told the audience a bit about the particular choreographer. We would dress Shirley as she spoke and change ourselves in preparation for the next section of dance. One segment was dedicated to Lester Wilson and the funk. In this section we wore fluorescent, oversized pimp hats and bright yellow suspenders. Larry helped Shirley into an orange, fluorescent, ostrich-feather bolero jacket, and I was charged with putting on her belt.

Alan had created a bit of business with that belt that always got Shirley an enormous laugh. At one end was a massive sequined medallion backed by Velcro. I had to stand behind Shirley while she spoke into the microphone, wrapping my arms around her waist and squeeze the Velcro-backed medallion to the other end of the belt so it attached. Three strands of beads, in different lengths, draped from the medallion at her belly and hung in a half-circle under the bottom of her ass. At one point in the dance, Shirley would turn upstage to the four dancers, her back to the audience, and shimmy her ass to make the beads dance as they slid up and down her bottom. It was like an early version of twerking. Audiences howled and Shirley knew how to milk it just right. Placing the belt around Shirley was, like everything else in the show, a tightly crafted piece of choreography, always timed exactly right so she could turn around, shake the beads, and work her magic. But it was not rocket science. It was Velcro.

Though her fabulous legs could have been insured with Lloyds of London, Shirley's body was shaped rather squarely. Her weight would go up and down week to week, and it would always reflect in her midsection, basically, her belly and waist. Unfortunately, the belt had been fitted to the thinnest version of Shirley. It only stayed attached by Velcro and, worse, the strands of beads were not strung on elastic. It had no stretch whatsoever. Depending on what was happening with Shirley's body that week, sometimes the Velcro wouldn't hold and the belt would fall. The gag would be ruined.

It was after Australia that the belt started to fall off during about 30 percent of the shows. We would all anticipate it when we noticed she had gained weight. Shirley's losing the biggest laugh in the biggest number of the show became solely my fault. I was now inept. I didn't know how to attach a Velcro belt.

It was a very simple fix. String the beads with elastic and add a little more belt length. Yet, I had no support in resolving the situation. No one wanted to confront Shirley because no one wanted to tell her she was heavier at times. I went to the costume designer, Bill Hargate, and made suggestions, but he wouldn't change a thing. I went to the road manager, nothing. I talked to Larry, nothing.

Instead, everything became about my inability to properly attach two pieces of Velcro. I was made to feel like an incompetent hack. Because of my ineptitude, I was now required to go to Shirley's dressing room before every performance for a "belt rehearsal." I had to perform the belt attachment as she talked with people and dealt with wardrobe, hair, and makeup. She would, of course, suck in her belly in the dressing room for all to see that she was right and I was wrong and the belt would stay on. I had to put the belt on her a dozen times, while counting, to prove that I could perform the task. The sole purpose of this "rehearsal" was to humiliate me in front of others.

On stage it was a crapshoot as to whether or not she'd remember to hold her belly in when she turned around so the belt wouldn't fall. If the belt popped open, she would blow up all over again. Everyone felt Shirley's wrath when the belt fell off. And everyone blamed me.

During what became my final performance, I solidly attached the Velcro around Shirley's waist. Then each dancer took a turn presenting an individual short solo. When Shirley's solo came, she turned upstage, pushed out her belly, and the belt fell off. We dancers were facing the audience and Shirley was facing me. Through gritted teeth, she said, "When are you gonna get this fucking belt RIGHT?" I had to keep smiling and dancing as she spun back around to the audience full of good cheer.

That night the road manager told me Shirley wanted to talk to me. I went to her dressing room. I will never forget her words.

"You're fired," she seethed. "You have absolutely no talent. You don't know what it means to be a professional. You will never, EVER, make it in this business."

I was devastated.

On the other hand, it was a relief.

About a month later, Shirley was back in Vegas and the dancer who was hired to replace me got the mumps. I received a call from the road manager. "We have a few weeks left," he said. "Shirley wants to know if you'll come back and finish out the show in Vegas."

I asked for twenty-four hours to consider it, my wounds still raw and stinging.

I agreed to go back but with a salary bump. I was rehired. I arrived in Vegas the next morning and learned two new dance numbers that afternoon. Shirley didn't rehearse with us. I worked with Larry, Claire, and Jamilah. I first saw Shirley that night when we walked through the new numbers on stage behind the closed curtain. She was pleasant and acted as if nothing had ever gone down, which made it easier for all of us. The curtain rose and I performed every number without a single hiccup. The belt stayed on. That night after the show, Shirley walked up several flights of stairs to my backstage dressing room. She kindly thanked me for saving her ass and replacing the sick dancer. She also told me I was a true professional. I finished out the run in Vegas without incident.

I was young. I was naïve. I don't know all the mistakes I made with Shirley's tour, but perhaps I was too eager to be the best I could be and maybe others thought I was very full of myself. We all have to be passionate and aggressive when we start out or we won't have the guts to try anything.

And there is a coda to this story…

Ten years later, I directed a Commitment to Life AIDS benefit at Universal Amphitheater. Bernie Taupin produced this star-studded event that featured Elton John, Liza Minnelli, Barbra Streisand, Johnny Mathis, Billy Joel, Natalie Cole, Kenny Loggins, Eddie Van Halen, Patti LaBelle, Sheila E, and Wynonna Judd. Bernie and I asked Shirley to host the show.

She was polite to me during rehearsals and, when the curtain fell, told me I was a fantastic director. I wondered whether she remembered what had transpired between us a decade before. I have the feeling she never forgets a thing.

Miss Diana Ross

AS A YOUNG TEENAGER in the late sixties, my major infatuation was an off-the-charts sexy diva, and if I had known back then I would one day work with her…I never would have believed it.

The Supremes were the ultimate girl group of the sixties. And when Diana Ross, the lead singer, appeared on *Ed Sullivan*, *Bandstand*, and record albums with her big Keene-like, heavily lined eyes, pouty lips, and asymmetrical haircut shaved in the back, teased high on top with the long spit curl by her left ear, I thought she was the hottest thing ever.

The first interaction I had with Diana Ross was in 1968. I was about to turn eighteen, and my mom asked me what I wanted for my birthday. The only thing I wanted was to see the Supremes at the Latin Casino Nightclub in Cherry Hill, New Jersey. I thought this would be an impossible request. Mom had very little money; we didn't even have a car. My mom was dating a man named Ralph at the time, and they surprised me with not one, but four tickets to see the Supremes and turned the evening into a double date. I brought a girlfriend who attended Sun Valley High School with me, Jeannie Melton.

When we arrived, we were told that our reservations couldn't be found and they were sold out. I was devastated. The ideal evening was dissolving rapidly as I thought, "My world is empty without you, Diana." Ralph, however, told us to sit tight. He disappeared inside.

Moments later, the maître d' appeared in his tux to escort Mom, Jeannie, and I inside. No Ralph. We followed our host, and Ralph was waiting at a table directly in front of the stage. He had told the maître d' that I was going into basic training tomorrow and would soon be shipped out to Vietnam. This was, of course, a horrific lie. But any ounce of guilt I may have felt quickly disappeared when the Supremes took the stage and the spotlight fell on the girl of my dreams, Miss Diana Ross. I knew in my heart of hearts that she sang every single song that night to me.

Fast-forward fifteen years to 1983. I had become a working dancer in Los Angeles and Michael Peters's protégé. Michael cast me as the love interest and dance partner to Diana Ross in her music video "Pieces of Ice." He choreographed the video, Bob Giraldi directed it, and we shot it in New York City. My character was an Arctic white wolf that turned into a heroic young savior to rescue Diana from her forlorn island of ice. I shared my Latin Casino experience with Diana and told her how her music was a momentous part of the soundtrack of my teenage years. Her response was cordial. Everyone in the cast and crew had to call her Miss Ross except Bob, Michael, and me. We called her Diana.

Diana wore a red sequined catsuit. The only unpleasant moment during the shoot was when I had to dance with her on my shoulders and the sequins ripped the skin on my neck and shoulders to shreds. But it was a small price to pay to get to work with the heartthrob of my adolescence.

In July of '83, Diana was planning her live concert in Central Park, and I was asked to reprise my role in her "Pieces of Ice" section of the show. It never happened. The concert did, but I didn't. I got strep throat and had to give up the role to my friend David Gibson. David was sometimes my dancing bookend as we were both six feet tall with light hair and blue eyes. It made it slightly less painful having my friend take over my role as I sat in my apartment and watched the performance on TV, crying through my antibiotics.

The third and final experience I shared with Diana was in the late eighties when I received a phone call from her, asking me to choreograph and direct her new world tour. She had seen my work with Michael Jackson, and they had obviously talked. I was flown to Connecticut where we sat in a beautifully spacious room overlooking her lush estate as she told me, "I loved Michael's show. I was hoping you'd direct and choreograph my new show. I really want to reinvent myself with the tour. You know, work some magic. How would you like to be the mastermind behind the new Diana?" she laughed.

Her voice reminded me of Michael Jackson's voice, soft-spoken and gentle, just a few decibels above a whisper. I was thrilled, inspired, and ready to get started, but there was a catch. "You're gonna have to put the show together without me at first. I have to go to Switzerland and have some dental surgery. But you can send me tapes and I can learn the show, then you can put me in it when I get to LA."

I made a monstrous error in not requesting a list of the songs she wanted to include in the show, but she never mentioned it, so I figured she was leaving it up to me. I went back to LA and got to work.

I began by brainstorming a list of songs I thought would be most theatrically effective for her show. When I shared my list with her musical director, he was thrilled. He told me how for years Diana had performed the same songs for every show. She also performed them at lightning speed so that the audience never had the chance to revisit the romanticism that the memory of each song could provide. Her fans were going to love this show, we were positive.

In my lineup, she would open with one of my favorite Diana Ross dance recording, "Love Hangover." The song begins with a slow, sensual rhythm and suddenly explodes into an infectious dance tune. Diana would emerge, center, in the midst of a luscious drape of red fabric that would cover the entire stage like an immense flowing gown. Larger than life, Diana would start singing the slow opening. Then, once the up-tempo kicked in, the whole dress would... *whoosh*...get sucked into the stage floor in a matter of seconds and reveal Diana with her team of dancers who had been under the fabric the entire time. This was ten years before Franco Dragone used a similar concept for the opening of Cirque du Soleil's water show "O."

I wanted to highlight Diana's career with a section on the Supremes that would begin with a lone dancer, center stage, watching the *Ed Sullivan Show* on a TV set. Ed Sullivan's amplified voice would introduce, "Ladies and Gentleman, The Supremes!" The sound of the Supremes hit "Come See About Me" would begin as they performed it on the show in 1964. The TV and the dancer would magically disappear as Diana and her two female backup singers appeared in a spotlight at the top of a long staircase. As they descended the stairs, the trio would sing Supremes' songs—"Baby Love," "Stop! In the Name of Love"—as Diana traveled farther and farther forward until they stepped off the staircase. Diana would move in front of the two Supremes as they sang "Someday We'll be Together," the last hit they made before the group broke up, illustrating Diana's journey from a Supreme to her solo career as Diana Ross.

Diana had been nominated for an Academy Award for *Lady Sings the Blues*, so I created a Billie Holiday section. A medley of three songs was set on a Harlem street corner with a streetlamp and a decaying wall of an old brownstone with a front stoop. Diana would appear as Lady Day, singing emotional songs like "Good Morning Heartache" and "Strange Fruit" with perhaps just a solo saxophonist and an upright bass.

I admired Diana so much. I wanted to create an evening that would cover her most popular songs but also incorporate songs that she didn't usually include in her live performances. For several weeks in LA, I continued developing the entire show from start to finish. The band would rehearse in one room and the dancers and background singers would work with me in another. I had one check-in phone call with Diana because she wanted to be assured everyone was working hard and to let me know she would be in LA soon to learn the show.

Everyone was happy. More than happy, ecstatic. Her managers were ecstatic. The musical director, her backup singers, and the musicians were ecstatic. The dancers were ecstatic. Everyone who knew Diana and had worked with her for years expressed to me that this was exactly what Diana needed to revitalize her career as a current female superstar. The show was fresh and would give both her traditional and newer fans everything they expected, as well as some electrifying surprises. She must have been curious about all the fuss because the next request I got from Diana was to videotape a rehearsal to give her an idea of what the show looked like and so she could start to learn the choreography from afar.

I borrowed a VHS camera and set it up in our rehearsal room, recording the sections we felt ready to share. I wanted to show her the basic structure of the concert and the range of musical selections. There was a minimum of choreography for her and a lot going on around her to make the show appear big. When we finished that day, I handed the tape to her management team who made a copy and sent the footage to Diana.

Three days later at the studio, there was a lot of whispered commotion among the musical director, some long-time band members, and Diana's management team. Certainly something was going down and none of us in the rehearsal room could figure out what it was. Someone from her management team told me that Diana was on the phone and wanted to talk to me. "Hi, Diana, this is Vincent. How is everything going?"

"What are you trying to do to me?" she screamed over the phone. "Are you trying to destroy my career? Where are my HITS?"

I was taken off guard. "Your hits? Well, Diana," I said. "ALL of these songs are your hits. They're all number ones. I haven't used anything other than your songs that people love. To me, any song you sing is incredible."

"I don't care about that. Where are my HITS???? My HITS????"

"Diana, I'm your typical audience, and these are the hits I'd want to hear you sing. I also thought it would be great to have you in some more theatrical moments…" I went on defending what I'd created and how much I thought it was exactly what everyone concerned wanted the show to be for her. She kept repeating over and over again, "Do you hear me? Where are my HITS???? My HITS???"

"Do you want to go over a list with me because you never told me what songs had to be in the show," I suggested, "I thought you would be happy with my vision."

"No," she said. "I'm not doing this show. We're gonna sit down and talk about this when I come to LA."

She stopped talking, and I handed the phone to her manager. He later told me, "Miss Ross said, 'Tell him to terminate all of the dancers. Then we'll see what his vision is.'" I sadly told the marvelous dancers that the gig was over. They lost contracts and money, and I felt responsible. They were as confused as I was as we hugged and kissed and they left the studio. I wondered why I hadn't been fired as it was really my fault. Then I remembered I was under a "pay or play" contract, meaning Diana would have to pay me whether or not I completed the job. I had a feeling our upcoming talk was going to be about whether or not she'd get her money's worth out of me or simply take the loss.

The following night I invited the recently fired dancers over to my house for a home-cooked meal to commiserate. They were very upset, as was I, and it seemed important that we all get together and provide mutual support. After dinner, we decided to watch the video that was sent to Diana.

Oh. My. God. As we watched it, we quickly understood what most likely prompted Diana's outburst. It's hard to say what was the most shocking section of the video we sent Diana. There was one ballad, lip-synched by one of the singers in the foreground of the image standing in for Diana. Unknowingly, in the background of the shot, two male dancers were practicing partner dance steps and lifts they would eventually perform with Diana in other segments of the show. They were taking turns playing Diana's part as they danced with each other. But now they appeared to be performing a gay, erotic ballet. So, yes, that looked ridiculous, especially if you didn't know it was a mistake. And how could she have known it wasn't choreographed this way? And there was more.

The dancers thought the camera had stopped recording. In a moment of innocent fun, several of them put on a huge Afro wig and performed impersonations of Diana. They emphasized calling themselves "Miss Ross," the Golden Rule they had to follow. One dancer captured Diana's diva stage persona in a *Saturday Night Live*-type sketch singing "Touch Me in the Morning!"

Miss Ross obviously did not see any humor in this segment of the tape. Perhaps she was never one to laugh at herself. I, unfortunately, never got to ask her.

I was paid my contracted salary without creating a single moment for Diana's tour that year. So I, too, was essentially fired. I was sad to not have had the chance to create what could have been a fantastic evening and perhaps one that would have presented Miss Ross in a theatrical, contemporary way. We'll never know.

Hal Prince

THE RIVALRY BETWEEN HOLLYWOOD artists and Broadway artists may not be as intense as it once was—now that Disney musicals occupy most of Times Square and movie actors star in Broadway productions—but during the eighties it was savage. New York City artists often had an anti-Hollywood attitude when it came to our work or us. Those who created for Hollywood—films, videos, tours, television—were often regarded by the NYC element as artists who had "sold out" and weren't as artistic as those who created for Broadway. I crossed that perilous divide in the winter of 1992.

Theater was my first love, from shows at my nan's house to junior high and high school plays, to Dickinson and Society Hill Playhouse—my time in the theater inspired all of my work.

When I got the call from my agent that *the* Hal Prince was directing *Kiss of the Spider Woman* and wanted me as the choreographer, I realized I was being invited into the exclusive world of Broadway royalty. Hal Prince was a creative God to me and was always at the top of the list as someone with whom I one day hoped to collaborate. He had brought to life some of my favorite musicals including *Evita* and *Cabaret* and had produced projects that Fosse had choreographed and directed. He was a visionary. The phenomenal team of Fred Ebb and John Kander was to compose the music, and the brilliant Terrence McNally would write the book. The legendary Chita Rivera was to play the Spider Woman. This was about as good as it gets on Broadway.

But I had a difficult decision to make. It was 1991. I had recently codirected and choreographed Michael Jackson's *BAD* Tour (which was a huge success) and with his star continuing to rise, Mike asked me to direct his second tour. The financial offer was extremely generous. But I had to choose either the tour or Broadway because they were happening concurrently.

I was becoming successful creating choreography for films and huge arena/stadium tours but theater boiled in my soul. Hal Prince had phoned me, complimenting me on all my work with the Blond Ambition Tour, and told me, "Broadway needs new blood." Hal and his A Team had recently concluded a workshop of *Kiss of the Spider Woman* at Purchase in New York. It was not successful. Susan Stroman, one of Broadway's reigning director/choreographers, had choreographed that workshop. Hal wanted a change.

"I'm looking for someone with some special talent," he said, reiterating several times, "Broadway needs new blood. I believe you can bring a fresh flavor to this new production of *Spider Woman*."

I have always tried to challenge myself, so I opted for *Kiss* over directing MJ's next tour, trusting that the universe had given me this opportunity to stretch myself in a new way. I also trusted that turning down MJ's generous financial offer would come back to me somehow with riches of knowledge since you don't ordinarily become wealthy by doing theater.

I'll never forget my first meeting with Hal Prince in New York. After an initial informative chitchat, he asked me point blank if I was gay. I told him that I was.

"As a gay man," he continued, "do you think Chita Rivera would be someone you would idolize?"

"Pardon me, Mr. Prince?"

"Do you think the gay character Molina in the prison would want to 'be' the Spider Woman if she is played by Chita? Do we need someone more glamorous?" Not a question I expected.

"I—I think Chita is incomparable," I said. "But I'm not sure if she's the type of woman that a gay man would idolize as *glamorous*, if you mean the Hollywood version of glamorous." Moments later, Hal brought me in to meet John Kander and Fred Ebb, two of the sweetest men in show business. After brief introductions and small talk, Hal announced to the room. "Vincent doesn't think Chita is right for the part."

I was speechless. What an awkward thing for him to say in front of these two men who grew up as friends with Chita since their youth. That was my introduction. I scrambled to clarify. "Uh, no," I said. "She's maybe not someone I would *consider to be a movie starlet* but she's a beautiful woman. She's Chita Rivera. She's amazing. But, Hal, you asked me if Chita was a glamorous idol. I said I loved Chita but didn't think of her as the Rita Hayworth, bombshell type."

"Well, then who would that be?" Hal asked. I was certainly not expecting this line of questioning, but I thought I knew what he was talking about.

"Well, someone like Vanessa Williams?" I said. The gorgeous, talented Williams had recently made headlines when she was stripped of her Miss America crown after some provocative photos had surfaced.

Hal replied, "You mean the woman who made the photos showing the little man in the boat??!!" It was an uncomfortable and disconcerting first meeting. Maybe that was Hal's objective. I came to understand over time that Hal Prince, in general, was not an admirer of choreographers. (Vanessa Williams did eventually take over Chita's role in the show. Hmm…)

The first day of rehearsal in Toronto, I was like an enthusiastic puppy. I arrived early at the Bluma Appel Theatre, part of the St. Lawrence Centre for the Arts, and plopped myself in the back of the theater in the shadows. Hal and members of the cast arrived, and Hal began to direct them from the audience. As I watched, Hal kept turning over his shoulder to look at me. I waved to him, "Good morning, sir!"

Eventually he turned around and said in an irritated voice, "What are you doing back there?"

"I'm watching what you're doing, sir," I responded, "so that I can get a sense of your style of the show. I want what I create to gel with your vision."

"Well, I don't want you in here," he said. "Go to the other room and create some dances." I followed his instructions. My assistant, Kim Blank, had come with me from Los Angeles. Neither of us was ever given a handbook about how to create a Broadway show. What kept ringing in my ears were Hal's words, "Broadway needs new blood." This seemed to me to be a confirmation of the only directive I had heard from all the megastars with whom I'd worked over the past decade in Hollywood and with whom I had achieved international success. "Create something the world has never seen before."

Since Hal passed on the talented Susan Stroman and could have had his pick of the Broadway choreography litter, my instinct told me he must not want the same typical movements that appear in most Broadway shows.

One difference I found in creating choreography for the theater was the luxury of time. I was given a week in Toronto to create a piece that I'd typically have a couple days to create in LA. As rehearsals in Toronto progressed, I would sometimes turnaround choreography so fast the rest of the team seemed baffled. For me, it was business as usual. A commercial shoot, a music video, a television taping—all my experience taught me to create work quickly, think on my feet, and trust my instincts. I was told that some people were talking behind my back, nicknaming me "the coke freak." This wasn't meant to be endearing and, for the record, was not the truth.

I felt some of the A Team began to equate speed with a lack of quality. "How could he compose quality work this quickly?" I also started to realize that Broadway, and more specifically Hal Prince, didn't want new blood at all, or a new style of choreography. He simply wanted a *new choreographer* doing the same old thing. I remember something he said to me that should have been a clue.

"Where's my kickline that's gonna stop the show?"

Reading the script and allowing myself to get inside the provocative music of Kander and Ebb, I didn't even know where a kickline would organically be placed. I had never created anything to manipulate an audience reaction, never designed a movement specifically for audience applause. Michael and Madonna always wanted to challenge the public and push the boundaries of performance. To create something to simply satisfy the audience with a cliché seemed like uninspired laziness to me.

Chita was a genuinely nice person and beloved in theater circles for being "just one of the gypsies." She was a legend. She was a prodigy ballet dancer before her life in musical theater. She rose to fame on Broadway as the original Anita in *West Side Story*. I wanted to do my best for Chita, because I adored her. I wanted to create movement as original for her as I had done for Madonna or Michael Jackson. Her energy was youthful, though her body had some physical limitations as she was sixty years old. I thought I was showing Chita off in spectacular fashion, but apparently others didn't feel the same.

Coming into the Broadway world inexperienced and fresh, I was too naïve to realize that the people coming to see Chita Rivera (and possibly Chita herself, though we never discussed it) didn't want to see Chita do anything new. They wanted to see her in a man's suit with tails, perhaps a top hat or a fedora, and dancing with a cane in her hand. They wanted to see her kick her gorgeous legs up in the air because that's what she always did in musicals. And that's most likely what the A Team wanted all along. But they never bothered to tell me! Perhaps they thought I knew. I didn't know.

The problems were mounting. I heard that I worked too fast. I heard that I wasn't creating showstopping moments. And the question kept being whispered, "Where's the kickline, for God's sake?" But no one told me any of these things to my face! Just a lot of murmuring in the shadows. I wanted so desperately to do my best. If someone from the A Team had just taken the time to tell me what they were looking for, if someone truly acted with the sincerity they all claimed to live by, I could have adjusted my choreography.

The shit finally hit the proverbial fan on a Monday morning. The prior weekend, Chita left Toronto to perform her successful one-woman show. While she was gone, I began choreographing the "Morphine Tango." It featured the male lead, Brent Carver, in a hospital bed having a morphine dream surrounded by other inmates. I was in the middle of creating this piece when we finished rehearsal on Saturday afternoon. We had no rehearsal on Sunday.

When Chita came back on Monday, she was flying high from the accolades she had received for her show over the weekend. I welcomed her back, it was all kisses and hugs and everything seemed more than pleasant. I explained that I was in the middle of the "Morphine Tango" and wanted to finish the piece while the muses were with me. I had nothing new to give Chita, so asked if it would be all right for Kim (my assistant) to work with her, refining the pieces she already had. Chita seemed fine with that.

At the end of that day, I was called into Hal's office. Hal began to lecture me that Chita came back from her short break ready to dive into *Spider Woman*, and she had no new work from me. And, he yelled, I "added insult to injury" by shuffling her off to review work with an assistant. According to Hal, Chita was furious—a total surprise to me.

Because Hal believed Chita was livid, Hal was beyond livid. He lit into me about not knowing how to work with stars, telling me I had no sense of professionalism and was nothing but an amateur. He then proceeded to attack my work. "If I had wanted the kind of choreography you're creating," he said, "I could have hired Paula Abdul!" Broadway royalty or not, Hal had made it too personal. He pushed the wrong buttons. I couldn't hold back.

"With all due respect, Mr. Prince," I said, "though you are undoubtedly the king of Broadway and have created unforgettable and outstanding work, more people have seen my work than have seen all of your work combined."

It was as if I'd punched him in the stomach. His face turned red. Beyond red. I could almost see smoke emanating from his ears. I don't know if anyone had ever spoken to him like that, but I was speaking the truth.

"When this project finishes in Toronto," he seethed. "You're fired." And he kept his word. I stayed until the show opened in Toronto, even though the rest of the rehearsal period was rough and emotionally hard to handle. Hal didn't want me to come onstage for a bow with the rest of the creators on opening night, but others on the team didn't feel this way, so I proudly took a bow with the creative team. I had worked hard, whether Hal Prince liked it or not.

When the show moved to London, Rob Marshall was brought in to create one more number: Chita in a man's fedora and white tails, dancing with a cane and doing high kicks. Obviously this was the song and dance the A Team wanted. The show ran for 390 performances in London and 904 performances on Broadway. All three leads won Tony Awards, as did the writers and composer. Hal Prince did not receive a Tony. I was nominated for a 1993 Tony for the choreography, sharing the nomination with Rob Marshall as the show's co-choreographer. Hal, Chita, and some members of the A Team stated in interviews that Rob had "saved the show" with his one number that was a take-off on so many numbers you've seen as a star vehicle on Broadway. My name remained as the principal choreographer on the credits.

Since *Kiss of the Spider Woman*, I've not only choreographed but also directed successful theater all over the globe, *except* on Broadway. Ironically, in 2004, I directed and choreographed my own production of Kander and Ebb's *Cabaret* in Berlin, first directed by Mr. Prince on Broadway. It was the first production of the show to be created in Berlin and the longest running show in Berlin's history. I directed and choreographed a highly successful *Evita*, another of Mr. Prince's original productions, at the renowned Ronacher Theater in Vienna. I was invited to direct because they wanted a director who could give Andrew Lloyd Webber's show a fresh vision.

What exactly happened from the point of view of others, I'll never know. There seemed to be a mismatch in creative energy between Hal and me from that very first meeting. I disappointed myself and I do believe I failed to a degree, even if only in my self-expectations. It all could have been avoided had there been more honesty and open communication among the creative team. They called themselves a family, but I never felt any kinship. The creative families I know and love tackle artistic endeavors with affection, dedication, and loyalty. They can be found anywhere in the world from a small town in Arizona to Hollywood or Berlin to Vienna or Buenos Aires. It's about the artists. It's about the creative heart. It's about love and communication and support. Not geography or egos.

6.

The Electric Socket of Creativity

SOMETIMES FANS WORSHIP CELEBRITIES (especially pop stars) thinking they are born with some magical power beyond the rest of us mortals. That might be true, as being gorgeous and having charisma certainly go a long way. But I'll tell you this…the good ones also work at it. Michael, Madonna, Shirley, Chita…they became icons because they worked hard and demanded it of themselves. They honed their artistic instincts.

As I reflect on all I've learned and all I've created, I believe more than ever that creativity and discipline are tools all artists have, it's only a question of whether or not those important tools for artistic expression are nurtured. When I feel creative energy in myself, I've always described it as "putting my finger into the electric socket of creativity." It's the best way I can describe it. It's almost something spiritual or otherworldly taking you over. It flows through you. But you have to learn how to plug in and what to do once you feel the energy. You also have to be exposed to what creativity looks like in a consumable form. I was lucky in that regard.

Music was always a part of my life. My dad adored jazz, my mom listened to Johnny Mathis, and my aunt Diane introduced me to Elvis. When times were good between them, my parents had often been the only whites at the otherwise all-Black jazz clubs in Philly.

Sometimes, their hip friends sat around our living room shooting tequila shots and playing music late into the night.

My maternal grandfather, Albert Chalfant, worked at the Sun Oil Company and played the violin in his upstairs bedroom late at night. He had his own love for music but was also thin, smoked a pipe, and eventually developed cancer of the jaw. The right side of his jawbone was removed, which frightened us grandchildren. Seeing him come down the stairs at night in a long robe with his white hair tousled always made us scream.

On the other hand, my mom's mother, Anna Dorothy Chalfant, was a short, fleshy woman with whom you could curl up and always feel safe. I called her Nan. The Chalfants lived in a two-story brick home built by Nan's father in 1900 near the dirty Delaware River. Nan's house was messy and overflowed with kids and cats. Lots and lots of cats. She came from red, white, and blue–blooded Republican Americans of Dutch descent.

Nan sewed and was a hoarder, with an upstairs junk room full of old clothes, a dress mannequin, assorted fabrics, and random "treasures" that she had collected over the years. One of my favorites was a cranberry velvet dressing gown that could be a magician's robe or the elegant costume of a Geisha. I cherished going up into that magical room to create anything I wanted, from haunted houses to beauty pageants, my imagination running wild.

Nan had a sweeping staircase that came down into the living room, a perfect stage. From the age of nine to age thirteen, I'd direct and choreograph fashion shows or lip-syncing spectaculars to popular music. "Itsy Bitsy Teeny Weeny Yellow Polka Dot Bikini" was a memorable early hit. I had plenty of raw talent in my eleven cousins and four siblings whom I coerced into starring in my theatrical presentations. Every show I created received a standing ovation from Nan, though I'm sure my aunts and uncles wondered what the hell I was doing and how I ever found my way into this family.

When I was thirteen, Nan took me to the set of Dick Clark's *American Bandstand* in Philly where I was allowed to watch the filming. I loved Motown and any music produced by Phil Spector. I thought Ronnie Spector was beyond sexy, and I had my huge crush on Diana Ross. When I heard the Beatles's music, I believed they were speaking to me personally. I had every Beatles album, every pin, and even a Beatle wig. I sent the Beatles a series of photos of a neighbor girl and me standing by the trashcans holding sheet music, suggesting they put the photos on their next album cover.

Everyone knew I was Nan's favorite, and I spent as much time at her house as my parents would permit. In Nan's safe harbor, I was truly happy. I was not only allowed to be creative but encouraged to develop my artistic personality and find out who I really was. I was always happy there.

My paternal grandmother, Wanda Paterson, was a second-generation Polish immigrant. We called her Bobby because as a child I wasn't able to pronounce *babcia*, Polish for grandmother. My paternal grandfather, Vincent Paterson, immigrated to the United States from England as a six-year-old in 1910. While crossing the ocean with his mother to reunite the family, she jumped off the ship in the middle of the night, lost at sea in the cold Atlantic. He would joke that we only had one "t" in our last name, unlike the common spelling of Patterson, because his Scottish great-grandfather believed that having one "t" would save so much money on lead pencils that he would become a millionaire. I often had to collect him from Joe's corner bar where I'd find him downing beers and staring into space with a smile. My Paterson grandparents lived in a lower-class immigrant neighborhood. They had bedrooms on opposite sides of their small brick row home, my grandfather's punishment for having fathered a child out of wedlock.

Unlike my loveable Nan, whose fleshy arms we loved to jiggle, Bobby was thin and the only person I knew who exercised daily doing Hula-Hoop, ab crunches, and toe touches. As a beauty regimen, she would cover her face with Vaseline. Once greased, we were only allowed to kiss her protruding lips: "Jus chiss me on the lips, chiss me right here on the lips," she would say.

Like my father, Bobby felt the world had not situated her in the socioeconomic class in which she belonged. She didn't have a cosmetician degree but made a little money giving hair permanents to the Polish ladies on the block. She was a shrewd businesswoman and socked away every penny that she didn't spend on designer clothes purchased from the clearance rack. She made us sit on the sagging velveteen couch as she presented fashion shows of her most recent purchases.

Fluent in Polish and English, Bobby taught herself French, Italian, and Spanish from ALM language records. She also wanted to visit those countries. My grandfather had no interest in travel but going abroad alone simply wasn't an option for a woman in the 1960s. Bobby needed a travel companion who could be her dance partner. I had a natural aptitude for dancing, and by sixth grade I was not only precocious but proficient at all the social dances. Back then, people of all ages gathered together on the dance floor. Every event had dancing—jitterbug, foxtrot, cha-cha, merengue, polka, the twist—and most people knew at least the basic steps. At baptisms, birthdays, graduations, weddings, backyard barbeques, or any social gathering, someone plugged in a record player and everyone danced. Bobby, using her saved pennies, booked a summer tour of Europe in 1962. So, at twelve years old, I went on my first trip (that was farther away than Philadelphia) as Bobby's travel companion.

We sailed the Atlantic on the SS *United States*, tourist class—a euphemism for third-class nobodies. But our lower-class travel status didn't stop Bobby. Every night she made us dress to the nines, sneak under the ropes into the first-class ballroom and dance the night away. The well-dressed, older woman dancing with the cute, young boy became the talk of the ballroom. Though it felt a little strange dancing with my grandmother, I loved the attention.

We traveled by train through Europe exploring France, Spain, Italy, Germany, Holland, Belgium, Scotland, and, finally, England to visit family. Wanting to taste how the other half lived, Bobby booked us into luxurious hotels. She relished attention and being partnered in all the first-class hotel ballrooms by a boy who could hold his own on the dance floor attracted people to us wherever we went. I would be exhausted from walking all day and dancing for hours.

"Bobby, can we go to bed now?"

"Not yet," she would say or, "Vincent, keep dancing. Smile. People are watching us." I remember her turning to me once, "I know you like your other grandmother better than me."

"No, I don't," I replied, frightened she might change plans and make us go home early.

"Don't lie to me," she said. "I know you do."

Bobby took me to the Folies Bergère in Paris, which was the first time I experienced the theater. The exquisite program included choreographed dancing, extravagant costumes, an orchestra, and real, live, bouncing naked breasts. She let me sip my first glass of champagne. She took me to my first musical, *The Sound of Music*, in London. She exposed me to languages, art, and architecture as she checked item after item off the extensive lists she had prepared before leaving Pennsylvania.

From Nan, I had learned unconditional love. She opened the door to my creative self. From Bobby, I learned about discipline and preparation and gained the love of travel. To this day, I still make lists.

Beginning with the shows at Nan's house, creating haunted houses in the neighborhood, making short cowboy films with our Kodak Super 8, and acting in school plays—I found avenues of creative escape all around me. Without realizing it, I was learning to "plug in." And when I was given the freedom to excel at Dickinson College, I did just that. I was also able to become a dancer after being told I was too old and had no talent. But you can't see the outcomes when you're in it. I think that's why I've always focused on the work at hand and trusted the creativity and the discipline would do the rest.

Bobby saw me act in college but died of cancer before I had any professional success. Nan saw all of my early dance performances on TV. She met Barbara Mandrell and Shirley MacLaine and gossiped with me about Madonna. "I read that Madonna gained thirty-five pounds! How can she dance that fat?"

I spent Nan's final ten days at her bedside as she passed from a stroke at eighty-five.

My grandmothers both fueled my passion to have a creative career. I would not be the artist I am without them.

7.

Santa Evita

Choreographers Don't Get Oscars

As I read Alan Parker's script for the movie *Evita*, the film played out in my head—the music, the scenes, the opportunities for dancing. *Evita* was one of my favorite musicals, having seen Patti LuPone on Broadway in the early eighties. The potential of a movie version had floated around Hollywood for years like an elusive, mythical unicorn. It seemed like it would never happen.

I was first invited to choreograph the film when Glenn Caron was set to direct. Then, when Oliver Stone became attached to direct, he also contacted me. He had written a script with the transcendent Montreal artist Louise Lecavalier dancing throughout the film as Eva Peron's alter ego. That version didn't happen. Now, Alan Parker was directing. The stars aligned as Madonna pursued the title role and was soon attached to play the iconic Eva Peron. I met with Alan in Los Angeles and agreed to do the film.

"Can I ask you how you see your role in the making of the movie?" he asked.

"Well, Alan," I said, "I wear both hats, director and choreographer, but I know how to wear just one. I appreciate being hired by you as the director, rather than have Madonna ask me. I'm excited to learn from you and translate your direction into movement. I'll make myself available any time you need me, not just for the dance sequences. Madonna respects my eye when it comes to any movement she performs."

Alan's reaction to my eagerness seemed lukewarm, something I had occasionally encountered with other directors upon first meeting. Directors can be control freaks and, unless they're extremely secure, they can view the choreographer as a competitor. It's partially because choreography can be an enigmatic art. I assured Alan that I would be *his* choreographer and work to bring *his* vision to the screen. We agreed we'd take things day-by-day once work commenced and by the time we parted, he seemed open and generous.

Alan and I began exchanging giddy letters about style, locations, and his overall vision for the project. I embarked on a regimen of regular tango lessons with my first choreography assistant, Miranda Garrison. I was thrilled to inundate myself with the physical and historical aspects of such a sensuous, powerful dance. As I realized the complexity of dancing the tango, one of my concerns was the short rehearsal period already scheduled. I expressed concern during my first meeting in London with Alan and his producer, David Wimbury—who immediately seemed smarmy.

"I've been taking tango classes and the tango is the most intricate partner dance I've ever done," I told them. "It might be a good idea for any actor who dances in the movie to take some classes before they get to Buenos Aires. It'll save a lot of time in rehearsal and on set. Especially with the rehearsal period being so short."

Alan and David emphasized how they wanted the dancing to feel "spontaneous, organic, not like a staged musical." They decided there was no need for much rehearsal because they wanted things to look "natural." I was confused. Alan had directed *Fame*. He knew about dance and the need for rehearsal.

"Alan," I pressed again, "all dancing requires hours of rehearsal to look natural. Partner dancing requires even more to look effortless, let alone natural. It's harder than dancing alone."

"I don't want anything looking choreographed, Vincent," Alan replied. "I know I'm going to have to pull the reins in on you on this one."

"Alan, I understand your vision. I do. I work from character all the time. But if you shoot a scene more than once, you'll need the actors to repeat the exact movement to match in the editing room." Finally, they acquiesced and opened up to the *idea* of additional rehearsal time.

Madonna phoned me from New York, beyond excited. I told her I was setting up private tango classes for her with a respected tango couple from Buenos Aires, Danel and Maria Bastone. I knew she'd take the classes and be a pro by the time she arrived in Argentina.

I spent New Year's Eve, 1996, at Madonna's exquisite home in the Hollywood Hills. It used to belong to the gangster Bugsy Siegel (and after Madonna to Joe Pytka). "Incredible, isn't it?" she said. "It's like an Italian gigolo. Too expensive to keep and too gorgeous to get rid of."

She had her hair styled to resemble Eva Peron. She was beautiful, sweet, and kind. She radiated differently in these personal moments. I wanted to tell her how much more powerful she was when she was just being herself, but I knew she'd laugh coyly and tell me pleasantly to "fuck off."

A few days later, I headed to LAX to catch my flight to Buenos Aires where I would make my temporary home at the Marriott Plaza Hotel. Miranda and I would arrive three weeks before the production team to cast and rehearse dancers. At the airline departure desk, I got my first inkling of the wild escapade to come. Lisa Moran, the associate producer, had already changed, canceled, and rebooked my flight several times in the past three days. And now we were told there were no tickets. I called Lisa in England. (Incidentally, she was also Alan Parker's new girlfriend.) "Lisa Moran is very sorry," said a nameless assistant on the line. "But you'll have to pay for both tickets, and you'll get paid back later." I plunked down the money.

It didn't take long for me to forget about the plane ticket ordeal. My room at the Plaza was sinfully beautiful and in the heart of the old city. It had high ceilings with bas-reliefs and a balcony that overlooked a quiet street where an old man sang opera on his balcony every night after dinner. Buenos Aires has breathtaking Deco buildings nuzzled beside glass and steel modern structures. My time there ahead of the others was inspiring as I walked among the people and the city, feeling the heartbeat of Buenos Aires: the tango.

One evening, I came upon an older couple in a busy square about to perform for the gathering crowd. They explained they were going to dance the tango in the *milonguero* style, the authentic tango, not the flashy, tourist-pleasing version. This couple, performing on a concrete sidewalk in front of a McDonald's, took my breath away. Their dancing exhibited a depth that went beyond the steps and revealed the heart of the culture. This would be the dance language of the film. No large *gonchos* or *sentadas*, no big leg extensions or upside-down flips. I understood how I wanted to translate Alan's vision and how to interweave the tango throughout the film.

I asked one of the local dancers I had hired, Carina Losana, to become my tango instructor and teach me that authentic style. "Close your ribcage," she would say. "Bend the knees, point the feet but step, ball then heel, be natural, strengthen your lead. Stop dancing what you *think* it should be. Dance what you *feel* it should be."

Casting began with sessions for locals of all ages. One day, I saw three hundred people. The next day, six hundred. The next, one thousand. They were from all walks of life because, in Buenos Aires, social dancing is woven into the fabric of life and everyone has some exposure to it. I was enthralled.

I had no idea if any of the principal cast besides hardworking Madonna could actually dance. I had not been part of the casting process, which was unusual for a musical film, and information was hard to come by. My nerves tingled with excitement at the thought of Madonna's arrival. I knew we'd have a rewarding collaboration, especially knowing how much Madonna wanted to be successful in this film. Receiving an Oscar had to be on her mind.

I spoke with Madonna before she left for Buenos Aires. "I've been rehearsing like mad with Danel and Maria. I've learned the tango, milonga, and the waltz cruzada." She was coming a week early to have conversations with a group of older Argentines who knew Evita. And she also wanted to be with me so we could rehearse, rehearse, rehearse. I relayed to her Alan's desire to have the dancing be "natural." With a sense of camaraderie in her voice she said, "Okay, Vincent, but please let me do a few fancy steps." The next day in the rehearsal studio with Miranda, I was madly analyzing everything I had created for Madonna. Was it difficult and interesting enough? Would it work for Madonna? Would it work, period?

When Madonna arrived, it was as if Buenos Aires was turned inside out. The city was rabid for the Material Girl. Some complained, "A video queen should not be playing Evita Peron!" Meanwhile, below Madonna's window, hundreds of young girls dressed as classic eighties Madonna look-alikes were dancing, chanting, singing her songs, and screaming her name. Madonna was staying at the Hyatt Mansion with private security at every door.

We first met in a marble-floored ballroom. "Oh, my God, Madonna," I said upon seeing her with tinted contact lenses. "How strange to look at you with brown eyes!"

"Wait until you see me with fake teeth," she said. "The problem with these lenses is that the whole world looks brown. It's so somber and dark. It's hard to keep my spirits up and not be depressed. And with all those screaming kids, I can't sleep."

We danced the tango and her form was beautiful. I had located a rehearsal studio for us outside the center of Buenos Aires. It was quiet, hidden, secure. Arriving before Madonna, I was working in the upstairs studio when I heard voices yelling from the street below. Madonna's black Benz was surrounded by teens on scooters and mopeds. Behind her were two dozen more cars filled with screaming kids, honking their horns. Two bodyguards stepped out of Madonna's car to escort her inside. By the time she got from the car to the studio door, the teens had become a mob, pummeling each other simply to touch her. The sleeve of her dress was ripped, she had a shoe yanked from her foot, and someone wrenched a small chunk of hair from her head. We held all future rehearsals at Madonna's hotel since taking her anywhere would require the national guard.

During our rehearsals, Madonna shared footage of her dance lessons and we discussed my approach to the dance scenes. She expressed the same concern that I had begun to hear from others: what was going on with Alan Parker, David Wimbury, and Lisa Moran on this project? There seemed to be no leadership. Only a handful of the creative team was getting input or creative feedback. There were few, if any, production meetings.

I scheduled a rehearsal with the men Alan had cast to dance with Madonna. The first actor I met was cast as Sr. Jabon and had five scenes in the film. In the longest scene, he had to dance with Madonna while she was singing. My first rehearsal with this actor was a disaster. The poor man hadn't read a script or heard the music. He couldn't dance and couldn't even keep time to the beat. He was never informed he'd have to dance or lip-sync in English. I spent four hours working with him. He left feeling like Baryshnikov. I left feeling like shit. I called Lisa in the hope to get through to Alan, but she thought it best that I not bother him with this "little problem."

"With all respect, Lisa," I said, "I need to talk to Alan about this. This is a creative problem, not a producer's problem. It needs to be a discussion between the director and choreographer." She hemmed and hawed. I pressed on. "If this is going to be a movie in which I'm not given access to the director when creative discussions are warranted, then I'm the wrong man for this gig. If this is a problem, you have a few weeks before principal photography begins to hire another choreographer."

She told me I could find Alan at the hotel bar with Wimbury. Off I went. Alan listened, then replied, "I thought I was doing you a favor, Vincent, by casting a man who had *Tango Forever* (a touring revue) on his resume." He never thought to ask the man what he had done on the show. Turned out he was the props master. I left that meeting tasked to find a new Sr. Jabon.

During auditions, I learned that most male tango dancers, called *milongueros*, do not follow choreography. The tango is totally interpretive in the steps and rhythms, like scat singing in jazz. I found one candidate who could follow choreography and had the right look—sort of Al Pacino meets Peter Sellers meets Ratso Rizzo. He also had some acting experience. The following evening, I was summoned by Lisa to meet Alan in his hotel room.

He lit a cigarette. "Well, you won," he said as he paced the floor. Alan continued with a long monologue, "I'll accept your new choice for Sr. Jabon, but I'm not at all happy that you couldn't make my original choice work. I pride myself on my casting and if I choose someone for a role it is for a specific reason and that person should be in the film. You're overqualified for this job as choreographer, really, but I'll let you use your casting choice because you have so little to do on the movie. And, actually, there's something more. I don't believe I trust you at all. I feel that you're dividing Madonna and me by creating two camps. As a director, you should know better. She's already difficult to deal with, and you're only making matters worse."

I sat in silence before responding. "Alan, I haven't been invited to one production meeting and, as my director, you've given me no creative guidance at all. Madonna and I are only professional friends with extensive work history. We're driven, like-minded artists. Remember, I'm here because *you* asked me to do this film, not Madonna."

I told him that if he didn't trust me, there was no reason for me to be there because trust is the foundation of collaboration. Silence.

He rose with his paunchy belly and stooped shoulders and walked to my chair. "I am totally in the wrong, and I apologize," he said. "I really want you on my team. I realize that I have pushed you away and have been falsely accusing you." We shook hands. We hugged. He kissed me on the cheek.

Rehearsals with Madonna continued with collaboration and success. I taught her the steps, then we would explore the scene—adding and discarding movement as Madonna owned the role. As I've mentioned before, Madonna can be brutally honest with no regard for tact or diplomacy. She challenges you at every turn. She listens when you speak and responds immediately. If you don't take her abruptness personally, your creative ego can match hers and you can collaborate. If you take it personally, game over. I was feeling good.

Once, I went to kiss her in the dancing scene I'd created for Eva and Juan, just an acting kiss. "You're funny," she giggled, as she turned her head away.

"What do you mean? And why can't you kiss me?"

"I don't think of you like that," she said.

"I don't think of you like that either, Madonna. We're acting."

Alan and the director of photography, Darius Khondji, finally visited and complimented us on everything we showed them. Madonna's dancing was perfection. We powwowed in an animated two-hour discussion about the Perons, the filming, and the style. It was everything we'd been longing to hear from Alan and stimulating to finally hear his thoughts and see inside his head. Madonna and I hoped this was a new chapter and these conversations would continue.

The next day, my rehearsal with the dancers confirmed why I love doing what I do. I was about to rehearse the "Requiem for Evita" with a multitude of tango dancers of various ages, shapes, and sizes. I described the scene as the moment of sorrow upon hearing about Eva's death. I wanted the tango to represent the sorrow of the nation. I played the movie soundtrack on the CD player. No one moved. An older couple said to me, "We can't dance the tango to this music. We dance only to tango music. Do you have any Gardel or Piazzolla?"

It hadn't crossed my mind that there would be any objection to dancing to the movie music that, admittedly, was far from tango music. I had to think on my feet. "As a lover of dance," I said, "when I watch you, the language of the tango is far more powerful than any music being played. When you move, your bodies express so many emotions whether there is pure tango music or silence. The only thing that is important in this moment of the film is how you illustrate the language of sorrow between you and your partner. I know it is unusual for you to dance to music like this, but I promise you, by doing it, you will allow millions of people in the world to experience the power of the tango."

There was still hesitation. "Let's just dance without music, in silence, listening to the beating of your hearts for rhythm." I realized many of the cast hadn't been born when Eva Peron died. She was only an idea, a myth, so I asked them all to dedicate their tango in this rehearsal and in their eventual performance to someone they loved who had died—a parent, a spouse, a family member, a friend. I asked them to put the face of that loved one in their head. If the image left their mind, they had to stop dancing and stay still while their partner waited, until the face came back into their mind. Then they could start dancing again.

It was a dark, overcast day, and it began to rain. I quietly put on the rich orchestrations of Andrew Lloyd Webber with the sung Latin eulogy created by Tim Rice. The people cast as husbands and wives, grandfathers and granddaughters, mothers and sons, danced the tango. Tears streamed down their cheeks as the rain ran down the studio windows. Some even sobbed. The dance became *The Requiem*. In the scenes in the film, in the shadowed ballroom, or walking in a line before the horses, the dancing is honest and touching.

After a month in Buenos Aires, I met Antonio Banderas. Beyond his devastatingly good looks, he had a warm sense of humor, an enlightened knowledge of theater, and just enough insecurity to make him vulnerable. A sexy combination.

Madonna had called me that morning. "Can you come early? I want to practice the 'Waltz for Eva and Che' before Antonio arrives. Then I'll go to wardrobe. When he comes, call me. I want you to dance it with me, not Miranda."

When Antonio arrived, Madonna entered, her arms demurely wrapped around her shoulders.

"Are you all right?" I asked.

"No," she said, pouting. "I need a phone." And she left the room.

When she returned, we danced the piece for him. Madonna apologized for all of the mistakes she had made, which amounted to exactly none. Antonio was apprehensive about dancing at first, which was the obvious result of the carefully executed master plan by Ms. M to keep her costar appropriately insecure by illustrating how good she was. But in a few hours, Antonio learned several sections of the "Waltz for Eva and Che." He brought a natural style to the piece. And they looked stunning together.

A few days later, principal photography began and rumor was that it went well. I remember thinking that day that our creative team was unbeatable, but if the film succeeded, it would be in spite of its producers. I left a note with Alan about hoping to attend dailies. I also congratulated him on now having two full days of shooting in the can.

But good feelings weren't the fashion with our producing team. I began to realize that I wasn't going to further my directing craft learning from Alan. You can't learn from someone who refuses to share anything. I received a phone call from David Wimbury about my request to see the dailies. "Alan is very superstitious," he began. "Every day on his way to the set Alan *must* sit between his director of photography and his camera operator. And Alan is only allowing those people on the set who are actually working at the time and the only people admitted to the dailies will be those people who have created the particular scene shown that evening. Do you understand? Could you please not hold it as a judgment upon Alan? Isn't this a great gig for you where you get to hang out in Buenos Aires and only have to come to the set those very few times when you're needed?"

I regarded this as bad-producer speak. I had no idea why I was being shut out. This was a musical *with dancing*. I hadn't anticipated these roadblocks but decided to wait before airing my thoughts.

The lack of direction from Alan kept me in an isolated bubble. On one hand, it afforded me the freedom to experiment, like the day with Madonna and Antonio when we dissected the "Waltz for Eva and Che." We started working through the lyrics as spoken words, just walking around the space. Then I asked them to sing the lyrics as they walked through the room and to combine the singing with the choreography.

"Eva, don't just yell at Che," I said. "Get him to understand your situation, don't defend yourself. Che, listen to her, don't be so quick to accuse. If you don't listen, you lose. Debate using your heart and your head. You both want to change the world for the better. You both care about the people. Because you despise and admire each other, there is conflict, danger, and risk here. Let's do it again."

It became more than choreography. The three of us were dissecting every scene that involved dance by shaping story, character, and intent. When Madonna, Antonio, and I reached the conclusion of the "Waltz," Alan's script read that Che would disappear. Then, all of Eva's past lovers would appear and partner her, the idea being that Eva succeeded only because of sexual exchanges. After several rehearsals, the three of us agreed it was more powerful when Che completed the dance with Eva, focusing on their conflict that drives the story. We brought the new idea to Alan.

"Oh," said Alan. "There goes Vince again, wanting more choreography!"

Antonio jumped to my defense. "This was not just Vince's idea," he said. "He created the ending first like in your script, but in rehearsals we worked on this version of the ending because it flowed better dramatically."

We showed him. Alan clutched my arm in excitement as they performed the scene, dancing and singing a sensual, ideological duel. When it was over, Alan decided to film Che and Eva dancing to the end, but since he might intercut scenes of her dancing with the various men of her past, he would film those moments as well. All in all, it was a good day.

Jonathan Pryce arrived to play the role of Juan Peron. He was so nervous I could see his hand quiver on Madonna's back when they first danced a simple rumba. I worked with him and Madonna was a champ, bringing him down to earth so he could be the Juan Peron of power and prestige. I was surprised at how sexy Jonathan was, even next to the steamy Antonio. Jonathan had a confident but quiet presence, virile and masculine. When he finally kissed Madonna in rehearsal, she practically melted. I suspect he took her by surprise, too.

I finally got to work on set when we filmed "Goodnight and Thank You" in the Odeon bar. Madonna was breathtaking. The combination of hair, wardrobe, makeup, lighting, sets, and, of course, Alan's direction was magical. Watching Madonna sing, I felt I was privy to the thoughts inside her head. The expertise she had gained in making music videos made her completely comfortable in front of the camera.

Later that day, we filmed one of the "Requiem" sequences in a beautiful, old, white-plastered parlor with light streaming through the windows. The dancers were emotional just as I had directed them to be in rehearsal. Some had tears streaming down their faces as they danced the tango in and out of the mottled light. Alan was like a jacked-up teenager, running around and getting all of his shots, oblivious to the overtime spent on the scene.

At one point, he was racing along with a crab dolly that traveled in a circle around a couple in their eighties. At the conclusion of the day, the man who had been dancing grabbed Alan's hand, "Muchas gracias por todo, Señor Alan," he said through his tears. Alan broke down and placed the sobbing man's head against his chest. The room was held in suspended animation for a few moments. When we wrapped, applause combined with enthusiastic handshakes and kisses on the cheek.

And just like that, Alan was my new best friend. "Hey," he said. "Do you mind giving up a rest day? I'd like you to come to the polo grounds tomorrow. There might be something you could help me with. If you don't mind."

"Of course. I'll be there. Thanks." I was jubilant to receive his invitation. I was on the 6:00 a.m. call sheet, but once I arrived at the polo grounds it was as if I was invisible. While everyone else ran around with purposeful urgency, I spent my time trying not to be in the way.

Alan came over. "So sorry for having you come all the way down here in this heat for nothing," he said. "I don't really have much for you to do but if you don't mind staying, I might be able to use you. You can always go back to the hotel whenever you feel like it, though."

"No job is too small," I smiled. "I could have helped you with that shot earlier, organizing the extras during the polo match."

"Okay," he nodded. "Great." He walked away. I spent the next three hours moving from the scorching sun to the shade, pretending to appear involved. I found a ride back to the hotel at noon.

With time on my hands, I took as much advantage of being in Buenos Aires as I could. I enrolled in a private Spanish class, visited the places Eva lived, and went to La Recoleta cemetery where she is buried. I went to milongas to experience dancing the authentic tango. I invited Madonna to a local milonga. It had a tiny dance floor and was packed to capacity. Madonna received applause as she entered. I became the ear to the queen, since I now spoke *un poquito de Español* and would manage the various requests that came to our table:

"Could I get an autograph?"

"Would she put a kiss on this champagne bottle?"

"Could I have my picture taken with her?"

"Would she be godmother to my child?"

"Could she put us on a lifetime pension plan?"

Madonna was as captivating and as charming as Eva Peron.

A few days later, I was admitted to dailies of Madonna and Sr. Jabon dancing together, followed by a scene from the "Requiem." The entire crew applauded after the dance footage and Alan yelled to me from across the room, "They don't give Oscars for choreography!" Ouch!

Another producer, Robert Stigwood, jumped to his feet in the rear of the room and yelled, "Bravo!" The entire crew congratulated me.

Prior to shooting part of the waltz in the slaughterhouse, I went into Madonna's trailer where Martin Samuel was beginning to do Madonna's hair. I asked them what style she intended to wear. "I think I'll wear it down, soft," she replied.

"I don't think so, Missy. I created this dance for you to carry the strength of Eva Peron. You need to pull it back."

"Don't go telling me how to wear my hair. Besides, you're the one who told me to approach this role with more vulnerability, remember?"

"Yes, but I meant the acting approach."

"Well, I'll wear it how I want."

"Well, let me tell you, if you come out of this trailer with your hair down, I'm turning you around and marching you right back inside for Martin to fix it."

"Oh, yeah, as if you really could." I left smiling. So was she.

Antonio was charming on set. But I didn't find it amusing when, after hours of rehearsal and exploration on the "Waltz for Eva and Che" he told Alan, "I don't feel organic while moving in waltz time. It feels more natural to me if I'm standing still."

In many ways, Antonio was polar opposite to Madonna. She was disciplined and methodical about practice and getting it perfect every time, whereas he would improvise, constantly looking for a new way to dance on the next take. I kept trying to bring him back to what we had discovered in rehearsal because his first instincts with physical expression were always the best. Alan allowed him to try his own thing on the last take. All Antonio did was walk in a circle around Madonna. Boring! I overheard Madonna tell Antonio that she liked what he did.

Alan found me the next day in the hotel lobby. "I just want to know if you're all right," he said. "I didn't know if you were mad when you left."

"I was frustrated," I said, "but not with you, Alan."

"Well," Alan said, "I'm pissed that I let Banderas look at the fucking monitor. Never again. I don't want you to be upset. Your work is perfect for this film."

The next day, Alan complimented me again as we watched more dailies of the "Requiem" footage. The dancers in torn clothing and broken shoes danced the tango among the horse stables as they expressed their grief. Alan was being congratulated on the footage when he turned to the whole room. "These tango scenes are the two most powerful pieces of film I've ever shot," he announced. "But I can't take the credit. Vince directed the dancers. He told them not to move until they had put a picture in their heads of someone who had died."

Madonna came over and whispered in my ear. "I want to apologize for siding with Banderas the other night," she said. "I thought it would make things easier. I love everything you're creating for this film."

Typical Madonna, fixing something after the fact. But I refused to get drawn into any mini-dramas. Because what I knew, and what Alan, Moran, and Wimbury didn't want to admit, was that this film was about Madonna's career. Our filmmaking team was plopped down in Argentina to move Madonna forward in the way *she* wanted to move forward. This was an Alan Parker film but more importantly, it was a Madonna movie. This frustrated and infuriated Alan as he was accustomed to being the star behind his movies. Here, he was just the director.

The Argentine government wouldn't allow Alan to film Evita's famous balcony scene at the actual Casa Rosada, the Argentine presidential palace. Alan and his production team had pleaded his case with President Carlos Menem. Menem had only one request. He would consider allowing the film to be shot on location if Madonna had dinner with him. Madonna told me, "Now they're whoring me out to get the Casa Rosada! But, fuck it, I'll do it. I'm going to be on that balcony if it kills me…or Alan." Madonna went to dinner and permission was granted.

One night, I took Madonna, her secretary, and our cinematographer, Darius, to Filo's, a trendy pizza bar. It was supposed to be a secret outing. We had a great meal with laughs and good food. Madonna was chatty. "They're kicking me out of my room at the Hyatt," she said. "Too dangerous. They want me to wear a bulletproof vest on the balcony of the Casa Rosada. But know what? It was a good day today, the pizza was great, and now I'm outta here like last year."

When we rose to leave, I noticed there were security guards at many of the tables. They were ex-CIA agents hired to protect Madonna. As we walked toward the exit, everyone inside began to applaud. Suddenly, one man jumped up and rushed for her. One of the security guards grabbed him and pinned him against the wall. Another guard called for our van to back up to the front entrance of the café. As we ran for the open doors, the angry man freed himself from the guard and threw a chair at Madonna. I blocked it from hitting her. It was like a scene out of *Dawn of the Dead* as screaming fans tried to wedge themselves between the top of the van and the café doorframe. We were pushed inside the van, the back doors were slammed securely shut, and we tore off through the deafening crowd.

I'm not sure if Madonna wore that bulletproof vest or not when she sang "Don't Cry For Me, Argentina." I didn't see the filming on the balcony of the Casa Rosada with the throng of 2,500 extras below. I had asked if I could be there as it was going to be an historic moment for the film and for Madonna. My request was ignored.

I asked Madonna how it went.

"Good."

"Good? You've just fulfilled a lifelong dream!"

"You're right," she laughed happily. "It was fucking incredible."

We were wrapping up filming in Argentina and plans were being made for the next legs of production in Budapest and London. Miranda Garrison, my assistant, had decided to leave the film, so

I asked to bring Carina, my Argentine tango instructor, to London as my new assistant. Lisa Moran let Carina's visa application fall through the cracks, so I invited my friend Kim Blank to assist me through the rest of the filming. We had a few rehearsals with Madonna in NYC, shaping the song "Buenos Aires" before she headed to cold, rainy Budapest, and Kim and I to London to cast the rest of the dancers for the "Buenos Aires" scene. Arriving at the London hotel, I received an urgent note to call Madonna in Hungary.

"Vince," she said, "I'm three months pregnant. I was pregnant when I saw you in New York. I wanted to tell you but was so nervous about it. I don't think the timing is perfect. My belly is beginning to get big and my tits are huge. I told Alan, and he kept denying it. I finally told him that we had to tell Wimbury and you. We've pushed up the ballroom scene with Che to this weekend because I don't know how much longer I can wear that slinky white gown."

I was making lists in my head of what needed to change if we had to hide a pregnant Madonna belly. We would be matching footage that we shot in Buenos Aires, so I had to be thorough. For her safety, I immediately wanted to amend some of the choreography.

"Don't change anything," she pressed me. "I'm fine. I run on the treadmill every day. What parts would you adjust?"

"The drop and the lift."

"No," she said. "It's perfect. Please don't change anything because of me."

"Well," I said, "it's a real blessing. You're playing the role you dreamed of and now you're having the baby you always wanted. You should feel very happy, honey. Enjoy it. I'll see you in a few days in Budapest. I love you."

"I love you, too," she said, as I hung up the phone. She had kept the secret but now that she was telling people, everyone was coming forward to support her in finishing the movie.

It was snowing when I flew from London to Budapest, cold, bleak, wet snow. As was typical on this film, no one gave me a call sheet or a schedule. I awakened a production assistant at 8:00 a.m. to discover I was to be on set at 11:30 a.m. It was not a happy set. The director sets the tone of the film, and Alan's insecurities were discombobulating almost everybody. He referred to the film as *his* film, never *our* film. Antonio was forbidden from attending dailies, which made the actor livid.

"Superstitious my ass," he said to Madonna and me. "Alan is just a fucking control freak. I spoke with my lawyer and from now on it goes into my contract in BIG PRINT that I get to see dailies."

Madonna and I were equally frustrated, but we focused on how to finish filming without resorting to a body double for her last dance sequences. "Vincent," she finally said, "maybe you better think about getting one. Can Kim do it?"

"No, Kim can't do it. You'll be fine. We'll just take it slow."

I put my attention toward making Madonna feel comfortable. The pregnancy took a toll on her stamina, but she still worked twelve-hour days, dancing in heels on marble floors. I think seeing the end of the film in sight kept her going. It had been whispered among all of us since leaving Buenos Aires that her performance was being praised as Oscar worthy. It had to be on her mind.

Having completed our work in Budapest, Kim and I headed back to London to cast and choreograph the bar scene for the song "Buenos Aires." For the choreography, I decided to not "clean" Madonna's movements to perfection. I wanted her to be the young Eva Duarte, innocent and naïve. I went into her dressing room before we began the shoot. "Please don't work so hard," I said. "I know you, and you'll go 'til you drop. Just tell me when you need a break, and we'll make it happen."

"I'll be fine." She squeezed my hand.

When "action" was called, it was as if we were in La Boca, Buenos Aires, 1939. Madonna entered the bar as an awestruck country bumpkin, Eva Duarte, and emerged ready to conquer the world. Alan pranced in the wake of the camera dolly. We shot all day and upon leaving, Madonna, though exhausted, thanked everyone.

Alan turned to me. "Do you believe it? She said, 'thank you.'"

"She always thanks us, Alan."

"Well," he replied. "That's the first time she's done it on set with the rest of us." I let it go. Just then a huge cake with blazing candles was wheeled onto the set. It was my birthday, and Madonna had done it again. She led everyone in singing "Happy Birthday" and gave me two tickets to see Matthew Bourne's *Swan Lake*. What a day!

I had one more day of shooting, a sexy bedroom scene between Eva and Juan Peron. Alan was charming and even generous. He gave me the floor as I finessed the romantic rumba bolero for Madonna and Jonathan Pryce. My work on *Evita* concluded on May 19, 1996.

Kim and I arrived at LAX, happy to be home. For forty-five minutes, I looked for the driver with the placard that had my name, but we couldn't find him. We called London. "Lisa Moran is very sorry," said another nameless assistant on the line. "She's been very busy and forgot to get you a car. You'll have to get one yourself and please send us the invoice."

The movie was released on Christmas Day in 1996 and made a killing at the box office, earning over $151 million worldwide. Madonna won the Golden Globe award for Best Actress and *Evita* won the Golden Globe for Best Picture: Comedy or Musical. The film received five Oscar nods: Cinematography, Art Direction, Sound, Film Editing, and Original Song (Madonna's solo, "You Must Love Me"), which won.

Madonna didn't win an Oscar for Best Actress. She wasn't even nominated. It felt unfair. She had created a superlative Eva. No matter, Madonna will always be linked with the film, *Evita*, and in some way with Eva Peron.

Choreographers are the only creative people on any movie set who don't have a category to receive an Oscar. Sadly, every choreographer's agent has to struggle with the producers to even get credit on the crawl at the end of the film. Main title credit is almost nonexistent for a choreographer, even on a movie musical. In

August, three months after returning to Los Angeles, my agent Julie received a note from producer, David Wimbury:

Dear Julie,
Re: Vincent Paterson Credit

Please confirm with Vince: As we have now completed filming, should his contribution still merit main title credit on the film?

Sincerely,
David Wimbury

My agent replied professionally:

Dear David,

As per our contract, yes.

Kind regards,
Julie McDonald

Though Julie and I had laughingly discussed sending this reply:

Dear David,

Are you fucking mad?

Kind Regards,
Julie McDonald

Neither the producers nor Alan negated my positive experience on *Evita*. I wish Alan had chosen to play more than a minor role in my experience but he didn't. It was the sensuality of Buenos Aires with the music on the streets and in the milongas, the warmth and beauty of the people, and the tango that got into my blood and rewarded me with a cherished life chapter. And the story of Eva Duarte Peron, a fascinating political pop star who constantly caused us to ask the question: good or bad, saint or sinner? And Madonna. These are the foundations of my memories.

After finishing my final rehearsal on set with Madonna, I went to say goodbye. A grand library with dark, wooden walls had been converted into her dressing room. Through a carved archway that framed her like a marble sculpture, sat Madonna. She was perched on a tall stool behind a makeup mirror in her white satin gown, illuminated with a ghostly light from the frosted white bulbs. Madonna's blonde hair was pulled back in a magnificent nest of curls encircled by an intricate braid. The bodice of her gown shimmered in the eerie light, and she appeared to radiate with an internal glow. The surroundings demanded whispered tones.

"Hi, honey," I said. "I've just come to say goodbye."

"I can see," she said. "When do you leave?"

"Tomorrow morning, early. Thanks for everything, Madonna."

"Are you going back to LA?"

"Yeah, sleep in my own bed."

Then she looked me in the eyes. "Thank you, Vince, for all of your help. You were wonderful." I kissed her on the cheek and left her with a goodbye note:

Dear Madonna, sister, daughter, lover, friend, partner-in-crime, finger sometimes on the same trigger...

What a pleasure to have completed this mad circle with you. Our collaboration has been an utter joy. It is not often I find a spirit to rival, challenge, and complement my own. I always seem to meet my match with you. Thank you for allowing me to be a part of your worlds—the personal, the professional, the historical.

Congratulations on your stunning work throughout.

Love,

Vincent

P.S. Remember, choreographers don't get Oscars.

8.

When Instinct Grabs You
by the Throat

Mike Nichols and The Birdcage

M Y HERO. I HAD BEEN a Mike Nichols fan for as long as I can remember watching movies. Never in my wildest dreams did I imagine I'd one day create by his side. When an almost-opportunity arose, I took the bull by the horns.

In late 1994, the entertainment magazine, *Variety*, published a blurb that Mike Nichols was directing a contemporary movie version of *La Cage Aux Folles*, or, in English, *The Birdcage*. It would star Robin Williams, Nathan Lane, Gene Hackman, Dianne Wiest, and Hank Azaria. Elaine May would adapt and update the script. Stephen Sondheim would compose the music. Tommy Tune would choreograph.

Stop the press!

My instincts told me that I was the one to choreograph this film. I admired Tommy Tune's work but making women look fab-u-lous was at the top of my list of skills. I called my agent.

"Julie, I want to choreograph *The Birdcage* for Mike Nichols."

"I think Tommy Tune is doing it already. Do you know Mike?"

"No, I know everything he's ever directed, but I don't know him personally. Julie, I *am* the person to do this movie. Please get in touch with his office and set up a meeting with him. I know this is meant for me. So, please, let's make it happen."

Next thing I knew I was sitting at a window table at Trattoria Dell'Arte Restaurant on Seventh Avenue in New York across from Mike Nichols. I could barely eat.

"You're not eating much, Vincent. The food is delicious here."

"Well, I have to confess that I'm a little nervous. I'm humbled sitting with you, Mr. Nichols."

"Mike, please. Well, stop it, please."

"Okay. Done."

"Now, my good boy, tell me why you feel you are right to choreograph this film. You know I have already asked my friend Tommy Tune to do it."

"I know you have, and I think Tommy's work is fantastic. But my career has often been about making women look feminine, classy, and sensual. I know how to make a woman's body sing. I taught Madonna how to drape in a chair and inhale a cigarette in a long cigarette holder. Simple movements can illustrate femininity. I've worked with some very sexy women—Sheena Easton, Whitney Houston, Sherilyn Fenn, Diana Ross, and Chita. *And* I've worn high heels before," I laughed. "I had to dance in high heels when I assisted Michael Peters in some all-female dance pieces. In this film, you need someone who can make male dancers and Nathan Lane appear to be *professional* female impersonators. I can do that. I'm such a fan of your work, Mike. It's so thorough. I'll give you more than what you want if you just give me the chance and your trust."

"Vincent, what do you feel about Sondheim doing the music? I've had a few talks with him, and he is very willing. Be honest."

"Mike, I'm a really honest person. So, to be honest…okay. I love Sondheim's work. But, if you're updating this to an upscale drag club in Miami, maybe you should consider having contemporary music. If you go to a drag club, the girls aren't singing Broadway hits. They're singing Donna Summer and Madonna, not Streisand, Garland, or

Minnelli anymore. Fresher, contemporary music would probably be playing in this club. But it depends on the kind of club you envision."

"Hmmm. Do you know anyone who could put this together musically?"

I did.

"Well, let me think about this, my boy. I think this could be a marriage made in heaven."

I got the gig. It *was* a marriage made in heaven. Every second. I cannot sing loudly enough the praise I have for Mike Nichols. He was the most knowledgeable actor's director that I have ever known. Mike met with my arranger friend Steve Goldstein and decided that Steve and I would work together on the music for the club, The Birdcage. Mike gave me creative freedom to cast the male dancers who would make the best drags.

Mike wanted me to be as much a part and presence on this film as I wanted. Eventually this led to creating dances and movement in places where no one had anticipated needing a choreographer's eye: for the two sets of parents dancing together at the dinner party, for Hank Azaria's ridiculous rumba to Gloria Estefan's song "Conga," for the reunion dance between Robin and Christine Baranski, as well as for all the performances in the club including Gene Hackman's finale in drag. And I conceived and choreographed what many find to be the funniest moment of the film, Robin Williams's "Eclectic Celebration of the Dance."

I had created with Robin several times before, and we were very comfortable working together. I had choreographed the opening numbers for *Comic Relief*, a television show that aired annually and where on-air contributions were given to global charities. These numbers always included Robin, Whoopi Goldberg, and Billy Crystal, and we always had a ball. I had also directed Robin in a fascinating documentary *In Search of Dr. Seuss*, for the Turner Network. Robin played a Seussian father who read to his own daughter and the daughter of director Chris Columbus.

On a break from the "rehearsal scene" in *The Birdcage* with Nathan Lane and Luca Tommassini, Robin pulled me behind the set.

"Vincent, HELP! I am dying here playing the straight gay man. I don't have a funny moment. I *need* a funny moment. But it has to be real. Can you think of anything that would fit in this scene? It has to happen fast."

"Wow, Robin, give me a minute. I'll think of something."

And I did. I put together the "Eclectic Celebration of the Dance," taught it to Robin on the next break, and he was prepared to do it on the next take. All was quiet on the set. "Action." The scene began, it came to Robin's moment, and he took it. He began with the lines Elaine May had written and then took a left turn into what I had created for him. The crew and Nathan lost it, laughing hysterically. Mike and Elaine were infected as well.

When Robin finished, Mike said, "That was just wonderful, Robin."

"Thank you, thank you. Vincent created that."

"Thank you, Vincent," laughed Mike. "Now let's get back to shooting the scene as written, please."

"Oh, Mike," begged Robin, as he crawled on his knees across the stage floor toward Mike, hands clasped as if in prayer. "Can't we do it again. Please. Pretty please."

"All right. Let's get one take we like as originally written, and we can wrap with adding this additional monologue to the scene. But I want you both to know, it probably won't be in the film," Mike smiled kindly.

Elaine May began feverishly writing some new dialogue lead-in lines and threw them to Luca Tommassini who played the dancer. What remains in the film is:

Dancer: "And what do I do? Do I just stand here like an object?"

Armand: "No, you do an eclectic celebration of the dance... You do Fosse, Fosse, Fosse... You do Martha Graham, Martha Graham, Martha Graham... Or Twyla, Twyla, Twyla... Or Michael Kidd, Michael Kidd, Michael Kidd, Michael Kidd... Or Madonna,

Madonna…" (And, I believe Nathan Lane came up with…) "But you keep it all inside."

I was in Buenos Aires with *Evita* when *The Birdcage* opened, so I missed the excitement. I got this cherished letter from Mike :

MIKE NICHOLS

February 21, 1996

Dear Vincent honey.

Sorry it has taken me so long. It is a madhouse here, but a very nice madhouse. Everything is going great for the movie, knock on wood. Our screenings are pandemonium, the reviews that come in are fantastic (two thumbs up, four bunnies, etc.) and the studio is all excited. I'm trying to be excited but may be too old.

I think often of you and love getting your missives from all over. Every day during mixing, etc., I look at your work and think how wonderful it is and how much you have given me and the picture.

Believe it or not, Orpheus is still being worked on. Apparently, the French are hopeless about rights, but slow headway is being made.

I hope we see each other soon and that life treats you as you deserve.

Love,

My story about *The Birdcage* used to end there. But it has developed a new wrinkle. I recently read an article in the *Huffington Post* entitled "25 Years Later, 'The Birdcage' Is Hollywood's Most Monumental Gay Movie" by Matthew Jacobs. In the very first paragraphs of the article, Jacobs states that Robin Williams improvised the now famous "Eclectic Celebration of the Dance," as written in the recent biography, *Mike Nichols: A Life* by Mark Harris.

Robin Williams improvised the now famous "Eclectic Celebration of the Dance."

My stomach turned reading and rereading this erasure of my contribution. I created that piece. I created it specifically for Robin knowing he would "werk it," and I was elated that he loved it. It wasn't improvised at all. In fact, knowing that both Robin and Mike were on set to witness my creation of this iconic dance piece for the film and would absolutely correct this misinformation, but are both no longer alive to do so—it was a sickening feeling.

I reached out to Matthew Jacobs, and we quickly unraveled that he cited as fact an incorrect assumption Mark Harris had written in the Nichols biography. When I clarified what really happened and that I had created that moment at Robin's request, Mr. Jacobs added a correction to his article. Mr. Harris, however, after correspondences from mutual artist friends as well as myself, never responded. This is not uncommon for choreographers. But we'll dissect this further in the next chapter.

Besides *The Birdcage*, I had the elation of creating with Mike on one other film, *Closer*. I got a call from him one day, "Vincent, how are you, my boy? I'm in London directing the film *Closer* with a brilliant cast, and I've run into a bit of a challenge that, for some reason, I can't seem to hurdle. So I thought of you. Are you available around now?"

"Sure, Mike. What's the situation?"

"Natalie Portman, who's a director's dream, has a scene with Clive Owen in a private room in a strip club. They have dialogue while she's performing a striptease or lap dance of sorts on a circular couch. It's a very sensitive scene because eventually, she shows him 'the goods.' I was hoping you might consider coming over and helping me with the scene, even directing it with me."

"Wow. Sure. Thanks, Mike. When? I'm there."

I flew to London and designed the scene with Natalie and Clive. Mike made some adjustments and then we shot it. Codirecting a scene with Mike Nichols even topped acting in a scene with Catherine Deneuve during *Dancer in the Dark*. Sharing dinner together, Mike continued to amuse me, discussing a crazy range of topics from heroin highs to Meryl Streep. Mike asked me if I would choreograph/stage a few other general scenes in the strip club as well as cast the girls. Certainly, I acquiesced. When he arrived in the room for the final audition for the strippers, I wanted to surprise him as well as have fun with him. I sat him in a chair in the center of the room and had each sexy female stripper give him a lap dance. From the color in his cheeks and the smile on his face, I don't think it's a memory he forgot for a long time.

He called me again, a few years later, "Listen, I want you to hear it from the horse's mouth. I am trying to have you involved in a new Broadway show I'm directing, but the producers are bending my arm to use a choreographer of whom they are very fond. I want you to know I am doing my best, but I am not sure how it will turn out. Let's keep our hopes up."

Unfortunately, that project never happened for me. But in 2000, what did happen was Mike, along with cinematographer Caleb Deschanel, sponsored me to become a member of the Academy of Motion Picture Arts and Sciences. There are only a handful of choreographers in the Academy.

A few times in my life I've had something said to me that has become an integral part of the way I create. Sometimes an integral part of the way I live my life. By now you know Michael Jackson's words, "Let the music talk to you. Let the music tell you what it wants to be," have become the standard for how I enter any project that involves music. From Mike Nichols, I learned another important lesson that I use constantly as a director.

Mike Nichols invited me to the first table reading of *The Birdcage* in a soundstage at Paramount Studios. Sitting at the table were some of the funniest and most talented actors and actresses in America: Robin Williams, Nathan Lane, Gene Hackman, Dianne Wiest, Christine Baranski, and Hank Azaria. The cast read the script aloud. They were hilarious. More than hilarious. Everyone was loud and big and inspired each other to heights of outrageousness. It was a laugh riot, and we were all exhausted with delight. Mike gave us a short break. When we returned to the table, Mike said, "Everyone, *that* reading was about as funny as it gets. Terrific work. Let's read it again, and this time let's try something a little different.'"

He gave the cast one direction. "Let's read it once again, but this time in '*close-up*.'" The second reading was just as funny, but more importantly, now it was honest.

9.

Choreographers Still Don't Get Oscars

The Case for Credit and Recognition

I ONCE HAD A life-altering experience that taught me an important lesson about trusting my instincts and overcoming the impossible. It's the story of how I lost part of my finger and grew it back.

In the eighties, Nautilus made popular workout equipment with exposed chains. While using one of those machines, one of my fingers got caught in the chain and was nearly torn from my hand. Blood gushing, I was rushed to the emergency room at Cedars-Sinai in Los Angeles. Ligaments and tendons were severely damaged, bone had been ground up and amputation of the remaining part of the finger was recommended.

I couldn't lose my finger. As a dancer, losing expression in my hand would make me feel incomplete. I simply refused the idea. I was determined to regrow my finger. When I told this to the doctor, he replied, "That's impossible." My instincts told me he was wrong.

I know it sounds crazy, but I was driven by the simple thought that I had grown this finger once in my mother's womb. Why couldn't I do it again? I visited nontraditional healers and meditation masters. I culled from their knowledge and created my own path to healing. I spent hours in meditation focusing on my damaged finger and visualizing it in perfect health, seeing the torn tissues knitting back together and the bone regrowing. I enlisted friends from all over the world to say aloud at noon each day, "Vincent's finger is as perfect as my finger." Within five months my finger had grown back. You can only tell it was damaged if you look closely.

I think about my miraculously regrown finger whenever I'm faced with something that seems impossible. I look at where I am in my profession and I look where I came from. That was possible. I moved to LA with almost nothing and, trusting my instincts, had a wonderful dance career. That was possible.

Throughout my choreography career, my agents and I have fought for credit, and fair wages, which we often received. But ownership of work, pension, health and welfare, royalty sharing? "Impossible." For three decades I have advocated and supported the establishment of a Choreographer's Guild for Electronic and Live Media. It's not only possible. It's long overdue. I believe if we can collectively envision a union for choreographers, it can happen. And it must happen because choreographers face significant inequities within our business, and it's only getting worse.

Remember *The Birdcage* story from the previous chapter? Where someone assumed Robin Williams had improvised something I had actually crafted and choreographed? Mike Nichols gave me main title credit on *The Birdcage*. That means I'm listed at the top of the film with all the other key creatives, including the movie stars. It wouldn't take much to fact check whether or not a film had a choreographer who could be tracked down and asked about their work. I was never asked about *The Birdcage* by Mike Nichols's biographer or the journalist doing the write up. I'm going to guess most choreographers in Hollywood with some legacy of work have dealt with this issue at some level. It all points to the gross injustice that exists for all choreographers working outside of Broadway: There is a lack of professional equality on every level for the choreographer. And it begins with perception.

```
                         ARMAND
         Celsius, look...this may be a drag
         show but it still has to be a good
         drag show, if possible--a great
         drag show...

                         ALBERT
         Yes!  And just because you're
         eighteen and hung doesn't mean
         you're qualified...

                         ARMAND
         Let me do this, Albert.
              (to Celsius)
         This is a complex number.  Full of
         mythic themes.  You were invented
         by the woman who's singing, you're
         her fantasy, this gorgeous fantasy,
         free and arrogant...and then,
         suddenly, you, the fantasy, see
         her, your inventor--and she becomes
         your fantasy.

                         CELSIUS
         I don't think I get it.

                         ALBERT
         Try more gum.

                         ARMAND
         Albert!  Well, you have to explore
         it, Celsius.  But start with the
         premise that, when you see this
         stunning, smoldering creature - she
         transcends your desire to chew -
         she electrifies you, something
         begins in your pelvis that travels
         straight to your heart - but hit
         the pelvis.

                         CELSIUS
         But what do I do?  I don't want
         to just stand here like an
         object.

                         ARMAND
         Do this!  5, 6, 7, 8!
              (he dances)
         And this!  Do a stunning
         eclectic, celebration of dance...
              (dances; to Albert)
         ...and you, of course, sing...
              (he dances on...and on)

                         VAL
         Pop!
```

Most everyone has some idea of what a director does. The director runs the show. The director is the team captain who guides and leads. In most cases, aside from the producers, the director has the final call on every aspect of the artistic creation. And even if he or she didn't make the final call, the director is usually held responsible for a project's ultimate success or failure. Most everyone has a general understanding of what the writer, actor, composer, costume designer, and editor does. If you run down the major categories of any awards show, you can see the list of the primary artistic leaders, and it's pretty clear what they each contribute to a project.

Choreography, however, is a nebulous art. Choreographers make up dance steps, right? Yes, but that's only a part of what we do. Moments of dance inserted into any genre require that they feel connected to the storytelling, the style, and the rhythm of the whole piece. The choreographer must know as much about the story as the director or risk creating movement that looks completely out of place.

I will often be handed a film or TV script that reads, "And now a dance happens." Or I'll be asked to create from commercial storyboards in which bodies in action are illustrated by vague line drawings. As a choreographer, often directors tell me to "create what you think will work." Now, my role as choreographer expands. For example, above is the original page from Elaine May's script for *The Birdcage* before I created the "Eclectic Celebration of the Dance" moment for Robin. Note the bottom section where it simply reads "he dances" and "he dances on…and on."

Or how about this page from Lars von Trier's *Dancer in the Dark*, where musical numbers are inserted as scenes with suggestions of action and lyrics but the actual dance movements will be up to me. You can see my notes in the margins.

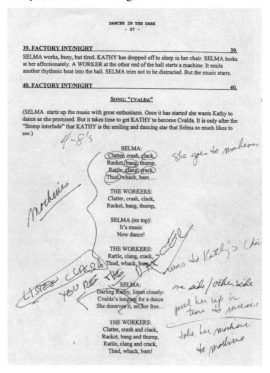

First, I *contemplate* the idea of the dance or dance/scene. What does this movement signify in terms of plot? How can the movement best convey the character or characters and the interaction between them at this moment? How can I use movement to help sell a product? How can I translate an idea into a physical reality? After listening to what the music tells me it wants to be, I *choreograph* the dance or *design the staging* that is created for a scene, though it may not be actual dance. An example of staging would be teaching Madonna how to look glamorous sitting on a divan and smoking a cigarette in "Express Yourself." The dance usually propels the plot, so I am also *writing*.

Second, in most cases, I select the dancers sometimes with or sometimes without anyone's approval. So, I am *casting*.

Third, I have to be as clear in my explanation of my physical intention with an actress like Kim Cattrall in *Mannequin*, as with Charles Barkley, with whom I shot several Nike commercials for director Joe Pytka. I *direct* the dancers or actors as to how their character portrays any dance or movement that I've created, handing the director a fairly finished product that they can then incorporate into the larger work. So, I'm *directing*.

In many cases, the choreographer will be asked to give valuable input about costumes/wardrobe, musical choices, sets, surfaces for dancing, and even the framing of camera shots. It's exciting to participate in all these elements and to utilize the knowledge many of us have in multiple areas of production.

But here's the rub, and it's a big one—in spite of all that specialized knowledge and responsibility to the storytelling, choreographers have no ownership of their work, no protection for their creations, no fair compensation, no definitive professional credit, and, consequently, lack widespread recognition. Choreographers, no matter how innovative or essential to a film, can't even win an Oscar.

There is *no union* for choreographers outside of the Broadway and regional theater arena. There is absolutely no one to assure us of any ownership rights, credit, or residual compensation for the creations we have made for film, TV, music videos, celebrity concert tours, commercials, industrials, cruise ship shows, ice-skating shows, circus tours, or theme-park shows. The choreographers who create for all of these venues don't have the same union protections offered to the writers, actors, directors, stage managers, and even animals on the working set. The consequences of this are shocking.

Let's first consider *credit*. Directors' and producers' names are prominent in film, television, and theatrical work. There are paragraphs in contracts dedicated to the billing and credit of actors, writers, composers, lyricists, cinematographers, editors, designers, animal wranglers, caterers, stunt actors, and stunt designers down to the size of the point type in programs or print advertising. These are the direct result of unions and guilds working for the rights of their artists. On most films, the choreographer's credit, if it exists at all, is on the final crawl of a film close to the very end. On television, it means trying to read microscopic credits that zoom by like a Tokyo bullet train. Again, if at all.

For my work on the Blond Ambition Tour, the *BAD* Tour, and all the music videos for Michael Jackson or Madonna, I had to share the credit with them as co-director and/or co-choreographer. Even *that* was unheard of at the time. The pop superstars nearly always took the credit for directing and choreographing their tours and fans were led to believe their favorite stars actually just "came up" with those dance sequences. Madonna did no choreography at all. Mike created his movement for his individual sections only. As generous as Mike and Madonna both were to me, I had to fight tooth and nail for credit whenever it was due. Their managers became the "bad guys," stepping in and making it clear that, though the predominance of work was mine, the legends were going to share credit along with me, whether they conceived the work or not. If I didn't like that, I would not be hired again. Even in the heyday of MTV's all-dancing videos, the credits on a card at the end of a video listed the name of the song and the artist, maybe the name of the director if it was a famous director. No mention of choreographers.

Think about how choreographers are recognized in popular culture compared to the other creative leads on famous movies or musicals. Ask someone in the general public to name one famous choreographer other than Bob Fosse. Some might mention a choreographer from the TV shows *Dancing With The Stars* or *So You Think You Can Dance*. But then ask them if they can name any famous projects Bob Fosse choreographed. Most people can't. But many people can, of course, name famous actors, directors, writers, and musicians as well as something specific those artists created. Being able to name them means they were properly credited. That credit gives their name a value, potentially leading to more paid work. It's nearly impossible for a choreographer to receive main title credit near that of the director, star talent, or writer, even for a movie musical that can be more than 50 percent dance sequences. Search a musical film on IMDb, check out the full list of cast and crew. Even a choreographer with main title credit on a film is buried somewhere with "additional crew" in the full list, if mentioned at all!

Imagine if a visual artist was never allowed to sign their works or we never knew who painted the Mona Lisa. Credit is important to all creative artists. It's our résumé to get the next gig.

Lack of properly defined *credit* promotes thievery, intentional or unintentional. Anyone can usurp our work, use it whenever and wherever they like, even credit themselves as the choreographer. There have been two Cirque du Soleil shows using work I created for Michael Jackson. Neither has given me respectable credit for my original choreography and neither provides me with any kind of financial royalty. And because it is legal, the producers feel it is justified. Fairness and morality never enter the equation. Not so long ago, the popular show *Dancing With The Stars* introduced another choreographer as having choreographed "Smooth Criminal."

The show not only misled a nationwide audience as to this other choreographer's false involvement in Michael's legacy but also ignored my agent's request to make a brief on-air announcement giving me the credit I deserved. It happened again, same show, two years later. One of the show's choreographers recreated the Marie Antoinette version of "Vogue" that I devised for Madonna. He used the predominance of my choreography and yet, again, I received no credit or compensation.

The lack of properly defined credit and no union to help arbitrate or mediate claims, encourages plagiarism. All great artists, from Picasso to Michael Peters, have been inspired by other great artists. As artists, we keep our eyes and minds open to inspiration anywhere we can find it. The difference is allowing a work to inspire you rather than plagiarizing iconic steps and claiming them as one's own. Plagiarism creates a paradox where it puts the choreography community at odds with itself, making it all the more difficult to come together to create an effective union. *Credit* for choreographers is a must!

There is also the issue of *ownership*. Writers, musicians, lyricists, composers, and some designers own their work. We've all seen lawsuits in the news where an idea is stolen and lawyers decide who was the original creator and a settlement is reached because that creation has monetary value. All written dramatic work can be registered with the United States Copyright Office and with the Writers Guild to help protect a writer's work. You don't even have to be a member of the Guild for the WGA to register your original work with them. You simply pay a nominal fee and your script or treatment idea is registered. Musicians have three entities available to them—the American Federation of Musicians; the American Society of Composers, Authors, and Publishers; and Broadcast Music, Inc. When you hear a famous recording artist on the soundtrack of a film or TV show, a producer paid money for the right to use that song. Musicians can sue for lost wages and royalties due to illegal use of their original work. Playwrights have the Dramatists Guild to offer legal advice on both contracts and potential rights violations.

But there is zero *ownership* for choreographers. Almost always a choreographer is hired as a "work-for-hire," meaning that all work becomes the property of the production company, the record label, or the musical artist. As the creators, we must give up ownership of our babies if we want to be employed. I don't believe Madonna has ever given ownership or royalty participation to her directors or choreographers, nor has Beyoncé or JLO or Rihanna or Miley Cyrus. I hope they prove me wrong. As a choreographer, I have signed "work-for-hire" contracts for every film, every commercial, every pop tour, every music video, every TV show I have ever choreographed, forfeiting everything for a one-time paycheck.

I own or co-own *nothing* I created for Michael Jackson. For MJJ Productions, I was always a "work-for-hire." Anyone can steal choreography and does. Dance teachers on YouTube teach my choreography. All over the globe, Michael Jackson tribute shows performed by look-alikes and grossing thousands of dollars use my choreography and that of Michael Peters. An actor that I recently directed in Vienna told me, "My boyfriend will be happy to meet you. He created a successful show called *Thriller Nights*, and he uses all of your choreography in the show."

We are not asked for permission to use the work—which is often bastardized. We get no credit. We get no royalty. It's as if we don't exist.

A new Broadway show, *MJ: The Musical*, is set to open in December 2021 under the producing banner of the Michael Jackson Estate. My agents and I are aware that, as of this writing, the music of "Smooth Criminal" and "Black or White" will be used. This is the credit my agent has been told will be listed in the program just before the cast and crew bios:

> *The Estate of Michael Jackson wants to thank the choreographers who worked with Michael on his short films, concerts, and live performances throughout his career. In particular, the*

Estate would like to acknowledge Michael Peters (co-choreographer on "Thriller" and "Beat It"), Gregg Burge (co-choreographer on "Bad") and Vincent Paterson (co-choreographer on "Smooth Criminal") whose original work with Michael was an inspiration for those production numbers in this show.

It took months of phone calls, emails, and meetings by agents, producers, lawyers, and me to achieve having this simple credit included in the program. We were never certain it was going to happen. More importantly, there was no union or other governing body to ensure this credit would have ever appeared in the program. Even though I am a member of the Broadway union, the Society of Directors and Choreographers (SDC), they cannot support me because I don't own my work. When one creates on Broadway, one owns his/her work, but you never own what you choreograph for music videos.

This *MJ: The Musical* situation prompts a troubling question for any future Broadway show that might use the work created by those of us in the electronic media: If Christopher Wheeldon, the Broadway director/choreographer, builds on top of my choreography from the Michael Jackson short films and calls it "inspiration," does he, as a member of SDC, now own my underlying work? Can he now win a Tony award for Best Choreographer with support from my and/or Michael Peters's choreography? Who will determine if he created enough original choreography to have earned a credit for creation?

We've already been told we'll receive no royalties. Ironically, if we choreographers were to take the dances we created and feature them in a Broadway show we produced ourselves, we would very likely be sued by the Jackson estate. And they'd win. *Work-for-hire*, are you kidding me? *Ownership*, yes!

How about the *financial* issue? A playwright is paid to write a play, then, when it is performed, that playwright is paid a percentage of the box office income called a royalty. Directors are covered by the Directors Guild of America (DGA) and receive royalties, salary minimums, highly visible credit, and ownership of their work. This is also the case for a composer or lyricist supplying music for any of the genres cited above. Also for musicians and their music, and actors and their performances. Broadway shows contractually give royalties to choreographers, but in every other case, choreographers do not participate in a royalty pool unless tirelessly negotiated by one's agent.

For example, there is a video game based on "Smooth Criminal" that uses my concept and choreography for the short film, including the lean. I have no union to assure I receive royalties or even credit for my original work now appropriated for a profit by people I've never met. A famous sculptor in China has created a piece of Michael in "the lean" from "Smooth Criminal." He is selling small replicas. This is my original concept, yet I receive no credit, no royalty. This injustice affects almost all choreographers whose names you know or don't know but whose steps you may have danced. Just think how often Michael Peters's choreography for "Thriller" has been used over the decades. He never received one penny as a royalty fee for that work. Had you heard of Michael Peters before reading this book?

Choreographers also receive no *pension*, *health*, or *welfare* benefits. Without a recognized union that encompasses all choreography work, it is impossible for choreographers to establish any such benefits.

Finally, there is the matter of recognition in the world of awards. Aside from the Tony Award situation I mention previously, there are inequities with awards across all mediums. And, yes, there is actually no avenue for a choreographer to take home an Academy Award for a multimillion-dollar musical film like *Evita, La La Land, Dancer in the Dark, Grease,* or *Dirty Dancing*. Choreographers also aren't included in the Golden Globes or People's Choice Awards. The Emmys has two categories for choreography, one for scripted programs and one for reality or variety programs. However, neither award presentation for choreography is televised on the primetime Emmy broadcast. They are presented at the untelevised creative arts ceremony the night before.

"Impossible!" has rung through our heads for half a century. How would it work? How would we organize? What would an all-encompassing choreographers' union really look like? How do you arbitrate ownership for dance steps? We've never done such a thing. Yes. It might be a challenge. And it's always easy to give up. But what's to gain?

I've learned through the process of growing back my finger, by working diligently, and by trusting my instincts that nothing is impossible. Voices are rising to create a Choreographers Guild for the electronic and live arena genres. Challenge inspires artistry and creativity. Choreographers must collectively visualize change, see a guild in our future, and correct this oversight in how the entertainment industry operates. This collective consciousness includes respecting each other so no choreographer feels replaceable if any one of us becomes too vocal fighting for what we know is equitable.

Dance is the gift choreographers give society. For many of us, our creations are our children. We should receive all of the benefits afforded other creatives—*credit*, *ownership* of our work, *royalties*, *pension/healthcare* benefits, and *award* recognition.

As a director, I will fight to give choreographers even more than what Mike Nichols, Joe Pytka, and (as you'll read in the next chapter) Lars von Trier gave me—creative support and credit for good work. The compositions of choreographers and the public's love for experiencing professional dance by capable performers are not going anywhere. Those who make it exceptional deserve a real seat at the creative artists' table. Some of them might also deserve an Oscar.

10.

A Danish, an Eskimo Pie,
and Buttons for Lunch

Lars von Trier's Dancer in the Dark

COCAINE. SCHNAPPS. KAYAKING. A little chaos and a shit-ton of imagination. This was a new recipe for working. At times maddening. At times electric. This was the world of film auteur and Danish national treasure, Lars von Trier.

I saw his 1996 film, *Breaking the Waves*, two nights in a row. Lars founded the Dogme 95 philosophy of filmmaking, which outlined definitive rules on how to create more organic films with an emphasis on actors and story rather than big-budget effects. "Dogme" had a philosophy and a strict list of rules—a manifesto—intended to empower filmmakers who might otherwise feel paralyzed by not having access to expensive cameras, lighting gear, or a large crew. Lars was one of the pioneers who blew the lid off independent filmmaking and truly challenged the form. I was an early fan.

When I experience an artist like Lars out in the world, someone with whom I want to create, I put their picture on my refrigerator. Then, as I pass the fridge every day, I visualize the person in the hope I will connect with their artistic thoughts on some astral plane. That it might bring us together to collaborate in some way. I know it sounds nuts, but it works.

In January of 1999, I got a call from my agent, Julie. "I know you only want to direct right now," she told me, "but Lars von Trier wants you to choreograph his new film, *Taps*, and it stars Björk. Vincent, both of their pictures are on your refrigerator."

Björk? AND Lars?

Taps was not going to be a Dogme film, but it was destined to be something special. Digital film technology was still new, and Lars wanted to use it completely for a feature film. The final cut was to be transferred to 35mm, but recording in the digital format allowed him to shoot lots of footage at very little cost.

I read the script but every musical sequence featured tap dancing...and I don't tap. (Recall my front-and-center faking it for Fosse?) Lars phoned me.

"Lars," I said, "I would love to work with you. But I don't tap."

"Wincent," Lars said. "Can you get someone to tap and you just point them around or something?"

"I don't work like that, Lars."

"Wincent, will you come to Denmark and talk?"

Zentropa is Lars's film company, housed in a former Copenhagen army barracks. I met Vibeke Windeløv, the film's producer, an intelligent and chic dirty-blonde. I liked her immediately. Lars was cheerful with a relaxed Danish thing going on. We talked for a moment, and then he dove into the script. "Wincent, tell me why you don't like the idea of the musical sequences being tap dance?"

"Well, Lars, first, I don't tap and I choreograph every step in my projects. Tap requires real technique, like ballet. You can't fake it. Björk isn't a dancer, and she'd never be able to carry off a film with only tap dances. I suggest the musical fantasy scenes be revisited based on the music Björk writes and allow each dance to have its own style."

Lars looked at me from under a furrowed brow. "Well, I don't want anything strange like people flying around. This is a very realistic story!" I turned to a page in the script where Selma, his lead character, dances on the ceiling.

"Lars, then what is this?"

He rose from his chair, walked in a little circle with his hands behind his back, returned to his seat, and looked at me. "Wincent," he said, "people don't say things like this to me."

"Lars," I said. "If we're going to work together, I have to be able to speak my mind. Americans aren't good at keeping our opinions to ourselves."

Lars left the room. "People don't question him," Vibeke said. "That's why you would be good for this film, Wincent."

The next morning, I met with Lars. "Wincent, you have worked in many musical projects. This is my first, and it will be a big musical, and it would be good to have you here. I also like that we could be brothers and talk together."

Negotiations were made, contracts signed, and I found myself back in Copenhagen with Lars, both of us a little drunk on schnapps. "So, Wincent, you think I should rewrite the script for Björk's music?"

"You've written Selma's fantasies happening at different emotional moments," I said, "so various styles of dance will give us the chance to be more specific about each emotional state."

"Maybe the final dance with her musical film idol Novy could be tap?"

"Perfect."

Lars decided we should go into seclusion to rewrite the script. We drove north to a tiny cottage that looked as if it had been plucked from the village of a train set under a Christmas tree. Snow wrapped the cottage near a bluff overlooking the North Sea. Inside, there were no heaters, only fireplaces, a few lamps, and several candles.

Time in this magical Nordic space with Lars was a dream fueled by vodka, cocaine, and schnapps. Not my usual way of creating, but it was perfect. While wolves howled outside, Lars and I discussed the script at length as we listened to the music that Björk had written. We devised a clever method for Björk to get into and out of Selma's fantasies, which were the musical sections.

On my way back to Los Angeles, I detoured to London to speak with Björk. We met at her apartment. "Björk, the music you've written for the movie is really inspiring," I said. "Lars wanted me to ask if you felt all right about cutting the songs down to a film-musical length."

"Well, Vincent, if that's what has to happen for the film, I understand," she replied. "These are working ideas, and I can make them tighter. Yeah." She was so easy-going, so chill.

By April, *Taps* had become *Dancer in the Dark* starring Björk and Catherine Deneuve. And I had discovered a great deal about my hero Lars. First, he'll only travel by car. And second, on her deathbed, his mother told Lars that the Jewish father who raised him wasn't his real father. So, on the same day he lost his mother, he discovered he wasn't Jewish and lost a lifetime of cultural heritage. It nearly shattered him.

He invited me to his home and showed me scenes from *Breaking the Waves* to illustrate the directorial approach he was planning, allowing the actors to improvise after the necessary takes were shot. He explained how he'd edit our film with jump cuts without regard to continuity in a scene. (Film continuity is having continuous action from one edit cut to the next to make it appear realistic.) Lars only cared about *emotional* continuity, not physical continuity.

"Lars, there's so much to do. When will the casting be done? I haven't seen any set designs, and Björk hasn't sent the music." I hesitated mentioning the lack of a musical supervisor. Lars replied, "Wincent, don't worry about anything!"

Of course, my first day in the filthy rehearsal room underscored my concerns. There was no constructed set or taped outlines of a set on the floor and no heat. I went to the Zentropa production office and clarified exactly what was needed. I think this first taste of American directness was like a kiss, a slap, and a bucket of cold water.

My assistant choreographer, Mette Berggreen, and I swept the floor, cleared out the cobwebs, and tossed out two dead pigeons. Over

Dad, Mom, Vincent. Chester Park, PA. 1951.
Photo from the author's personal collection

Vincent as Sacred Heart Boy. Our Lady of Charity School. 1964.
Photo from the author's personal collection

Karen MacDonald, Vincent. Michael Peters Workshop. 1980.

Photo by Kim Kaufman

Bill Goodson, Michael Peters, Tony Fields, Vincent. Michael Peters Workshop. 1980.

Photo by Kim Kaufman

Linda Klein, Frances Conroy, Vincent. Dickinson College. 1971.

Photo by Don Moll

Miss Piggy, Vincent. *John Denver and the Muppets: A Christmas Together*. 1979.

Photo from the author's personal collection

Vincent, Michael Jackson, and cast. "Smooth Criminal." 1988.
Photo by Sam Emerson

Michael Jackson, Vincent. "Smooth Criminal." 1988.
Photo by Sam Emerson

Vincent, Michael Jackson. "Thriller." 1983.
Photo from the author's personal collection

Vincent, Michael Jackson, Joe Pytka. Sanyo commercial. 1988.
Photo by Sam Emerson

Madonna. "Vogue." Commitment to Life. 1990.
Photo by Harold I. Huttas

Vincent, Madonna with the cast of Blond Ambition Tour. 1990.
Photo from the author's personal collection

Madonna, Vincent. My fortieth birthday. 1990.
Photo from the author's personal collection

Barbara Mandrell, Vincent. *Barbara Mandrell and the Mandrell Sisters*. 1982.
Photo by Ric Boyer

Vincent, Olivia Newton-John. "Totally Hot." 1979.

Vincent, Kim Cattrall, Andrew McCarthy. *Mannequin.* 1987.
Photo from the author's personal collection

Paul McCartney, Vincent. "Stranglehold." 1986.
Photo from the author's personal collection

Diane Day Crump-Richmond, Sara Miles de Levita, Jamilah Halvorson,
Vincent. "To Be Or Not To Be." 1983.

Vincent, Mel Brooks. "To Be Or Not To Be." 1983.

Photo from the author's personal collection

Vincent. *Rolling Stone Magazine: The 10th Anniversary.* 1977.
Photo from the author's personal collection

Juba Lucas, Vincent, Weird Al Yankovic, and the cast of "Eat It." 1984.
Photo by Jon "Bermuda" Schwartz

Van Halen, Vincent. "Hot for Teacher." 1984
Photo from the author's personal collection

Kim Blank, Madonna, Alan Parker, Vincent, and the cast of *Evita*. London. 1996.

Photo from the author's personal collection

Vincent, Michael Jackson. "Blood on the Dance Floor." 1997.

Photo by Bill Nation

Lars von Trier, Vincent, Catherine Deneuve. *Dancer in the Dark.* 1999.
Photo by Zentropa

Angela Winkler, Anna Loos, Peter Koch. Rehearsal for *Cabaret*. Berlin. 2004.
Photo by Joachim Gern

Anna Netrebko. *Manon*. Berlin. 2007.

Photo by Enrico Nawrath

Anna Netrebko, Vincent. Rehearsal for *Manon*. Berlin. 2007.

Photo by Enrico Nawrath

Vincent, Joe Masteroff, Joel Grey. *Cabaret*. Berlin. 2004.
Photo from the author's personal collection

Back: Maurice Bejart, Jean-Christophe Maillot, Bill T Jones, Sidi Larbi Cherkaoui, Akram Khan.
Front: Vincent, William Forsythe, and Marcia Haydee
Photo by Karl Lagerfeld

the next few days, I designed rough choreography for six dance scenes using incomplete music tracks because that's all I had to work with.

After a week or so, Björk arrived, and we got to work. I thought I would open the film with a tap step or two, so I taught Björk a simple time-step and a shuffle-ball-change. I began to create a dance style utilizing Björk's idiosyncratic movements, a mixture of child-like whimsy and naïveté. She moved like a marionette or a loveable cartoon character. We had so much fun.

To our first rehearsal of "My Favorite Things," she wore a calf-length, long-sleeved, red gingham dress over a pair of jeans. On her feet were little red patent leather shoes with taps. In the opening scene, fluttering her arms like a flying goose, I had her finish with a few tap flaps. As she exited backward through the stage left door, she flashed me a Forty-Second Street grin, exclaiming, "Now, that's entertainment!"

I was in the rehearsal room, designing a scene for *The Sound of Music* section where Selma/Björk comes to a theater rehearsal. In the scene, the rhythm of the drumsticks on the piano seduces Selma into a fantasy as she sings and dances about her love of musicals. The scene is called "In The Musicals Part I," and Lars came to watch. Samuel, the theater director, dances with Selma until the police arrive. I asked whether he had cast Samuel. I had been partnering Björk in rehearsals but would need two days with the actual actor playing Samuel. The script described Samuel as "sixty years old, rather urbane," and I had seen some of the headshots of actors under consideration. Older. Jewish.

"Wincent," Lars said. "I've found my Samuel. I'm very happy about it."

"Great!" I replied. "So, he'll be here by Thursday?"

"Oh, he's here now."

"Even better!"

He put an arm around me and took me to the rehearsal mirror and gestured toward it. Toward *me*. "Here he is, Wincent."

"Oh, Lars, I don't think so. I haven't acted in a long time. I made the decision to stay on *this* side of the camera as a choreographer and a director."

"But, Wincent," he continued, "you'll be my perfect Samuel. I've had a smile on my face since I thought about this last night. You must be Samuel!"

How could I refuse?

After feeling alienated by Alan Parker during *Evita*, working with Lars was the opposite. He observed rehearsals, totally engaged, watching us wade through the scenes for the first time. He asked me to simplify the dances. I told him, "The way I work, Lars, is to throw a lot of ideas on the canvas then scrape away the excess. I promise you that the final version of the dances will feel appropriate." He trusted me.

The choreography in *Dancer* is motivated by two things: 1) a rural community's theater production of *The Sound of Music* and 2) the musical fantasies where Selma escapes the overwhelmingly harsh real world. I told Lars, "I want the dance fantasies to feel as if Selma choreographed them, not me, so they'll have a raw and natural feel."

Lars adores dance, and I caught him on a break one night doing the line dance from *Saturday Night Fever* with some of the crew. Whenever he described a specific step or attempted to demonstrate some choreography he envisioned for the film, I found a way to incorporate it. I loved the pleasure on his face when he recognized it.

Since Lars was an advocate of creating dogmatic philosophies and cinematic rules, I created my own work manifesto as the choreographer on this project.

My Manifesto

1. *Allow the director's vision to speak through me.*
2. *Be true to my artistic heart and voice.*
3. *Ask questions, then ask more questions.*
4. *Listen with patience and understanding.*
5. *Instruct gently and clearly with inspiration and kindness.*
6. *Remember to say, "Thank you."*

7. *Continue to ask, "Have I taken enough risks; does the work scare me?"*
8. *Allow change and be grateful for it.*
9. *Learn something.*
10. *Enjoy myself.*

Catherine Deneuve arrived at her first dance rehearsal looking spectacular. She hadn't danced in a film in over thirty years, her last musical film being *Les Demoiselles de Rochefort* in 1967. She was beautiful and tough. She smoked a lot and got out of breath quickly, but I gave her plenty of breaks in between working her ass off. She learned my choreography through sheer determination. She and Björk portray best friends in the film, factory workers. In one song, "Cvalda," Selma leads everyone in a "Stomp"-like dance full of intricate, percussive rhythms. It wasn't easy. After that first rehearsal, Catherine got a standing ovation from all of us.

Lars, Björk, Catherine. It's a wonder to me how these three talents, each so different yet great in their own way, came together on this project. And how did I find myself able to relate so easily with each one? Part of it might be my overall connection to the story we were telling. We were filming on the other side of the world, but the story actually takes place in Washington, USA. The entire world of the film is a rural area of blue-collar workers in the 1960s. A place not much different from where I grew up. And Selma, Björk's character, is a single mother in this world doing everything possible to make a better life for her son. She actually resembled my mother in those ways.

After Mom divorced my abusive father, we were still an emotional family, but rage and anger were replaced by love and passion. Everyone kissed each other on the lips. My brothers, sister, mom, and I all developed distinctive, unapologetic, infectious laughs. (In fact, mine is the first human sound you hear in *Dancer* since I was now playing the role of Samuel.) Growing up with a young single mom meant one moment she was the disciplinarian, the next we would all be rolling in gales of laughter—each fighting to get to our one bathroom before we peed our pants. I credit Mom for my sense of humor. She was always ready to laugh. And laughter has saved me more than once while working with the found family that usually evolves on a film set.

But that carefree openness was Mom at home. Out in the world, though her laughter in a crowded room was unmistakable, she refused offers to dance at parties, didn't attend PTA meetings, and was even uncomfortable meeting my friends' parents. Having five kids by twenty-six must have been a challenge; we never had much money. Even when they were still married, she stretched my father's meager earnings, and there was even less after the divorce. But she worked hard to put food on our table and dress us all perfectly—shirts and socks had to match. This could also be one reason I had an affinity with both Catherine and Björk, even though they were so different as performers, they were both that kind of person who doesn't simply get dressed...*she puts herself together*. That was definitely Mom.

Unlike celebrities who get comfortable in front of cameras, Mom never seemed to recognize her beauty. This conflict of striving to look beautiful yet being so timid made her a greater riddle to me than the Sphinx. There was a back and forth with her: confident, shy, confident...then shy again. Like the character of Selma, Mom lived life as two different characters.

Catherine was the true legend of the film—a bona fide, megawatt movie star. She treated us as her equals, while working just as hard. One night, Mette and I drove Catherine back to the Hotel d'Angleterre. We laughed at Catherine's story about her volunteer assistant from Zentropa who got her driver's license two days before Catherine arrived. The assistant drove Catherine to her hotel in a tiny VW, stalling out at every corner. At one point, the car wouldn't move. "Sweetheart," Catherine said, reaching between the seats, "it works much better if you take off the fucking emergency brake."

We agreed that Zentropa's lack of production savvy was a fair trade for a production team that was appreciative and kind. When we arrived at Catherine's hotel, I walked her to the door. "Vincent, stop," she said. "You don't have to do this. You're such a gentleman."

"My mother taught me well," I said.

Mette and I watched her walk away in her black jeans, black blouse, cashmere plaid shawl, and black shoes with the slightest of heels. Totally put together. "Wow," I said. "We just drove around with Catherine fucking Deneuve!"

When I returned to my apartment, Lars called. "Wincent, I must tell you how much I love this new piece, and Catherine told me she had a great time. She said that it was good to dance again, like therapy for her."

Two days later, I met him in the sink factory where he illustrated a "sexual, writhing, people-machine" using naked Barbie dolls. Frustrated that he couldn't make their unbendable appendages entwine, he ran over to the large, green, cutting machine that I intended to use as a structure upon which the dancers would stand. He began an energetic monologue about Catherine being thrown into the center of a group of people and clinging to them in near-impossible configurations. Some bodies could turn as if on a spit while others would be pulled up and down by their ankles. Eventually, all the people's hands would connect to Catherine's hands and a pulse of life would emerge from her fist. I told Lars I would let his engaging marriage of Hieronymus Bosch's *Garden of Earthly Delights* meets Picasso's *Guernica* inspire me.

I wanted Björk to have moments of raw weirdness in her movement. I called them "Björkisms." The beauty was in the uniqueness that *is* Björk and in her truth of character. After a rehearsal, Lars told me how much he loved Björk sticking her tongue out while she danced. "Many people do this as a nervous habit, Wincent, but I don't think anyone has ever gotten it on film," he said. "I'd be most pleased if you could incorporate it into the choreography."

May arrived, and I began the "107 Steps," where Selma takes her final walk to the gallows. I sketched it like Christ's walk toward his crucifixion, dark, melancholic, and disturbing. Brenda, the warden, counts Selma's steps to the gallows, creating a rhythm that transports Selma into a blissful fantasy. She enters the cell of an angry prisoner, sits by his side, and strokes his hair. A guard violently yanks her into the hallway and pushes her into the arms of six sex-starved male prisoners who molest her through the bars. In her fantasy, Selma believes she is receiving the stigmata, in a state of heavenly bliss. Another guard shoves her toward the stairway leading to the hanging chamber.

When we walked through the movement, Björk began to cry. Her two friends were sobbing in the corner. Lars joined us and watched the piece twice.

"Wincent, this is very surprising."

"Well, Lars, is it a good surprise or a bad surprise?"

"A good surprise. But can I ponder this a while and then tell you what I'm thinking?" We broke for lunch. Lars found me later.

"Wincent, I was not expecting to see something like this. It brought up many emotions in me, and I had to go outside because I wasn't expecting to feel these many emotions. This is very good, what you've done."

Then he offered a twist. "Wincent," he said, "maybe the guards also dance with Selma so that in her imagination everyone is kind to her, the star of her own musical fantasy?" Of course. OF. COURSE. I created tango-inspired moves for the guards so Selma interpreted their angry manhandling as a dramatic partner dance and the piece became even more surreal and haunting.

Because the Zentropa production team was not experienced in an undertaking as large as *Dancer in the Dark* there were constant challenges. On my first day seeing the moving train on location for "I've Seen It All," I was told that several of the dancers I had cast had been changed without my knowledge. Also, I had planned that the eighteen dancers and Björk would dance from car #1 to car #5. But late in the process, I was informed that car #4 would have a house-sized trailer on it. Without consulting me, the production crew decided that when the dancers got to car #4, everyone could simply walk sideways, single file and start dancing again when they got to car #5. I received this information sopping wet, standing in the sleeting rain, after working out train timings for four hours. I was not happy.

Meanwhile, in the rehearsal room, the props for the dancers playing loggers were *actual lumberjack tools*: extremely sharp axes, dangerously large saws, sledgehammers, chainsaws, and four sets of steel leg-bands with metal teeth. Of course, all that had to go. I now had three hours to create a solid sketch of the dance. Oh, and Lars wanted another minute of movement added to the sequence. The most vexing aspect of all these challenges was the impossibility of getting angry with anyone in production because *they were all so nice!*

I opted for dinner alone that night, searching for peace. I was sipping a cognac when Björk shyly asked if she could join me. We shared my dinner and dessert, talking about life, love, friendship, and art. She brought me back to the land of the living, an angel in a brown, wool sweater with multicolored rabbit fur sleeves.

The next afternoon, I finished the five-minute dance in spite of the setbacks. Since there was no musical director, I taught the dancers the lyrics to the song. By the end of rehearsal, we ended up with something special and unique. The lack of polish provided by all the challenges actually supported Selma's story, while the setting would illuminate her vision of life as a movie musical.

I took the cast on location to rehearse "I've Seen It All." The train track ran through a valley of pine trees and through a trestle bridge, which crossed a river. The train had a yellow and green engine followed by a dozen rusty coal cars followed by five open, flatbed cars on which the dancers performed. In the final film, the loggers dance with axes and saws—props this time—as Selma and Jeff (played by Peter Stormare) walk beside the moving train. Hoisted onto the train by two loggers, Selma and the eighteen loggers dance a punk clash of ballet and Björkisms. They run to the end of the train, holding Selma out over the tracks like the figurehead on the bow of a ship.

We filmed "I've Seen It All" on a gorgeous day in May in three takes. With each take, Björk shed layers of emotional skin. By the third, Selma emerged, creating a blissful utopia through the rhythm of the rolling train.

In a small house in the Swedish woods, I created "Smith & Wesson (Scatterheart)," Selma's escape fantasy after she murders her landlord Bill (played by David Morse). I used circular movement to portray two energies orbiting one another as Selma attempts to receive forgiveness from Bill. Mette and I danced the piece for David and Björk. Bill starts on the floor, dead, while Selma sits in a chair beside his body. When it was the actors' turn, I couldn't find Björk. She had found a little cubbyhole and was sobbing her eyes out. Watching the movement sync to her music and Selma's story had overwhelmed her.

The first day of shooting "Scatterheart" was disappointing. It had been over a week since we rehearsed and the performances lacked magic. There were several twenty-minute breaks for technical reasons. The actors kept asking for an opportunity to build momentum. Just as we completed the first take in which a spark of magic happened, lunch was called. When filming wrapped, Lars asked, "Wincent, how do you feel?"

"Frustrated, Lars," I replied. "We have to change the way we shoot these dance scenes. I need time to review the dances with the cast and run them until they feel organic again before we shoot." He agreed, and we adopted this process throughout the rest of the film.

I had been eager to watch Lars direct the acting scenes. "Wincent, you can come whenever you like but I assure you it is not very exciting. It's all in the editing." In that same little Swedish house, Lars shot the dialogue scenes with one digital camera, which he operated himself. He asked the actors to first use the dialogue he had written and then improvise with the dialogue as they saw fit. He gave direction while he kept the camera rolling, collecting hours of footage to take into an editing room and create his story.

I got to know Lars better during our conversations at the end of the long days. I had noticed tension between him and Björk. He kept telling me there was another side of her that I hadn't seen. I hadn't. Lars has fears and phobias that run hand in hand with his genius. I could see how Björk's uninhibited free spirit might throw his world out of alignment.

I was asked about casting the role of Oldřich Nový, the Czech Fred Astaire whom Selma idolizes. I suggested the musical legend Joel Grey. Joel had won a Tony and an Oscar and was on my refrigerator, somewhere near Lars and Björk, as the emcee in the movie *Cabaret*. (The power of the fridge endures!) Joel arrived to record his courtroom duet with Björk in a small Swedish hotel room. It was nearly a disaster. Lars, Björk, Joel, and I were in the room. Joel began to ask musical questions. Lars got up and left to have a beer. Joel began to address his questions to me. Björk was exhausted and not helping clear Joel's confusion about the unusual syncopated rhythms she had composed.

"Björk, can you sing the notes for Joel, maybe?" She smiled oddly at me. "Well, could you both try speaking the lyrics to each other?" Nothing. Finally Björk blurted out that she was upset because she had been promised a day of rest, and it was unfair that she had to be creative right now. She didn't want to be there. Poor Joel! On top of this, the room was so tiny that the only place for him to record his vocals was in the shower. He began to find his character and speak with an accent, Björk perked up. "What country are you from?"

"Ohio," he joked. It broke the ice. I coached Joel and when the session concluded, Björk threw her arms around me. "You saved the day, Vincent! I didn't know where to begin. Joel is so elegant. Thank you."

Noticing the differences in their body language as they worked together, I decided to create a piece that would highlight Joel's gracefulness. Selma would get to become a dancing lady with a star partner, and Lars would get his wish of a tap duet.

But just when things would come together, it seemed new things were falling apart. When I returned to the studio in Copenhagen, the courtroom set was not built as scheduled and the music wasn't ready. Björk now didn't want to come to work. She had been promised weekends off and never got them. We had been plowing ahead at full steam and without interruption. She was justifiably exhausted and decided to take a three-day break leaving Joel with Mette and me to rehearse the courtroom dance scene without her.

Joel kept telling me he was not a dancer. All the while his elfin body breathed movement. Like Banderas in *Evita*, Joel questioned the thoughts behind the choreography. When I directed him from a narrative perspective, he felt clearer. Working together, I realized his body sang more vibrantly with tighter, percussive movement, so I altered some of the choreography for his duet with Björk. I held the first rehearsal with the sixty cast members for the courtroom scene in the lovely old gymnasium.

"I think this is the most interesting project on the planet," I said, "and I hope you'll forgive the inconveniences. Where else could we be in a film with Catherine Deneuve, Joel Grey, and Björk? Look around. We have teachers, students, choreographers, modern dancers, hip-hop dancers all together. Let's have fun!"

I proceeded to teach the choreography for the courtroom, breaking it down slowly. Catherine sidled up to me. "Wow. I had never seen you work with a room full of people. I really enjoyed myself today."

Catherine accepted every challenge and was patient with the lack of production savvy on the film. She's a diva and deservedly so. She was constantly late for rehearsals in the morning, she came back late after lunch, and she always required more than the five-minute rest break given to the rest of the cast. It was just her nature: I've-been-Catherine-Deneuve-for-so-long-I-don't-know-how-to-not-be. I appreciated Catherine a lot.

The courtroom scene choreography and rehearsals, "In The Musicals Part II," came together in just three days. All sixty-two dancers learned the four-minute extravaganza precisely, then, like Lars with the actors, I allowed them to improvise it. Each could decide which way to turn or which arm to extend into the air first, making it feel as if it had been created by Selma.

When Björk joined us, she gave light and discovery to every moment. She was the gem of the movie and the duet of tap dancing with Joel played well on the desk of the presiding judge. Our first run-through was met by applause from the crew and production team, jammed into every available nook and cranny of the set to watch.

Lars pulled me aside. "I want you to know I have realized clearly that there is no other person in the world who can do what you do. I am very impressed and very glad you are here."

"Lars, I couldn't do what I do as well as I am doing it if you were not as generous as you are. This is your baby, and you have trusted me without knowing me. How could I not blossom in this atmosphere?"

I began to see a glimpse of that "other side" of Björk that Lars had mentioned. But my understanding of it was slightly different than his. With each rehearsal, I noticed Björk would seem to fall in and out of focus. Catherine could take a note, and I'd see her immediately incorporate it into the scene. That used to be the case with Björk, but now—over a month into filming and two months since our first rehearsal—it took longer and longer for Björk to digest a note and make it part of her performance. This made everything more difficult. We needed to see a solid rehearsal to know if something worked, otherwise we were flying blind. She would always be brilliant once the cameras started rolling but getting there had become a nail-biting experience. However, I didn't see this as some innate personality flaw or difficulty on Björk's part. I saw this as someone acting for the first time in a demanding role where she was pulling out all the emotional stops. She was diving off an emotional cliff headfirst in playing Selma. I saw an artist stretching herself to the limit.

Mine was a tricky position to be in, and I felt my role expanding to peacemaker. I didn't mind. I loved them both. The tension building between Björk and Lars is not entirely uncommon on a film set. Stakes can be higher when working creatively and collaboratively because the artists involved bring their passion to each moment. Everyone was enthused for our first day of filming back in Denmark, June 23, in the sink factory. Lars gave me control of the set, interjecting his notes and opinions in the appropriate places with impeccable timing. The dancers transcended the dirty factory, the metallic dust, the cacophony of grinding machines, and gaseous exhaust fumes from the forklift. Björk reigned supremely eccentric. Catherine was sensational, even though she forced us to wait an extra fifteen minutes for her to return after each break.

"Fifteen minutes?" someone from France said. "Do you know how much she must respect you? I've been on productions where we've waited for three hours!"

Both she and Björk gave inimitable performances and, after I called "wrap," I led the applause for Catherine then Björk, who was hiding among the dancers. "I'm embarrassed," she confided sheepishly.

"Take the love, take the love," I whispered in her ear.

"Just a different culture," she replied, uncomfortable with the display of affection, even from her supporting cast.

The day to rehearse as Samuel, I arrived on set as the theater director of *The Sound of Music*, not Vincent. Lars shaped the scene on the stage of the little theater.

"What is your job, Samuel, when you're not at the little theater?" Lars asked.

"I teach junior high school. English and English Literature. I throw small game parties. I have a book-discussion club, which meets every fourth Sunday in my home for brunch. I collect LP's of musicals and a little bit of jazz. I like Rodgers and Hammerstein. I was born in Pennsylvania but moved to Washington after graduating college. I'm attending summer programs to acquire my master's degree. I would like to have my own theater company one day. I'd like to fall in love because I am a romantic at heart."

"That's very good, Wincent! I mean, Samuel." Lars asked us to improvise the dialogue for a few rehearsals, and I asked if he wanted any of the original dialogue. "Just the idea of the lines," he said. "Then, I'll tell you if any important information is missing that I need."

I felt my character Samuel possessed immense imagination and frustration, directing and choreographing *The Sound of Music* in a tiny town of the Pacific Northwest in 1964. I was constantly flipping between my role as Vincent, the understanding choreographer, and Samuel, the community theater maestro. "I've always wanted a schizophrenic friend," Björk said to me. "Now I've got one. You."

There were more rumblings growing between Lars and Björk. A rumor began circulating that Björk had flipped out during the last shoot in Sweden. She had been doing a special effects shot, crushing Bill's head with the metal moneybox he had stolen from her. The actor, David Morse, had been replaced with a dummy. The story went that Björk got completely carried away, throwing the metal box through a wall. The Danes were horrified at the expression of raw, unbridled emotion. Lars loved it. When I asked him if the rumor was true, he said, "That's Björk, you know. She must turn the tap on fully, or off. She never does the in-between."

A couple days later, Lars confided in me that he had spent a sleepless weekend worried about his fraying relationship with Björk and its effect on the film. He divulged, "Björk has been nothing but harsh with me, and I can no longer feel that the movie's future depends on if she'll commit or not. She called me 'the meanest person in the world' and 'a coward.' I am not a coward." He canceled the day's filming. That evening he would discuss with Björk and Vibeke how to continue. Time to establish some rules.

I also felt for Björk. She had been totally independent for years, answering to no one. She now had to become a team player in an unfamiliar arena. She wasn't trained as an actress. Selma was a gut-wrenching role that would test the mettle of any accomplished performer. Selma is going blind, works in a factory, escapes into musical fantasies, slaps her son, kills a man, receives a death sentence, and is hanged for her crime. Björk hadn't the technique to shake Selma off or leave her on the Zentropa lot. It must have weighed heavily on her.

The next day Björk called in sick. We lost another two days. Then she decided to take off Friday through Monday, so another four-day break. No one wanted to be upset with Björk, but it seemed as though she had lost interest, which cast despair on everyone. We were left in the dark as no one explained Björk's reasoning to us. We still had several fantasies to film, there was much more work to be done.

The "little theater" scene was finally shot but the night got off to a tense start. Everyone was on set when we were asked to hold, as Lars and Björk were having a conversation. That "conversation" concluded with Lars throwing a chair through an expensive video monitor. Lars came back, and Björk skulked in behind him. Björk asked me, "What scene are we doing?"

There was no rehearsal, no blocking or reading the lines through. Lars made a few general comments to Björk, Peter Stormare, and me, "In this scene, Selma wants to leave and Samuel must make her stay. I am not so concerned with the dialogue in the script."

I was nervous about Björk, but we started filming and she was flawless. Sometimes Lars directed us and sometimes he didn't. There was never a concern about continuity. I began each scene a little differently, changing my position in the rehearsal room, or talking to a different person. The *idea* of the scene was the only important thing. My primary direction from Lars was to be less professional as Samuel. Lars also had me work with Björk in varying shades of compassion or impatience, giving himself editing options. Afterward, Björk hugged me, "I know nothing about acting but you are a generous actor."

On the day we were supposed to shoot another scene between Selma and Samuel, Lars came running up to me. "She ate her shirt," he said.

"Excuse me?"

"Björk. She just ate her shirt. She hates this shirt she was supposed to wear so she ripped it apart with her teeth in little pieces and then ate it. Buttons and all," he said. "Then she went running away and climbed over a barbed-wire fence into the woods and no one can find her."

I couldn't believe my ears.

"Wincent," Lars continued, "I've got a whole new respect for her now that she has eaten her shirt."

I didn't know if this was true or not, but nobody could find Björk. The schedule was being reworked as people searched the woods. Lars wanted to jump ahead to the gallows scene, worried Björk might lose it before he was able to finish his film. Poor Lars. Poor Björk. What a mess. Two hours passed with no sign of her. I went outside where characters dressed in sixties wardrobe wandered, searching for Björk. It looked like an Easter-egg hunt out of *Edward Scissorhands*. We were frustrated with her and worried about her. For the first time, I had the soul-crushing feeling that this film might not be completed.

In some ways, Lars and Björk were both living on the edge of lunacy with their individual strains of creativity as their outlet. I confess that I sometimes envied their artistic insanity. I think genius lives on the rim of reality, always teetering between the world of sanity and the nether regions of madness.

Björk's manager arrived with a list of demands that had to be met before Björk would come back to the set. The first was that Björk wanted total artistic control and final cut over the musical dance sequences in the movie. Björk and her manager thought it was already in the contract, and since it wasn't, that was the first demand. No director gives an actor final approval over a part of his movie, and

Lars would never do such a thing. The cast and crew were dismayed. None of this was a good sign.

Catherine invited me for coffee and spoke a mile a minute. "They coddled her much too long," she said. "They should have put this in the hands of lawyers at the beginning. Now they better have the lawyers come in and let her see the amount of money this is going to cost her. Perhaps, if after two weeks she had decided she didn't want to do the film—that is one thing. But you don't make a decision like this when the film is two-thirds complete. And what does she think this does to all of us who have worked so hard, flown across the globe to do this film? This is a huge film, not some music video…"

I took a more aggressive role in this power struggle between Björk and Lars because all our work was too important to be destroyed over a personal feud. I found Lars roaming the lot. I put my arm around his shoulder, "Lars, we have to talk."

"But, Wincent, I have to…"

"Come on. As your friend and brother, I need to talk to you." I spoke to him about the magnitude of what had been created, reminding Lars that the film was greater than Björk or him at this point. I implored him to find love for her. If not, it would show in what he shot. For the audience to love Selma, Lars must love Björk, at least for another month. The performance Björk was giving was a gift for him to capture on film. He would never tame her, and he should stop trying. I told him he understood all of these things, but sometimes we just need a friend to remind us.

The lawyers did their thing and soon Björk was back on the courtroom set getting ready to shoot her scene on the witness stand. I whispered in her ear, "I know how hard this is for you and the next two weeks are going to be even more difficult with the reading of the verdict, the time in prison, the hanging. This is bigger than you or Lars; it's greater than all of us. We have to finish this film and give it to the world. We don't have a choice. If you need a hand to hold, a shoulder to cry on, someone to laugh with…I'm here for you."

"Thank you, Vincent. I so appreciate that," as she kissed me on the cheek.

The courtroom filming was highly successful. Björk was stunning on the stand. Catherine was brilliant. Joel spoke so softly that every attendee leaned forward in their seat, straining to hear Novy's testimony. And when he and Björk danced together it was magical. When Joel departed the set, he was given a standing ovation. As he strode down the aisle, beaming, he came over and hugged me, "That's a trip. Thanks so much." Everyone applauded until he left the room.

For the gallows scene, Björk sang "The Next to Last Song" a cappella. Watching Björk lip-sync to a track was mesmerizing, she was so good at it. But hearing her sing live and unaccompanied was cathartic. She was strapped to a board, her delicate neck in a noose, holding her son Gene's glasses in her hands. Selma was letting her son know she can only sing him a "next to last song." A mother's dying words to her son.

Because of all she seemed to be experiencing the past few weeks, it was difficult to decipher whether it was Selma or Björk who was losing control in the scenes. When Selma got hysterical, we all became nervous. Was it Selma or Björk? Thankfully, it was always Selma.

Toward the final days of filming, I thought things had been repaired between Björk and Lars. Sadly, I was wrong. It was my last day and the final musical piece of the film—Selma in her isolation cell singing "My Favorite Things." The filming was supposed to begin at 2:00 p.m. but, at 5:30, Björk had still not come out of her room. Word spread that, although she had been warming up her voice at the house all morning, she didn't want to do this scene. She would come back in a month and do it. Lars was furious. The depressed crew sat in the blazing sun at café tables in front of the cantina. "How could she do this on the final day of shooting?" It was impossible for us to return to do it in a month.

Finally, there appeared a spark of movement across the parking lot. Björk was coming to set. Everyone scattered. Lars grabbed me.

"Wincent, let's watch the monitors." We hurried into a side room as Björk walked to the center of the small sound stage and into the claustrophobic holding cell. It had gray walls, one metal bed, a toilet, a sink, and a shelf. She sat on the bed. This piece was experimental. There was no choreography, no direction. Selma would sing the song in her cell after listening to the sounds of a prison church choir emanating from the ventilation grill. We put the headsets on our ears.

In front of Björk was a glass wall. Behind it were the one hundred cameras in ten rows of ten. The assistant director, Anders, whispered, "Action…"

The only sound was Björk crying. Lars looked at me with sad puppy eyes. Björk continued to cry. Maybe it was the confident, shy, confident, shy, sad, and broken woman I remembered as my mom when I was young or maybe it was simply the close relationship I'd developed with Björk. Either way, I thought I could help. I ran out to the set. I went to the outside wall of her prison cell with a ventilation grate in the upper corner. *"Raindrops on roses and whiskers on kittens,"* I whispered. She continued crying. I continued, *"Bright copper kettles and warm woolen mittens. Brown geese that fly with the moon on their wings, these are a few of my favorite things…"*

Silence.

"Sing, Selma. Use your voice. Make yourself happy," I whispered. Though there was no audible response, her crying had stopped. *"Raindrops on roses and whiskers on kittens…"* I began again.

Suddenly, I heard the door to the cell fly open, and Björk ran out of the building. I caught up to her, wrapping my arms around her and kissing the top of her head. "This is insanity," she wept. "This is like being in a fucking cage on display. This should be a crime against humanity. Someone should take behavior like this to Amnesty International!"

"Björk," I said, "this is what an actor does. Your feelings can be Selma's feelings. An actor would give anything to be going through what you're experiencing right now. This is a gift."

"This is horrible, Vincent," she cried. "I can't do this. I just can't."

"Yes, you can. How do you feel as Selma, alone in an isolation cell? Your son's far away; you're about to be hung. Sing it from your heart. It doesn't have to sound perfect. It's about how Selma feels."

Only the assistant director and the sound crew were on the stage. Lars was off in the shadows. I walked Björk back into the room. "You can do this. I'm going to stay right outside." I closed the door.

Through her crying, Björk began to sing, *"Raindrops on roses… and whiskers on kittens."* She pounded the wall with her fists, once, twice. She began to sing the entire song through her tears. Then silence. She began a second time. Again, silence. I opened the door a crack and saw Björk's reflection in the glass, "Sing, Selma," I whispered. "It's your gift. Sing to make yourself free." I closed the door.

She began to sing in unintelligible Icelandic, a haunting melody in a celestial voice. She grabbed the blanket, threw it over her head and crawled across the floor. Singing this strange tune, she laid down on the bed and covered herself with the blanket. Then one final time she sang "My Favorite Things" all the way through.

I looked at Lars, and he nodded to the assistant director to stop filming. I opened the door and walked Björk off the set and across the meadow to the entrance of her dressing room. "Sometimes a film can change people's perspectives," I said. "You possibly just made people realize what sadness and isolation a human can feel awaiting the barbarous torture of the death penalty."

"I don't know why any person would want to go to that place," she said. "I'm just not suited for this. I never will be." I can't be sure if it was Selma or Björk in that cell—I'm not sure if she knows. Or if it matters. None of those things matter in the high-charged moments. When I think back on all this now, I can see the connection to my teenage years as the man of our house, the deep emotional support I developed with my mom out of necessity. The caretaker role I had adopted as an eldest child now playing out on set to bring Lars and

Björk together as artists. But at the time, I only knew it was everyone's efforts that finally got us over the finish line.

I met Vibeke on my way back to the set. She told me Lars thought that what Björk had done was sensational but feared it would bring the audience too down *before* the hanging scene. Lars spoke with Björk, and it was decided that she would do another version, which they eventually did. In the distance, I saw them laughing together, being friendly with one another. I had finished my work on *Dancer in the Dark*. I was overwhelmed with the melancholy of departure. I walked up to Vibeke, "I have to go, Vibeke, I have to leave now. I hate goodbyes."

She hugged me tightly. Lars was walking toward us. "Come and join us in a schnapps! You must!"

We walked to where Björk and Lars were now sitting on the grass. I opened the bottle, pouring each of us a glass of the potent liquor that had become our communion drink when the going got rough or a celebration was at hand.

"To the end of the film. And to you, Wincent," Lars said. We toasted. Björk stroked my hair and kissed the side of my head. Vibeke sat beside me. I drank my schnapps and rose. "I have to go. I love you all very much."

As I walked away, Lars called out, "You are my friend, Wincent!" In the rear-view mirror, I watched them clustered in a tight group on the green lawn.

Björk was an artistic treat with whom to collaborate. I can't imagine another actress bringing the truth and power to *Dancer* like she did. She should have received more international recognition. Her struggles with Lars seemed to always be about her music and that is understandable. Björk is music incarnate. She eats, breathes, and sleeps music. Her naïveté about who controls the music in a film broke her heart, and she defended her position like a warrior. Every moment spent with her was a joy, and I appreciated all of the work we created together. From our first encounter, Lars treated me with an open spirit and a generous heart. He allowed me to be as complete a creative entity as I dared to be. He collaborated without egocentricity. He never held onto titles, never asked me to qualify anything I created or any method I chose to adopt. His self-assurance and casual belief in his own talent afforded all of us the opportunity to appreciate our own. I will carry the knowledge I acquired from him into every creative situation for the rest of my life.

"Choreographer and Dance Director: Vincent Paterson." That was my main title credit on the film. Dance director credit was given to Hermes Pan, Fred Astaire's choreographer. As payment for playing the role of Samuel, I was sent to the Cannes Film Festival with all expenses paid. That was an unforgettable occasion, walking the red carpet with Lars, Björk, and Catherine.

Dancer in the Dark won the Palme D'or, the Best Film, at the festival. We were like a creatively eccentric, dysfunctional family of sorts, living and working so hard together. We created this film because of and in spite of ourselves. I would never be the same again.

10½.

One Hundred Cameras. Really.

Making History with Dancer in the Dark

Although *Dancer in the Dark* was not going to be a Dogme project, Lars's joy for making rules was no different on this film. Here are some of Lars's original rules for shooting *Dancer in the Dark*:

—*The dialogue scenes will be filmed with the digital technology of 1 HD camera.*

—*Actors will follow script dialogue once and then improvise with original dialogue.*

—*The dance fantasies will be filmed using 100 mini-DV8 cameras.*

—*Handheld or tripod cameras for close-up shots on the singers are prohibited.*

—*Each musical sequence will be filmed only once.*

—*There will be no moving cameras in the dance scenes.*

Lars had the novel idea of shooting the dance scenes with 100 mini-DV8 cameras placed all around the environment. Because Lars would be busy operating the camera for the dialogue scenes, he and Vibeke decided that since I created the dances and because I had directed cameras before, I should lead the 100-camera technical crew. This meant designing the placement of the cameras and determining the framing of each one to capture the dance sequences.

Peter Hjorth, Charlotte Kirkeby, Edvard Friis-Møller, and I became the crux of the 100-camera team.

No one had ever used 100 individual cameras to shoot a scene, so we were making this up as we went along. For each dance location, we would capture the musical number from 100 angles, first placing the cameras based on the planned choreography. Next, each camera would be framed to capture different size images. Finally, all of the cameras would be cabled to one port and, by pressing one button, all of the cameras would record simultaneously. This allowed the dance to be captured from one hundred perspectives in one take. Performing the dance only once meant a lot of preparation for a small crew, but the amount of time, effort, and money saved during filming was a producer's orgasm.

Of course, our first venture with the 100 cameras was the most demanding musical fantasy to film: "I've Seen it All," with the action on a train as it traveled through the lush Swedish countryside. Lars wanted us to capture it all—the lake, a married couple hanging laundry in the backyard, grandparents dancing near a herd of sheep. He suggested the dance on the train be shot from two perspectives: 1) on the first day from the train looking out—using eighty cameras; and 2) on the second day from the countryside looking at the train—using fifty cameras. So, in the end, this song was actually shot with 130 cameras.

Peter, Edvard, and I decided where the cameras should be placed. Camera mounts had to be welded on the train cars. Train floorboards were replaced with Plexiglas for cameras to capture images from underneath the train. Miles of video and audio cable ran through the valley, attached to a central bank of monitors. The sound design team placed speakers throughout the countryside. Fortunately, we had mounted and framed most of the eighty cameras on the train two days before filming, because when we showed up to finish on the day before shooting, the weather was icy, cold rain. Being summer in the land of the midnight sun, we worked frantically until the wee hours and returned at dawn, only four hours later, to wrap up the framing.

And then we made history. Björk and Peter Stormare took their opening positions on the bridge with the dancers on the train and in the countryside. And where did we hide while all this was being filmed? Good question.

Zonja was the large, metal room built to house the A/V equipment, twelve video monitors, and members of the team including Lars, Robby Müller (director of photography), Peter Hjorth, and me. On day one, Zonja was placed on a flatbed car on the train. We sat in front of ten video monitors each capable of flashing the images of ten cameras, one image for each of the one hundred cameras. Monitor eleven showed three cameras on tripods that captured Björk's lip-sync. This was the first of Lars's rules to be broken: *Handheld or tripod cameras for close-up shots on the singers are prohibited.* Lars realized he couldn't have a musical film without close-ups of the actors singing the lyrics. Monitor twelve displayed a visual journey of Björk's route throughout the song assembled in mostly wide shots.

Watching it all inside Zonja felt like NASA. Mette and Anders Refn (assistant director) remained outside the train to yell the cues through loudspeakers for the cameras to begin rolling, for the train to begin moving, and for the music playback and talent to commence. Lars was as excited as a little kid. Under Zonja, the train began to roll as music filled the landscape. Inside Zonja, the images on the monitors started to play a mesmerizing narrative. After approximately eight minutes of holding one's breath, Lars called "cut."

In one take from eighty cameras, we had captured over ten hours of mini-DV8 video footage. We all sat silently, stunned. "What just happened?" Lars asked.

Lars quickly reneged on another of his rules: *Each musical sequence will be filmed in only one take.* "Wincent, we must do another take, don't you think?"

"Absolutely, Lars." We did two more.

When Anders called "wrap," everyone was exhilarated and physically exhausted. I ran into Björk at the hotel that night. "How do you feel?" she asked.

"Like a glorious train wreck. You?"

"Like a glass of champagne that's been sitting out on the table for a week."

On the second day, the sky was azure with Oklahoma white clouds. Without telling anyone, I grabbed Robby Müller and we ran to change the frames on a couple of the cameras that were low along the train tracks. We had to capture that exquisite sky. Just as we adjusted the cameras, the train began to roll. Once the train moved, we'd be completely visible in the shots of the fifty cameras placed in the landscape. "Hit the dirt!" I yelled, and we dove on our bellies into the high grass. Lying there, we looked up at the train rolling by with Björk and the loggers dancing as black silhouettes against the blue sky. We turned and smiled at each other like five-year-olds playing soldiers in a foxhole.

I rode home with Lars in his camper that day. "Wincent," he said, "I hate to say this, but I think we've created a classic."

We learned more about designing the cameras with each dance fantasy. Eventually, the prep to shoot every musical piece followed the same plan. The 100-camera crew would visit the set as Mette and the dancers performed the choreography. Lars would devise a concept for the cameras, then he and I would place them. The cameras would be mounted and framed over several days, and then we'd shoot.

"Scatterheart" was filmed in a house in the Swedish woods. For the house interior, Lars decided the cameras should be framed as extreme close-ups or with a surveillance camera-like POV. Lars and I walked from room to room as I described the action, and we played the camera-placement game. I would throw out an idea. Lars would throw out a stranger idea.

"An extreme close-up (ECU) with the camera on the floor of Bill opening his eyes when Selma touches his hair," I suggested.

"Three cameras from different angles getting extreme close-ups of the needle stuck at the end of the record," Lars said.

I would suggest an ECU on Selma's hand pushing a hanging lamp; he would top me by suggesting an ECU on the brass ball above it. Outside the house, I suggested putting a camera on Gene's bike. "Wincent, that is a terrible idea. That is totally against the rules," he smiled. He reminded me: *There will be no moving cameras in the dance scenes.*

"But, Lars, the camera is moving organically. No one is moving the camera. If it was mounted on a tree limb and the wind moved the branch, would that be against the rules?"

"Yes, Wincent, it would." When it came time to film, he changed his mind and decided a camera mounted to the bike was organic, so it went back on.

After we finished, Lars turned to me. "This is wonderful," he said. "Now, I can go home and sleep." He borrowed a kayak, and off he went for a glide down the shallow stream.

After the cameras were mounted, Peter and I sat in Zonja, in ninety-degree heat, framing, focusing, and setting the f-stops on each camera. Mette had two stand-in actors move through the space so we could follow them. This took about two days.

The crew told me they had chills as we shot the song in the house interior. The next day we prepared to film the exterior shots of "Scatterheart." Selma ends in a cold creek.

"Vincent," Björk said. "I was wondering if you would mind if we didn't over-rehearse this part. I want to feel my way through it a bit."

"I'm fine with that," I said. "Let's just walk it once from the top and stop before you go into the water."

"And I was hoping you could help make the cameras move more quickly so there is not so much time between each take," she added. I asked the crew if we could please move with lightning speed from take to take. And to please make every effort to quickly dress Björk in dry clothing after she stepped out of the stream.

We rolled cameras. On one take, while Björk stood in the middle of the creek singing, "*I just did what I had to do*," it seemed as if she was going to sink under water. It was haunting and everyone in Zonja held their breath.

"In The Musicals Part 1" took place in a small theater with a tiny stage. We put the cameras in the ceiling, on the sides of the stage, in the back of the theater, and drilled holes into the wood-paneled walls to hide the cameras inside them. The holes would disappear in postproduction through digital effects (Paintbox).

For the courtroom scene, "In The Musicals Part 2," the art department again drilled holes in the walls of the set to hide the cameras. We placed cameras under desks, in the jury box, on the pole that held the US flag. The more outrageous the placement, the more excited Lars became.

On the "Cvalda" song in the sink factory, Lars wanted each camera's image to contain elements of factory machines in the foreground to highlight the lyrics, "*Clatter, crash, thump...*" and the driving rhythm of the machines, the doorway into Selma's fantasy.

In "107 Steps," Selma walks from her death row cell to the gallows. Lars wanted the cameras at or below eye level. This was a perfect idea because the only rhythm for this piece came from Selma's footsteps down the hallway and Brenda, a prison guard, counting Selma's steps as she goes. But it became too predictable, and we also placed some at different levels.

The final 100-camera sequence we filmed was Selma in her cell trying to change her frame of mind by singing "My Favorite Things." Lars and I decided to mount the cameras on a grid as the front wall of the cell, a menacing, inescapable wall of cameras that almost drove Björk insane. Watching the images on the monitors reminded me of a David Hockney Polaroid collage with beautiful fragments composing a full image.

So many catastrophes were averted because of the 100-camera crew. They welded camera mounts in every conceivable location from factory to treetop and then connected video cameras to them, ran miles of video and audio cables through houses and valleys, arrived earlier than anyone on the set and worked long after the rest of the production crew had finished for the day, helped set f-stops on the lens for each camera, covered and uncovered each camera because of weather challenges, disposed of the empty battery packages, even brought coffee.

By the time I returned to Hollywood, I had framed over 1,000 camera shots. I gained more knowledge than I ever could have hoped to acquire on this film. One of the crew told me, "You feel art from the heart, Vincent. We like your style of taking care of business while taking care of everyone."

This incomparable team gets a standing ovation from me.

11.

From Russia with Love

Falling for Anna Netrebko and Opera

W HAT THIS MAN DOES is not art and should not be considered art! It is commercial! It has no value and none of us at this table consider it artistic on any level! Can we move on, please?" That was once said about me by another director. Loudly. In front of a room full of people.

It was December 2001, at a Nordiska filmmaker's seminar in Lillehammer, Norway, where I lectured on "the conception, creation, and capturing of dance in contemporary films." At a Q&A session, I was seated among several "dance" filmmakers, mostly from England. The students directed most of the questions at me, probably because of my association with the most prominent video and musical stars of the time. Everyone knew Michael and Madonna, *The Birdcage* had been a huge hit, *Dancer* won Cannes—and in 2001, that wasn't even half of my resume.

The haughty director who tossed those words my way had created a pseudo-artsy film in which birds performed their mating dances to Beethoven. I knew it was just pettiness. But I still almost melted beneath the table with embarrassment.

But then a Frenchman, with the impeccable demeanor only the French can have, rose from the audience, "How dare you speak about this man like that. What Vincent has created with Michael Jackson alone has brought dance back to the world. The world dances now! Men dance now! What he and Michael Jackson are doing is not only valid, it's invaluable!"

The Frenchman was Patrick Bensard, the director of the dance film archives at Paris's Cinémathèque Française. Over the next few days, sharing stories over meals and attending the same lectures, I got to know Patrick. We became fast friends. He would eventually play a crucial role in what I would call my "resurrection" the following year.

During 2002, I had a perplexing, soul-searching period. Some of it is still a blur. Some of it still scares me. I was not getting hired. It was as if I had never existed and no one had ever heard of me. I didn't understand what was happening or why. I had a solid body of work, some of which was already being labeled "iconic." I knew there were jobs available, but apparently not for me. I contacted some directors I knew, but networking was never my forte. I stopped conversing with ex-collaborators for fear of sounding desperate, which can become your death knell in Hollywood. I felt myself starting to spiral downward. Why was this happening? Why now?

I don't often dwell in darkness, but I've certainly traveled down that path a few times and sadness has been a companion to me all my life. I know I'm not the only successful artist who has experienced a severe dry spell. For many of us, the fear of not working again always hovers in the shadows. And even though I worked hard to create an adult relationship on my own terms, I always knew my abusive father continued to have an impact on me. It seemed living in the shadow of his chaos embedded faint feelings of worry and insecurity inside me, even when things were going well.

I felt the darkness around me growing. Was it all over for me? I was becoming seduced by paranoia. My confusion about losing my professional life carried over to my personal life. I was embarrassed to share how far into the depths I was falling even with those close to me. I lost perspective, and the belief that "all things happen in their

right time" sounded like complete bullshit. I fell into a depression
that not even a letter from the sagacious Mike Nichols could help:

Dear Vincent,

I miss you too. I'm sorry to hear you are going through a valley of doubt
and worry. I just want you to know that for all of us in our profession that
is part of it. Part of the luck, that waxes and wanes, part of growth that
happens while things are scary. I asked George Wolf to talk to my acting
class for their graduation a few years ago. I figured he knew a lot about
anger and I wanted him to discuss it's uses. He got up to talk and he said,
Mike wants me to talk about anger but I think I'll talk about failure. I've
had four big successes lately and I have realized that the last time I
learned anything was the last time I had a failure.

So true, so important to remember. My advice is do something small
without salary or for very little dough. Do something that is exactly what
you want to do that has nothing to do with making money. Every time I
have pulled back and worked for the sake of the piece, not my price or
the industry, everything has come back and in spades. The studios, and
all that goes with them, are soul destroying. The only way to survive is to
do something else, to remember what it feels like to be an artist, away
from the money machine. What you are experiencing is growth.

Anyway, my two cents. I send my love and my confidence in you. You are
enormously talented, whether it is what you brought me on BIRDCAGE, or
your directing, or the way you shaped your scenes in DANCER, or the
truth and insight you brought to those scenes and to your work always.
What you feel goes with being first rate. With the French pronounciation, I
say to you - Courage. You will come back stronger and better than ever.

Best,

Mike

One of my agents actually suggested I get out of the business for
a while. Hearing this, instead of helpful advice on how to change the
situation, I freaked. Even with loving friends and family, it had become
impossible to share how I was feeling. Paralyzed. Hopeless. Worthless.

I bought a revolver at a gun shop on La Brea Avenue in
Hollywood, drove to Santa Barbara, and checked into a hotel on
the beach. I loaded the gun, convinced I had no reason to live. I got
into bed, leaning against the headboard. I put the gun in my mouth.
I closed my eyes.

The phone rang. The jarring sound pulled me out of my head
and back into my body. I took the gun from my mouth and picked
up the receiver.

"Will you be needing any ice?" a voice asked.

"What...?"

"Will you be needing any ice? We're about to close the front office for the night."

"No, thanks." I hung up the phone. And then I laughed, hysterically. I put the gun away and slept for about sixteen hours.

The next day I drove home. The exact moment I walked in the door, the phone rang. It was Patrick Bensard calling from Paris, "Mon ami, Vincent. *Comment ça va*? I am hoping you are well, yes?"

"Yes, Patrick, I'm fine," I lied. "How are you?"

"Busy, crazy like I always am. Vincent, what do you think that we would make an evening of you presenting your work at the Cinémathèque with the films of Michael Jackson and Madonna, your commercials, movies, whatever you feel? We can fly you to Paris and put you in a hotel. We will have a fantastic time, my friend."

"Patrick, thanks so much. This would be such an honor!" He was saving my life, and he didn't even know it.

On December 2, 2002, I presented my evening at the Cinémathèque Française in Paris with my friend Maxine Taupin on my arm—Elton John's "Tiny Dancer." The evening was a thrill. The reception by the French public made me feel like an artist again. After the presentation, a tall, thin man shook my hand. "My name is Bernie Fleischer," he said. "I'm from Salzburg. I grew up knowing all of the moves you created for Michael Jackson. I loved them all. Can I ask you what you know about opera?"

"Well, Bernie," I said. "Maria Callas…Plácido Domingo. I think I could tell them apart, if I saw a photo." We both laughed. "I really don't know much about opera, why?"

"I met a young Russian soprano with an exceptional voice. She'll never sing anything but opera, but she watches MTV all the time. She knows all about you."

"Okay…"

"I'm a producer. I would like to produce a DVD of about five arias from her first CD, *Young Heroines*, that you conceive and direct in the music video style. Opera for a younger audience. Nothing like this has been done in the opera world. Would you be interested?"

"Well, thanks, Bernie. I'll listen to the CD and tell you what I think. What's her name?"

"Anna Netrebko."

I'm now going to ask you to stop reading and, if you've never heard of her, look up Anna Netrebko. She's not only beautiful, she's magnetic. And above all, she can sing. From the first note of Anna Netrebko's voice, something stirred within me. I knew practically nothing about opera, but I was hooked. And I couldn't wait to work with her.

Anna had a unique sound. She had a rock/pop feel with an operatic tone. I told Bernie I would direct and choreograph the DVD we'd eventually call *Anna Netrebko: The Woman, The Voice*. We'd interlace the videos with interviews I'd conduct with Anna in my living room. She was on the cusp of becoming one of the greatest, most popular, and well-loved sopranos in the history of modern opera.

The budget for the project was tight, yet Bernie inspired us with a revolutionary spirit as the opera world frowned upon anything outside the traditional. After speaking with Anna on the phone, I deciphered through her thick Russian accent that she was willing to do anything that made her, and me, and us, happy. "And, Veencent, I LOVE clothes and shoes! Pleeezzzeee. I want to look beautiful!"

I had chosen arias from *Faust, La Bohème, Don Giovanni, La sonnambula,* and *Rusalka.* Some of the settings would be realistic; some, whimsical. Knowing Anna adored fashion, Bernie's wife, Michaela, and I sprinted to Salzburg's famed opera house, the Großes Festspielhaus. One of its stages was used in *The Sound of Music*, where local legend states the real von Trapp family sang before slipping away through the stone tunnel passageway to escape the Nazis.

Our mission was slightly less dire. We met Dorothea Nicolai, the wardrobe supervisor for the opera house, to rent costumes for the video. To break the ice, I related that my mother shared her name. I showed her the tattoo of a dot on my wrist, representing my mother's nickname, Dot.

Dorothea and my mom could have been soul sisters—she'd have been right at home next to my mom and Nan back in Brookhaven, creating the latest fashions from magazine photos and pulling together fantastic looks from bargain basement racks of cast-offs. Mom even turned her eye to our home's interior, always curious about the latest trends and fashions. Returning from a visit to any friend's home, Mom would grill me, "What'd the furniture look like? What color were the rugs?" I would train myself to take mental pictures. I can thank her for my attention to detail because I got pretty good at it.

Dorothea became my new best friend, giving us a tour of every costume room, wig room, makeup room, even every catwalk high above the stage. "Just pick whatever you like," Dorothea said. "I'm sure it will be fine." She spoke about each costume in specifics, knowing who wore it and for what show. "That's Jessye Norman's" or "That would fit Anna Netrebko." With each article of clothing she sighed, "What a life and story this one has to tell."

We still had more wardrobe to find, so we hired a local costumer, Frank Oberberger. Three days after meeting on the phone, Frank brought in two racks of haute-couture wardrobe—jaw-dropping ball gowns from period films, a breathtaking aqua rag dress, a lavender gown inspired by an Austrian drape and soft as a cloud, a metallic gray gown with Swarovski rhinestones, and a black gown with a collar of black feathers that resembled monkey fur.

We headed to our first face-to-face meeting and wardrobe fitting with Anna at Salzburg's Hotel Sacher. As we carried armfuls of gowns down the hallway, Anna leaned out her door in her robe and yelled in her Russian accent, "I can't get MTV in this hotel!" I yelled back, "Then throw the television out the window!"

She looked stunning in every dress she put on, and she knew it. "No, ees not possible to wear thees one. I look like big Russian bear in thees." She looked sensational. "Pleeze, not make me wear thees one, Veencent. My ass looks like…like I don't know what, even."

"Frank, throw it away!" We all laughed hysterically.

Anna was certainly not what I expected in an opera star. She wore thousand-dollar jeans and rapped along to Eminem's greatest hits. She was a mix of sophistication and rebellion, which perplexed the opera world but inspired me. I knew the camera would love her.

Before shooting any of the arias, Anna and I worked alone. She was nervous, having never been in front of a camera. I sat her on a chair in the center of the rehearsal studio.

"Anna, let's try this without music, speaking the libretto of the aria. Then sing the song but more intimately than you would on stage. Be honest, as the camera picks up the thoughts in your mind. Do you know the American actress, Glenn Close?"

"Yes, I know who she is."

"She's the perfect example of honest work on film because whenever the camera captures her in a close-up, she always has a very specific thought in her head."

I moved around the room having her direct her performance toward my fist as if it were the camera. She was open and receptive with a formidable desire to be the best at her art, while maintaining a saucy happiness about being here, being young and slowly becoming very famous in the opera world.

We found locations, built sets, cast, and rehearsed the performers and filmed in Salzburg and Munich. Harry Geyer and Eva Baumann created the sets and set pieces. Harry has a farmhouse in the Austrian countryside outside Salzburg. Entering his attic was like being back at Nan's in my creative "junk room." It was a treasure trove of spinning wheels and sewing machines, Seussian musical instruments, and sundry thingamajigs. Eva and Harry worked magic. Eva created arms made from tree limbs for the cast in the aria, "Non Mi Dir" from *Don Giovanni*. When I had created "Like a Virgin" for the Blond Ambition Tour, I wanted to use tree limbs for the male dancers. Later, I tried to sell the tree-arm idea to Josh Groban for one of his tours, but he couldn't grasp the concept, "Men wearing tree limbs for arms? I'm not sure." Anna loved the idea.

Our aspirations for these music videos were higher than our budget, but if I ever felt discouraged, Anna's performance piloted me through. With Bernie Fleischer's determination, we completed what we felt was respectable, if not occasionally inspired, work.

Not everyone thought so. MTV-style videos for opera arias was a foreign idea to the opera world and some of the reviews of *Anna Netrebko: The Woman, The Voice* were scathing: "The only passable sections in this otherwise awful DVD are the interviews that show Netrebko as a vivacious and beautiful woman who is still trying to cope with sudden stardom. The five lip-synced arias are an absolute outrage. Staged like second rate fashion shows, they are a pinnacle of bad visual taste and an insult to the music. The director, Vincent Paterson, should perhaps stay with his former subjects, Madonna and Michael Jackson."

Yet, on the other side: "This DVD is the first 'opera music video' ever made, and so far the only one, so it cannot be compared to anything. And neither can the incomparable, sensational Russian soprano, Anna Netrebko. She's the best thing to happen to opera since the nineteenth century...I hope Ms. Netrebko and Vincent Paterson have another opera music video in the works!"

Anna Netrebko: The Woman, The Voice became the highest grossing classical DVD to date. After airing on French television, it was nominated for the Rose d'Or at the Montreux Festival, 2004, in the category Television Arts and Specials.

I loved being involved with the opera world, and I adored Anna Netrebko. Not long after completing the DVD, I was approached by Anna's manager about directing an opera for her at Los Angeles Opera. Anna and the tenor, Rolando Villazón, had become an electrifying operatic duo and had performed Gounod's *Romeo and Juliet* at LAO to tremendous success. Plácido Domingo, the general director at LAO, offered Anna the opportunity to perform at the Dorothy Chandler Pavilion with an opera of her choosing. She chose Massenet's *Manon*. Plácido greeted me in his downtown office with the warmest smile, "So, Vincent, Anna would like you to direct *Manon* here next year. What do you say?"

"Sir, I am flattered. We had an extraordinary connection on a project we recently finished, and I would love to work with her again."

"That sounds wonderful. Do you know the opera?"

"Yes, I've listened to it many times."

"I think it needs cutting. It's way too long. Feel free to go through it and cut what you think is extemporaneous, then show it to me. It's too long to let the story be told clearly. See what you can do. I love Anna and Rolando, I want to conduct this for you."

"Wow. I can only say 'thank you, maestro.'"

I lived with the libretto and made some cuts. Plácido not only liked them but also asked for more to allow the story to be told more succinctly for a contemporary audience.

I met with Christopher Koelsch, director of artistic planning for LAO. We discussed designers. I wanted Susan Hilferty to design the costumes. Her designs for *Wicked* alone informed me that she had the sense of glamour, fashion, and humor I wanted for *Manon*. We invited Duane Schuler to design the lights. Chris suggested Johannes Leiacker, a German set designer, and I agreed. I asked Christopher if I could "shadow" a director of an upcoming opera to learn the ropes of the Los Angeles Opera.

"I have a suggestion, Vincent. Garry Marshall is going to direct Offenbach's *The Grand Duchess*, and he will need a choreographer. Would you be interested?" So, one year before directing *Manon*, I choreographed *The Grand Duchess* starring opera diva Frederica von Stade. It was a great education and a delight working with Mr. Marshall.

I began my opera homework. I attended seven live operas that year and watched over a dozen on DVD. Some directors had shifted the time periods from the opera's original time frame. Sometimes this worked, sometimes it didn't. I decided to move *Manon* from the period of French wigs and powder to the 1950s. I had two reasons for doing this. First, Manon's story held up when moved to the 1950s. Second, I loved the look and glamour of the female movie stars of that time period. Their dress, hair, and style highlighted the female body in sensual fashion. I knew Anna would carry off this era with aplomb. I believed that updating the look of the opera, combined with Anna and Rolando's youthful spirits and good looks, would make the story more relatable to a younger audience. Being a French opera, I followed a French idiom: *Plus ça change, plus c'est la même chose.* The more things change, the more they stay the same!

Manon is the story of a teenager being sent to the convent for being "mischievous." She has grander dreams than those of most rural young women. She crosses paths with a wealthy young man, des Grieux. Manon declares, "When you are young and beautiful and nineteen, you should have everything!" Is this so far-fetched for the attitude of a strong-willed girl in the 1950s? Like Manon, Anna fearlessly followed her dreams to get what she wanted from life.

I created a Manon who reads fan magazines, seeing herself as the star of her own life-film. As she travels up and down the ladder of success, she copies the visual style of iconic stars of the fifties that depict her physical and emotional state at each phase of her journey. On her train ride to the convent, she presents a waifish Audrey Hepburn persona. Falling in love with des Grieux , she is as fresh as a young Natalie Wood. As her social star rises, she strolls the Cours-la-Reine with a Count on her arm, emulating the look of Gina Lollobrigida as men fall at her feet. Persuading des Grieux to not enter the priesthood, she appears at the sacristy gates in a blood-red coat looking as breathtaking as Liz Taylor. She arrives with des Grieux at the Hotel de Transylvanie gambling hall resembling Marilyn Monroe. Finally, imprisoned and dying of tuberculosis, she resembles a broken Jean Seberg.

I cherished every second with Anna and Rolando. They are actors as well as singers. They both loved exploring story and character. Anna was a dancer in her youth and knowledgeable about the power of movement. Rolando Villazón epitomized the smoldering passion of an ill-fated lover with his expressive eyes, his agile body, and his touching tenor voice.

I have two favorite moments of this creation. A young Manon sings an aria, "Adieu, Notre Petite Table," reflecting on how much she will miss her life without des Grieux. Manon is alone in their Paris apartment sitting at the dining table. As subtext, Anna and I surmised that Manon and des Grieux had probably had sex on this table. Anna's Manon wore a robe and slip as she gently ran her fingers across the tabletop, erotically climbed upon it and finished the aria on her back. There was not a sound until after her last note when thunderous applause erupted from the audience.

My other favorite moment is when des Grieux is to be ordained into the priesthood. Manon confesses her love for him while he pleads with her to leave him to God. He paces behind the sacristy wall like a trapped tiger in a cage. She clutches the hem of his vestments through the iron gate, then, defeated, walks away. Unable to live without her, des Grieux throws open the sacristy doors and grabs Manon, pulling her into an embrace on the sacristy stairs as the set disappears upstage into the darkness. Audiences of all ages screamed and stomped as if they were at a rock concert!

The sold-out shows ran during September and October 2006, in Los Angeles. It was a joint venture with Berlin's Staatsoper, so in April 2007, we took *Manon* to Berlin. It was Netrebko's premiere opera performance in Berlin and the city was crazy with expectation. The brilliant artist and humanitarian Daniel Barenboim conducted the opera. I remember an amusing incident with Maestro Barenboim. During one rehearsal, I stood beside him as he gave the singers notes about the libretto. With each note, they smiled a little larger.

"Why is everyone so happy?" he asked.

"Well, Maestro," one of his singers replied, "We are finding it amusing that every comment you are giving us about the approach to the libretto is almost word for word what Vincent told us during our blocking rehearsals."

Constructing the show at the Staatsoper was not the walk in the park it had been in LA. The talk among the crew was that the artistic director of the opera was on some mind-altering substances most of the time. The sets had a hard time fitting this opera house stage. Cast members missed rehearsals regularly. Regardless, we opened to exuberant response. The positive press was unstoppable, though a few critics ranted that my *Manon* had a Hollywood touch.

European audiences are very frank in letting the director know immediately how they feel about the work. Many new directors at the Staatsoper had been "booed" rudely and loudly. On occasion, Barenboim had to accompany the director during curtain calls to calm the people down. I was nervous.

When the opening night curtain closed, deafening applause began. When it opened, the entire chorus, then principals, then Barenboim took their bows. The heavy gold curtain closed then reopened as the orchestra stood with Barenboim. It closed again and Anna brought me out, then she left. I was on stage taking a bow. Alone. I bowed with the biggest grin imaginable and was excited, but the applause continued for fifteen to twenty minutes as the full cast returned to the stage again and again. Later, several people told me I had probably broken history at the Staatsoper. There were no boos for me. None.

Being accepted into the opera world, as someone from the commercial world of Hollywood, fills me with a major sense of accomplishment. It also lives with me as a reminder to all the joy I could have missed out on had my dark moment in that Santa Barbara hotel room gone differently. Things can get bleak, but I've since learned more than ever to trust the universe. The universe, after all, brought Patrick Bensard into my life, defending me from a potential Q&A assassin and then leading me to Bernie Fleischer, who then entrusted me with a talent like Anna.

In fact, one of my most prized possessions is a photo taken from a helicopter high above the Staatsopera where twenty thousand people filled Unter den Linden, the main street in East Berlin, watching our opera production playing on a seventy-square-meter screen while it was being performed live inside. Not a ticket to be had, so *Manon* took to the streets.

12.

Come to the Cabaret

Vincent,
Your Berlin Cabaret will be astounding.
May you be blessed by the angel.
—Glenn Close

IN 2004, I FLEW TO Berlin to meet Lutz Deisinger, a German producer, and his resident director, Julian Kamphausen, to discuss the first theatrical production of the Kander and Ebb musical *Cabaret*, to be created in Germany. They knew my work from *Dancer in the Dark*, for which I had choreographed and directed the dance sequences. We met at Bar Jeder Vernunft, an original German mirrored-tent from 1912, located on a wooded lot in central Berlin. Lutz and his partner, Holger Klotzbach, found the tent in the German countryside. They bought it, had it sent to Berlin, and transformed it from a frankfurter stand to a famous cabaret theater.

Stepping through the flaps of the tent is like going back a century in time. It's a circular space with mirrors lining the inside canvas walls. There are two levels: dark wooden booths and tables on the top tier, and small, circular café tables on the ground level. Poles of mirror-covered wood support the spiegeltent. The space seats 250 guests during a performance. The dressing room is an old "gypsy" caravan trailer set up behind the tent. Without doing a single thing to the space, you feel like you're in a 1920s German cabaret.

I was inspired immediately. To direct the first original production of *Cabaret* and to do it in Berlin—the city in which the musical takes place—and to be the first "book" musical presented in the tent…how much better could it get? But then, the catch…they had chosen a Finnish director who had never directed a musical, and they wanted me to choreograph only. Big breath!

"Well," I said, "This is one of the most magical spaces I've ever been in. I would want to put my spin on the entire story and would become frustrated just choreographing. I'm honored, but I'll only be involved as the director *and* choreographer. I could create one hell of a piece."

Julian said, "We've already made an agreement with the Finnish director."

"Well, thank you anyway," I said. "I wish you the best, and I'm sure you are going to have an incredible show."

A week later, Lutz phoned, "In my heart I know you are the man to direct and choreograph this show." I was off to Berlin.

The "cabaret" songs of the musical were to be in English but the rest of the songs and the dialogue would be in German. I spoke no German, so I took a crash course and by the time I arrived back in Berlin to hold auditions, I knew some colors, numbers, and the conjugation of three verbs: I am, I want, I have.

The night before auditions, in my surgically clean Berlin hotel room, I awoke with a sobering thought, "What the hell am I doing? I am directing this show entirely in German. Am I out of my mind! I need to call my agents right now and tell them I can't do this!"

Instead, I breathed, took *zwei* (two) Tylenol PMs, opened the window, and tucked the comforter around my feet. *Auf wiedersehen*, fear!

Mette Berggreen, my Danish assistant choreographer from *Dancer in the Dark,* joined me again. We began the casting process. I like dancing that is sensual, specific, and narrative, and I relish the audition process. At every dance audition I say, "Pull me toward you when you dance rather than push me to the back of my seat. Use your eyes to project your story. Imagine the room is filled with billions of bubbles and, when dancing, move as few of them as possible."

When casting actors and dancers, I have a solid sense of what I am looking for but always hope a performer will walk in the room and change my mind. Good actors and dancers must project self-assuredness in their audition. There is so much pressure when directing or choreographing, I want a cast I won't have to babysit. Because of my German classes, I was able to introduce myself at my auditions: "*Mein name ist Vincent Paterson. Danke dass Sie da kommen sind. Ich habe nur safe sex.*" (My name is Vincent Paterson. Thank you for coming. I only have safe sex.) It broke all tensions immediately.

Mette, Julian, and I selected the Kit Kat Girls—a *zaftig* Slovenian, a Danish drag queen, a Swiss Kewpie doll, and a Berlin beauty with just a hint of cellulite. I needed to select a "swing" who would learn all the parts to cover the dancers in case of illness or injury. I chose a blonde floozy-type who Mette thought too animated and couldn't imagine seeing her being content with sitting in the wings every night waiting to go on. But I liked her *because* she was hungry to go on. I imagined her keeping sushi in the sun then offering it to the other Kit Kat girls as a snack at intermission. I knew she would keep the others on their toes.

The mix of actors I cast was eclectic, to say the least. Sally Bowles was a film star. Fraulein Schneider and Kost were the leads at Brecht's Berliner Ensemble. One actor was a performance fire-artist who spent a year in Berlin never being seen without a lit candle on his bald head. One actor was an ex-soap opera star who had been imprisoned for trying to escape from East Berlin when the wall was still up. One was a respected drama teacher. The emcee I cast was a dancer who had never acted before.

We had assembled a stellar production team for a relatively small show intended to run for one season. Julian became my assistant director and dramaturge. Adam Benzwi was my musical director. Adam is an American, a brilliant pianist and musical director, who had moved to Berlin several years prior. We decided to have a small band that would include a tuba, a toy piano, and a singing saw.

I met set designers. I passed on Jurgen, the brawny bald stereotype who saw the entire show being done in black rubber cubes. I passed on Heinrich and Ilsa, the couple who saw lots of flowing silk drapery and ramps, ramps, ramps! Momme Röhrbein had a more flexible perspective. I told him I wanted the sets to feel inexpensive and handmade, minimal, yet clever. The tent had such an "atmosphere" that I wanted the sets to be true to the historical charm. I decided the band should sit off the side of the stage, meshing the actors and dancers with the musicians. Also, on this miniscule stage, I wanted to open the story with a moving train.

Momme designed an enchanting set with sliding curtains that the actors moved during transitions to change the environments, and a minimum amount of furniture. A 3-D cardboard train had a light in front and smoke coming from the stack. When it came through the stage left curtains on a turntable, it took your breath away. As the turntable circled, the train, which was constructed in perspective from big to smaller in proportion, gave the sense of moving into the distance.

My costume-design team was Fiona Bennett and Nicole von Graevenitz. I met them in Fiona's East Berlin apartment for an awe-inspiring journey of their ideas. They had done impressive homework; however, there were too many ideas and some were just too "good" for my vision of the show.

Dear Ladies,

Thank you for your work. Every idea is unique and more than good, though some costumes are too good for this production. I would love you to consider every costume being the cheap version of your dreams.

I love the gorilla costume you created with the sculpted latex face, but my instinct tells me it's too perfect. How would this company of players have afforded that costume? Is there a way to make it as good as it could possibly be without much money?

The show should appear to want to be bigger than it can afford to be. Each character, except for Sally onstage, should have only one or two costumes. Sally's costumes should feel like they're assembled on a shoestring budget with ingenuity, uniqueness, and zaniness. I cannot imagine two more perfect designers to do this than you.

—Vincent

The production crew for *Cabaret* was small, and I developed a relationship with the entire team from stagehands to props people. I learned everyone's name as a matter of respect. Feeling like a family gives every person the opportunity to take personal pride in their contribution. And you never know when you might need to call in a favor.

I came to Berlin having done my homework. I had sketched out the dances at Alley Kat Studio with LA dancers Suzi Lonergan and Bonnie Story. I had staged the dramatic scenes on paper, though Julian informed me that German actors like to "experiment" to find their own blocking. I believe that as there is dialogue, music, and lyrics, there is my staging. If something feels unnatural, I'll change it once it's mounted.

The full company met around a rectangle of tables in our rehearsal hall, scripts in hand. Everyone, to my relief, spoke English.

"Welcome, everyone," I greeted my cast. "When I first walked into Bar Jeder Vernunft, it was love at first sight. I want our version of *Cabaret* to be presented in a voice like the bar's: historical and magical. Our gift is that the situation with the bar, as in any smaller theater—lack of budget, lack of staff, small stage, no back dressing room, no understudies for most roles, no great salaries—perfectly mirrors the real lives of the characters in *Cabaret*.

"As the director, I'm willing to go wherever you want to go, explore whatever you want to explore, as it regards the play. But if your personal life is a drama, put it to brilliant use on the stage or leave it outside the door. I want to get the show on its feet in one month so we can see the entire show in a complete but rough form. Then we'll probe deeper into the scenes, the characters, and the songs. Let's read the play."

Two cast members, Angela Winkler and Margarita Broich, raised their concern that the second act got too dark with the Nazi themes. They told me they had had this crammed down their throats forever and that Germans were a little tired of it.

I replied, "Prejudice, racism is a global concern. Perhaps Germans have lived and learned this. Each of your characters believes he or she is right. Each believes they will survive. Each lives with hope. If you live your character's truth, the play will have a resonance that addresses the beauty of the human spirit as well as the nature and injustices of mankind, not just Nazism."

As a director, I often work with a model of the set and small figures that can be moved from scene to scene. I photograph them in every new position resulting in a simple version of a stop-motion animated film. These storyboards allow me to be explicit with my vision of the show with the cast as well as the designers. My first scene rehearsal began with Angela, one of the top theatrical actresses in Germany, who seemed like an innocent from another world, like Björk. I shared the photos with her so she would see what I envisioned.

Blocking the scene was difficult because Angela was accustomed to creating her own stage movement through experimentation. I gave her my blocking and, after running through the scene several times, gave her permission to change what felt uncomfortable or unnatural. It was an immediate collaboration filled with love. By the end of our rehearsal, Angela sang "Na Und?" or "So What?" and finished by spinning with glee.

"Vincent," she laughed, "I've let something go!"

"Angela, I'm so happy," I replied. "There's plenty of room for individuality inside what might seem to be cloyingly specific." Julian told me that Angela had mostly worked with one director for the last fifteen years. He was a sadist who wouldn't allow actors to look him in the eyes. Julian said that this rehearsal with Angela was like letting an animal off the leash for the first time.

Cabaret was a crash course in directing an eclectic cast in a foreign country. I learned how to succinctly communicate with actors of different backgrounds, how to guide the actors to answer their own questions, how to challenge them to make the most dangerous and personal choices to keep the stakes high. Each actor worked differently, and I pulled all kinds of tricks out of my bag.

I regard musicals as seriously as I do dramas because the human stories of struggle, pain, desire, love, and achievement are what I love to tell. If a story is worthy of the stage, it must, in some way, reveal truth. Whatever language I direct in (I've since directed in English, French, German, and Japanese), I am always looking for truth. I found it fascinating that, though I heard the dialogue in German and was familiar with the English text, I absolutely knew what was working or not working as truth for each scene.

Some actors came in for the scene blocking with all of their lines memorized, and with these actors I could begin to delve and probe sooner. Others took their time learning the dialogue. It was all part of various processes. All fascinating.

The first note I always give to actors is to find elements of the character that they see in themselves. Second, every action in life, as well as in the theater, is about *getting what you want*. I expect actors to know the answers to the following questions:

—*What do you want from the other character or the audience?*
—*What are your obstacles to getting what you want?*
—*What do you have to lose?*
—*Are you using every tactic to get what you want?*
—*Where are you? To win you must "own" the space.*

I also encourage them to keep their character's secrets to themselves, so they don't lose their power.

For every project since "Smooth Criminal," I have each cast member write a brief bio about their character and ask them to track their actions from the beginning to the end of the story. Everyone came in with a biography filled with fascinating, intricate stories.

Every dancer wrote a bio that mingled her life with other members of the Kit Kat Club. When working on a scene, I could refer to their bio material, "And how does that childhood friend Karl figure into this feeling you have?" It was also a learning curve in trusting myself. Drawing on my knowledge from the classes I had taken, the directors I had observed, the great teachers I had had, and because of the homework I had done, the communication flowed easily.

Peter Koch (as Herr Schultz) and Angela (as Fräulein Schneider) had some serious breakthroughs. Angela was struggling to find the difference between the serious work at the Berliner Ensemble and being in a musical. I kept reiterating, "If the musical is well-written, it's the same. You seek the truth in your character and each situation."

It is thrilling to witness an actor's discovery during the rehearsal process. Angela and Peter were interpreting the "Pineapple Song" as a sweet love song. We broke it down into acting beats. I had them sit back-to-back and sing the song as if every word they sang came out totally wrong. Embarrassingly wrong. I had them sing it again back-to-back as if every word the other person sang was not what they wanted to hear. They experienced a gamut of emotions, exploring the plethora of thoughts that go through our heads while having one brief conversation with someone. The song became filled with colors of seduction, secrecy, honesty, fantasy, frustration, and love.

On another day we worked on the last scene in the show and one of the principal actresses was causing a disruption. We got through half the scene when she hollered, "I don't think I should have to say this line. *'They have all the money, the Jews!'* Two hours of building a character and this is what she gets to say? I don't think this is how people should remember her. I don't want them to think this about me. Maybe I can say it in a nice way."

I took a breath, "This is an important line because many people actually think this way. This is not your personal sentiment; this is the sentiment of your character."

When we went through the song again, she yelled out something about the last two lines being terribly written.

"You know what," I said, "maybe we should just throw this script out and let's do *Heidi*!" I put down my script and walked out of the room.

Adam came out and caught me laughing. "Sometimes, the director needs to be a little dramatic," I said. "That probably shook them up!" We went back into the room. I gave the actress a hug and told her how much I appreciated her and loved her work. I did love her work.

Besides my first cast, there were swing actors who would take over roles during the first few weeks. Maria Körber, Angela's understudy, would do two of the preview nights. Maria told us that she remembered being on her balcony as a girl and hearing the marching boots of the Nazis coming down the streets, "one thousand men, and two thousand boots. Marching, marching." She said, with tears in her eyes. "It was a frightening sound and one that I can still hear." Once, Hitler picked her out from her classmates and had her sit on his lap and sing a song. Her father was a famous film director and directed movies for the Reich, including a notorious anti-gay propaganda film. Not long before I met Maria, her filmmaker brother went hunting for a Nazi officer who was hiding out near Berlin. He found him, tied him to a chair, put the camera on, and beat him mercilessly until the man confessed. He edited the footage, produced it, and marketed it. It was fascinating working in Berlin, getting inside the stories and places where so much tragedy occurred.

Anna Loos played Sally Bowles. Anna, a successful TV and film actress, was nervous about showing her sexuality, though she was a strong and sensual woman. I created "Mein Herr" as a naughty Weimar S&M number. Throughout the song, when I directed Anna to put a sexual thought in her head, she began to laugh. So I stood directly in front of her and had her sing the song into my eyes. When the choreography took her to the floor, I got on the floor. As she crawled on her knees, I crawled beside her. I encouraged her to think erotic thoughts with a smile behind her eyes. She had to be the dominatrix in this number, controlling but with humor. When we finished the song, Mette said she wished she'd had a movie camera because it was an amazing dance watching the two of us work like spiders.

Our first run-through rehearsal was frighteningly bad. I wrote on a piece of paper to Julian, at my side, "I am going to SCREAM!!!!!!" I felt everyone had forgotten everything that we had worked on. When it was finished, I said, "Well, that was horrible."

Anna, who was playing Sally Bowles, looked at me, "Horrible?"

"Yes, horrible," I said.

I gave notes. I told them it was difficult watching great actors do bad work, especially if they didn't recognize it. Angela, usually so silent, spoke up and said they had only worked on some of the scenes that day and needed time to let the notes sink in. I reminded her they had been given the option of using their scripts to walk through the new work just to remember it, even if it was not heartfelt. Anna, in tears, told me she just didn't know how to make a specific grand entrance that was troubling her. I told her she was giving it too much weight and to throw her shyness away, she must believe she's a major diva. I suggested she imagine that she was Marilyn Monroe in *Gentlemen Prefer Blondes.*

"I don't know how to play a diva!" she said.

"You're a celebrity in Berlin, Anna! Pretend you're at the opening of one of your films with the paparazzi flashing cameras in your face! You know this girl. She has a lot of you in her. Find it!"

When I got home that night, Adam called me and told me he was so happy I told the cast they were horrible. I asked him why he hadn't chimed in. "Because I want them to think of me as the good guy!"

"Fuck you," I laughed.

We finally moved rehearsals to the tent. I had forgotten how small the stage was. When everyone arrived, I asked them to crowd in close together for a group hug. Then we ran the show. No costumes, sets, props, or lights. Only four chairs, two small tables, and Adam on the piano. Magic happened.

It was two weeks until opening. In "Money," which "makes the world go 'round," I asked the singers to visualize a spinning globe in the distance and to send their voices around the globe, caress it, and travel back. Adam looked at me with a strange look on his face after they sang it, "Somehow that works."

Immediately after the song "Heirat" (in English "Married"), Schultz proposes marriage to Fräulein Schneider. I asked the actors to think about the last lyric, *"My dreams are taking me to the marriage altar."* I directed them to sing their last line with hope but with the fear that something might not allow this to happen because if, at the end of the song, we know she will accept his marriage proposal, there is no need for the proposal scene that follows.

For one of our final rehearsals, I put the chairs in a circle. I directed the cast to spit out the dialogue of the entire show at lightning speed, no pauses, no worries about emotional interpretations. We began. I acted as the game show host, and when an actor would flub a line or forget one, I gave a loud buzzer noise and said, "There goes the microwave!" or "You just lost the BMW!" It got faster and louder and everyone was sweating to keep up the pace. It was another way to get the company pulled together as a team and to have the actors hear the dialogue with new ears.

Three days before the opening preview, the costumes and wigs weren't finished. The set was falling apart and the scene changes were noisy. One of the actors leaned on a table and the leg broke out from under it. Anna went on a paranoid crying jag, freaked out that her costumes weren't done for her to feel her timing, her wigs weren't finished, and she feared she would lose her voice.

I spoke to everyone about being polite and speaking to each other and the crew with respect. Then I yelled at crew people who walked out of the theater for a smoke and weren't there for a set change. I was frustrated with the lighting designer. Sometimes he would tell Julian that something I desired was impossible, then he would create that design in another scene without realizing it. The light board was so inappropriate for a musical that it did seem like the 1920s. Every change or new cue took hours to put into the system. And changing one light cue seemed to affect every other light cue in the board's memory.

I was nervous for the first preview performance in front of an audience. We hadn't had one run-through of the show that took less than six hours because of the set problems. The morale of the actors had sunk to an all-time low. Even Julian, my strong, young, stalwart companion, had been reduced to tears.

Yet the magic of the theater prevailed, and the first preview was sensational. While putting on her makeup, I had given Anna five pages of notes for Sally, all saying the same thing: "Have fun! Lighten up! Stop letting me see you think! This is not Jessica Lange doing Tennessee Williams! Enjoy!" And that night she showed me the Sally for whom I was searching. Angela proved to be a dream. Watching her process was an education. Her performance as Fräulein Schneider was as raw and as unique as Björk's performance in *Dancer in the Dark*. She was my dream actress, my Glenn Close. Margarita began to glisten, being funny, sexy, pouty, and defiant as the prostitute, Fräulein Kost.

We needed more time but it was preview week. The band was inconsistent. When the musicians were on target it was heaven, but when they were off, it was a minor train wreck. Lutz told me that during the preview shows, the audience likes to have the director stop the show and work directly with the actors, or the lighting, or the sound. So I did some hands-on work with Eric Rentmeister, the master of ceremonies. This was his first acting role and every night in front of the audience, he got warmer and wiser, more relaxed and more mischievous. He took advantage of his dancing skills to create a hypnotic body language as the host of the Kit Kat Club.

As the play closes, Cliff heads out of Berlin on the train remembering and writing lines of dialogue spoken by characters he has met. I placed the actors throughout the tent, reminding them that this was political theater in 1918 and that at any moment the Gestapo might enter and drag them off to a concentration camp. While speaking their lines, they moved to the stage like ghosts surrounding Cliff as he jotted down his reflections of the dangerous, political times he had witnessed in Berlin.

On opening night, we were graced with the presences of Joe Masteroff (the author of *Cabaret*) and Joel Grey, who won an Academy Award for his role as the conferencier at the Kit Kat Club. We received two extraordinary, eight excellent, and two so-so reviews. I was told this was a phenomenon as the German critics were barbaric. The BBC did a twenty-minute, highly flattering piece on the show. We were headlined in every Berlin paper. Headlines like, "Anna Loos, the new Liza Minnelli!" "Forget every *Cabaret* you have ever seen. Don't miss this one!"

I had no idea that this small show would have this sort of notoriety. I thought I was going to Berlin to do a small musical in an intimate tent with little notice, an opportunity to hone my directing chops. The show was intended to run from October 2004 until March 2005, but it was extended to May almost immediately. It was eventually moved to a larger theater and has become the longest running show in the history of Berlin…over fifteen years.

Our *Cabaret* had been blessed by the angel as Glenn Close wished.

13.

More Michael

DURING "SMOOTH CRIMINAL," MY friendship and intense working dynamic with Michael Jackson had found a tempo. No one I had ever worked with mastered the electric socket of creativity quite like him. He was constantly plugged in. It makes sense to me now, when I look back on the whole of my time with Mike, always scattered between other projects either he or I were off doing. Every time we reconnected, it would reenergize my passion for this crazy business. No matter where I was in the world, I always looked forward to getting back into the studio with Mike.

The Way You Make Me Feel

THE FOOTAGE FOR "SMOOTH Criminal" had been "in the can," which literally meant in 35mm metal cans, since around April of 1987. When "Smooth Criminal" became part of *Moonwalker*, I also choreographed "Speed Demon" and "Dirty Diana."

In late August of that year, I got a call to meet Mike at Debbie Reynolds Dance Studio to discuss another short film. When I got to the rehearsal hall, Mike gave me a warm hug and an adorable smile. He looked relaxed in his black pants, red corduroy shirt, and loafers. He told me, "I was thinking I might not do much dancing in this one.

Maybe you could choreograph something for the end of the song. We can add a dance break if we want."

"What's it called?" I asked.

"'The Way You Make Me Feel,'" he said.

"And you don't want to do just a little dancing with that title, Mike?"

He paused. Then said, "Yeah, let's do it. We can kill it." We listened to the song. Mike shared the video's concept: A street gang is trying to pick up girls. They make fun of Mike because he's shy. An older man advises him to be himself. Mike pursues a stunning girl, played by Tatiana Thumbtzen, until she falls in love with him.

Debbie Reynolds Dance Studio had become a home for us. "Beat It" and "Thriller" were rehearsed here and now it was our base for "The Way You Make Me Feel." We began to experiment with Flamenco silhouettes and other movements. At one point, I was lying prone on the floor and pounding my fist while I did a pelvic pump that can only be described as fucking the floor.

"Ooooo," Mike gave his signature squeal of joy. "Ooooo. That's nasty! You are so nasty!"

"That's not nasty, Mike." I said with a sly smile, "That's fun."

"Ooooo. Okay. Show me."

Mike enjoyed pushing the "nasty" envelope sometimes. We called some dancers to join us—Eddie Garcia, LaVelle Smith, Art Palmer, and Sean Cheesman.

A few days later, I met Mike and Joe Pytka, who was directing the short film, on the set at Culver Studios. This was the first time I had met Joe. At a tall, lean six foot seven, he was physically intimidating.

I was given some sage advice from a friend who worked for Joe, loved him, loved me, and knew we were about to meet.

"Listen," my friend said, "Joe is a really tough character. He's a pussycat at heart but he's a lion on the outside, and if you show him any weakness, he'll eat you alive. He *loves* dance. Oh, yeah, he says 'fuck' like every other word! And he's got a great sense of humor. Like you." Joe's also Polish, like me.

"I thought you weren't doing any dancing in this," Joe boomed at Mike.

"Well, Vincent and I got together and started playing around," Mike responded. "I'm adding some music at the end, and we're gonna kill it."

Joe said he wanted to walk me through the set and pick my brain. He and I started talking.

"I'm bringing in some gang members to do some freestyle movement and give the piece some authenticity. I know you can move Michael down the street and find things for him to do. You and Michael've done great fucking work. I'm glad you're here."

I decided to have some fun. "Well, thanks, Joe, but I'm a little surprised," I said. "I was actually called by your office a few months ago to choreograph a commercial, and I was asked to hold some dates. I held those dates and yet you filmed the commercial after hiring a different choreographer. No one bothered to tell me about it. That's really fucked up, man! And on top of that, you're a fucking Polack!"

"Hey! Hey!" Joe stopped in his tracks, pissed as hell. "No one calls me a fucking Polack!"

"Unless you're another fucking Polack," I said. "My paternal grandmother is first generation. Borkowski!" Joe's face froze, then he smiled. It was the beginning of a long and beautiful friendship that continues today.

For the short film, I wanted Mike's fans to see the more relaxed Mike that I knew in rehearsals. I choreographed his character in "The Way You Make Me Feel" to be sexy, fun, and masculine. The video concept supported Mike looking like a regular guy.

"You know, Mike," I said. "I love how you dress in rehearsals. I think it would be cool if you wore something like you have on now. That corduroy shirt looks great on you, man."

"Really?"

"Yeah. That blue's a really good color. Just something like that with a T-shirt under it."

For the short film, Mike did wear his blue shirt. He also used a necktie instead of a belt, inspired by Fred Astaire, always putting his spin on every look he wore. I sketched Mike's journey through the set, finding crazy actions for him like leaping through the backseat of a car trying to get Tatiana's attention.

Something extraordinary happened for all of us when Mike began to sing. There was silence on the set as Mike coolly walked toward Tatiana, snapping his fingers. He walked in a tight circle around her, then stopped behind her. He broke out in full voice, "You knock me off of my feet, now, Baby. HOOOOOOOO!" The playback was supposed to start immediately but everyone was so enthralled in the magic of hearing Michael sing so powerfully, that we all stood frozen. Mike looked around at us. "What?" he said shyly.

Everyone exhaled. "That was incredible, Mike," I said. "You blew us all away and no one could move." Mike giggled like a boy, the opposite energy of the powerful, sexy man who had just knocked us off of our feet.

At the MTV Awards, choreography was the only nomination that "The Way You Make Me Feel" received. I didn't win, though, and it was a disappointment. But I was elated when Joe Pytka shared a letter he had received from Steven Spielberg after the video aired.

March 8, 1988

Dear Joe,

Now that I have watched "The Way You Make Me Feel" video numerous times I still feel as I felt the first time Quincy Jones showed it to me...I can say with no doubt that it's the greatest lesson on how to design and stage a song and dance number since the Golden Age of the MGM musical.

For me, as well, it surely is the best video ever made.

Please accept these late congratulations...

...and when are you going to direct your first movie?

All my best,

The BAD Tour

In late 1987, Mike presented his first solo concert, the *BAD* Tour in Japan and Australia. It would be his first tour since the 1984 Victory Tour with his brothers, The Jackson 5. When the show returned to the States in January of 1988, Mike's manager, Frank DiLeo, called me to direct and choreograph a more spectacular version. We put the show together in Pensacola, Florida. For his first tour, the intention was to showcase Mike as a formidable entertainer, a solo performer, separate from the Jacksons.

Mike and I wanted to grab the audience's attention from the top of the show and take them on a high-powered journey. For the opening, a seven-foot-high video wall that ran the length of the stage slowly rose from below. On it appeared Mike's distinctive silhouette walking across the screen, stopping, spinning, then flipping up onto his toes. With a thunderous chord of music, the wall became a blaze of blinding light. As it slowly lowered, Mike was standing center stage with his four dancers behind him—Eddie Garcia, LaVelle Smith, Dominic Lucero, and Randy Allaire. The audience went insane. After his infamous Motown Special performance, after the short films "Beat It," "Thriller," "Smooth Criminal," "The Way You Make Me Feel," here was Michael Jackson live. First time out solo. Pure Michael.

Mike wanted the new-at-that-time giant jumbo trons—giant video screens on either side of the stage so every fan could see him. I showcased the choreography that had become world famous through Michael's short films. Sheryl Crow, before she was *the* Sheryl Crow, was the female back-up singer for the *BAD* Tour. She was delightful, and I cast her as MJ's love interest in the stage version of "The Way You Make Me Feel." During the tour, Sheryl would hibernate in her room and write her own music. It wasn't long before her stupendous career took off.

For the recreation of "Thriller," Greg Phillinganes, the musical director, helped create a fun illusion by being Mike's body double.

Greg has a small frame like Mike and, when he ran onstage in streams of light wearing a werewolf mask, the audience thought it was Mike. In a blast of smoke, Greg vanished from the stage, and, in another, Mike appeared on the end of a long, metal arm riding over the heads of the audience.

With this tour we set precedents that became signature elements for Mike, like ferocious wind and smoke blowing up from grates in the stage accompanied by piercing beams of white light. And we discovered what Mike and I nicknamed "the magic moment." Michael had a huge respect for showmen like Sammy Davis Jr. and James Brown who came from the old-school world of one-man shows. During rehearsal, Mike came to me with an idea.

"Vincent," he said, "I want to put some stops in the show…like James Brown did. Magic moments. I want to see how long I can be with the fans in a magic moment."

"Okay," I said. "When we run the show, find the places where your instinct tells you they should happen."

Mike got such elation from striking a pose and unflinchingly holding it while the crowd screamed and chanted, "Michael! Michael!" He'd move the slightest bit, freeze, and the ear-splitting screams began all over again, sometimes for over three minutes. It was mesmerizing how he could keep the fans in his control. It was Mike's tribute to James Brown, as both icons knew the art of affectionately teasing their adoring audiences.

I didn't travel extensively with the *BAD* Tour, though I flew into NYC to make sure it was all going to pop at Madison Square Garden. The reviews were raves. I caught up with the company in Rome to make adjustments to the show when the concert moved from an indoor arena to an outdoor venue. While there, I met up with an artist friend from New York at an outdoor café. His young friend, the actress Helena Bonham Carter, joined him. After finding out what I did for a living, Helena asked, "Do you want to go with me to the Spanish Embassy tomorrow night for a Flamenco party?"

"Sure. I love Flamenco music!"

The memory of that party is splashed with washes of sparkling rose-red sangria, enticing rhythms of a battalion of Flamenco guitars, hypnotic hordes of stomping feet, the thunder of clapping hands, and Helena's radiant face. Neither of us had ever danced the Flamenco, but we poured our hearts into every step, defying anyone who told us that we had absolutely no idea what the hell we were doing.

Mike's opening night in Rome, May 23, 1988, remains one of the most vivid memories I have of a Michael Jackson experience. The outdoor concert was at the Flaminio Stadium under the stars where Mike, the dancers, and the musicians made magic for the thirty thousand fans that filled the stadium. After the show, the entire company was invited to a private castle in the middle of Rome for a banquet in Mike's honor. It was like stepping back in time. The castle interior was lit by candlelight. A long hallway ran the length of the castle, with rooms off to one side. On the stone walls hung centuries-old tapestries and antique oil paintings in elaborate wooden frames.

As we were led to our tables, we passed room after room of elegantly dressed guests at huge banquet tables filled with decadent spreads of food. And I'm not talking veggie trays and Swedish meatballs. It was the sort of feast you'd see in a sixteenth-century painting or in Peter Greenaway's movie, *The Cook, the Thief, His Wife & Her Lover*. There was a monstrous boar with an apple in its mouth; multitiered cakes with white, silver, and gold icing; stuffed pheasants and guinea hens; overflowing fruit bowls; lavish arrays of vegetables; and candles glimmering in silver candelabras.

The dancers, the musicians, and I were led to our table in one spacious dining hall and instructed to wait before eating. We heard faint applause in the distance that became a roar of cheers as it traveled down the long hallway like a tsunami. Mike, wearing a red, military jacket with gold braiding was escorted by the host of the evening into our banquet room. Looking like royalty—he was the King of Pop after all—he greeted the applause with grace.

In his dark sunglasses, Mike was acting cool and politely hiding a huge smile. When he saw us, he broke into a giggle and, as he gave us a little wave, he was ushered in to the next room. I felt caught in an anachronism where unimaginable wealth and untouchable privilege were surrounded by Medici-like decadence and the King of Pop just happened to drop in for a night with over one thousand intimate friends.

It always warmed my heart to see Mike revered in that way. He deserved every accolade. The *BAD* Tour represented the best of Mike in live performance. His precision, his focus, his talent. It was a great show. London's Wembley Stadium had a quota for the amount of shows anyone could perform there, so Mike could only do seven sold-out nights. He broke Madonna, Genesis, and Springsteen's records for audience attendance.

At the time, the *BAD* Tour put Michael Jackson in the Guinness World Records as the most financially successful tour ($125 million) and for performing to five million fans, the largest number for a tour to date.

The Grammy Awards

"This is the greatest awards show performance of all time. Know that."
—Rembert Explains the '80s: Michael Jackson at the 1988 Grammy Awards
by Rembert Browne, February 28, 2013

MIKE HAD NOT BEEN winning Grammys. Politics? Jealousy? I have no idea the real reason and for those of us who were Michael Jackson fans, it made no sense. It seemed spiteful. In 1987, Mike's album *BAD* had five number one singles, was nominated in five Grammy categories, and won nothing. In 1988, he had only one nomination, Record of the Year, "Man in the Mirror." But Mike kept on pushing in spite of whatever was going on around him. Caught in a tornado of God-like admiration by his fans, as well as constant badgering by the tabloids, he kept creating, kept performing, and kept the world on its toes. And I thrived with the creative freedom he gave me.

He was invited to appear on the televised 1988 Grammy Awards at Radio City Music Hall in New York and given an unheard of *ten minutes* for his performance. We decided to put two songs back-to-back: "The Way You Make Me Feel" and "Man in the Mirror." For the show, we flew in Tatiana to reprise her role. Mike, Michael Bush (Jackson's stylist), and I loved the idea of Mike appearing in the blue shirt again. We decided Mike would open in silhouette behind a screen, performing some of his lightning-fast improvisatory poses. Then, cooler than any of the Rat Pack, he'd breeze leisurely down the steps, singing the opening of "The Way You Make Me Feel" in a slow, swinging tempo with a sultry tone in his voice. When Tatiana appeared, the song would kick into a hot rhythm and the dancers would join in.

With the opening refrains of "Man in the Mirror," the tempo would change for an emotionally raw performance by Mike. The principal singers entered first and, on a dramatic key change, the soulful choir of New Hope Baptist Church of New York appeared from out of the darkness.

Mike and I created a handful of moves in rehearsals for him to use at his disposal. It was a spiritual experience being in the rehearsal room. Imagine being surrounded by the voices of Andraé Crouch and his choir, Siedah Garrett who cowrote the song, Táta Vega, The Winans, and Michael Jackson. Blessed.

When I left rehearsal, the Grammy producer, Ken Ehrlich, rode with me on the elevator. He had seen me hand Mike something before we split, and he asked me what it was. I told him it was a wooden microphone for Mike to use to rehearse later when alone. Ken was blown away, saying that while most of the other nominees would be celebrating the night before, Mike would be in his suite rehearsing the songs and choreography.

The night of the performance, Mike employed every idea we had played with, pulling each out at exactly the right emotional moment, not as a trick, but as an expression of how he was feeling. As the song built, he went crazy—spinning, jumping like a Maasai warrior, skipping across the stage like he was in a Southern Baptist Church, and dropping to his knees. At one point, he stayed on his knees until a male backup singer came over to assist him to his feet. He ended the song in his Christ-on-the-cross, heart-exposed-to-the-heavens pose.

The Grammy audience of musical luminaries gave Mike a standing ovation. Mike gave them a ten-minute performance that had Little Richard, Stevie Wonder, and Billy Joel yelling their hearts out, and winning the hearts of the nearly thirty-seven million viewers who were watching on TVs around the world.

Mike later told me that, though he was elated with the response toward his performance, he was very sad about not winning the Grammy Award. "Man in the Mirror," his powerhouse tune about introspection and trying to make the world a better place, lost the Grammy to the lighthearted, carefree "Don't Worry, Be Happy." He cried in the car on the way back to his home.

Black or White

IN 1991, I GOT A call from Mike's team asking if I could meet him at Debbie Reynolds Dance Studio again, this time with John Landis, who was directing Mike's new video, "Black or White." Mike had on a red satin mask, a black cape, and a black hat with pieces of his hair hanging on the right side of his face. We spoke about the concept for the short film while we listened to the music. "If you're singing about Black or white, you're celebrating many ethnicities of the world," I suggested, "So, what if you performed different dances with dancers from around the world. We could have African dancers…"

"Oooh," Mike replied quickly, "I like that Indian movement with your head moving on your shoulders. I'm gonna work that step, Vince. And *American* Indian dancing, too. It's almost like that going-to-church step. Maybe I could wear a feathered headdress. That would be…oooooooo…"

So, I cast the video and worked with the various artists to bring authenticity to the movement, taught them to the dancers, and was ready to rehearse with Mike. He got a small dose of believing his own myth on this gig. He kept missing rehearsals with me because he was often playing video games with Macaulay Culkin. When he finally showed up, he realized the choreography was more complicated than he had anticipated, and he couldn't learn it all in a day. It was a lesson in humility. "Am I bad if I don't want to do things some days?" he asked me.

"You're not bad, Mike. But it's not cool for your people to call every two hours and say that you're going to be late. Then you don't show. Just take the day off."

We started working together. We talked on the breaks. "You like working with Madonna?" he asked.

"Yeah. She's a ballbuster, but she works really hard, and she's inspiring."

"I don't trust her. She told me I should do the video 'In The Closet' in drag, and she would play a man."

He also completely pranked me. He said, "I was thinking, since we're doing 'Black or White,' what about a section with Black people in the South picking cotton for a white slave master?"

I gulped, "Well, maybe…" He slapped me on the arm and laughed out loud, telling me that he couldn't believe I thought he was serious.

When I brought the dancers to rehearse with Mike, the room ignited with the mix of world dance styles and Mike's edge. As we ran each section several times, MJ began to put his spin on the global steps. I cherished watching him learn my choreography then make it his own. All went great in rehearsals, so I was taken aback when I stepped into Mike's trailer on the first shoot day and he was really down.

"Vincent. I don't know what to do about this. This is what John wants me to do."

He handed me the storyboards. Part of John's concept was inspired by a collection of stark but elegant photo portraits by the artist Irving Penn. Like Penn's portraits, all of Mike's dancing would be filmed against a solid gray backdrop.

"I can't do this," Mike confided in me. "This is not what my fans expect. I don't know what to tell John. We gotta come up with something because this won't work." Though we loved many of John's ideas—walking through fire, the Statue of Liberty, the kids with Macaulay Culkin, the morphing of faces at the end—Mike was right about the dance scenes.

"Well," I said, "let's go crazy and throw ideas back and forth. Right now. We could have different backgrounds for each dance. Maybe the American Indians' dance can be out in Vasquez Rocks and some can ride by on horseback…" We were feverishly brainstorming. We were inspired to do a riff on John's image of a baby holding a snow globe.

"Mike, what if you're dancing with Russian Cossack dancers and at the end of the dance it starts to snow and you'll lose your balance. Maybe John can have the snow globe being shaken by the baby with you all inside…"

Mike and I were so animated as we envisioned where we'd showcase each group. We spent a couple of hours mapping it out before we invited John into the trailer. To give John due applause, where some directors would feel their vision had been completely undermined, John was ready to change on a dime. He sat through our presentation, listening carefully.

"Okay," John said. "Maybe I was thinking too stylized. I like this. Let's make this happen." It was a beautiful collaboration that took Mike all over the world with dance. When I got home that Friday night, there were two packages at my front door—a video Walkman with four rechargeable batteries and a box of movies. There was also a note:

"Dear Vincent, Thanks for everything, Michael."

John Landis often treated Mike and me like we were kids, though he was always complimentary about the work and, admittedly, we sometimes acted like children. Once Mike called me to come up on the roof of the sound stage with him and Macaulay. He had had someone bring a box of water balloons up to the roof and the three of us threw them, bombarding the unsuspecting people below. And, yes, there was a pie-throwing party with John included!

I remember telling Landis that Mike liked to shoot five or six takes as he was warming up. John said, "That's just wasting film."

"But John," I replied. "He's paying for it, and you never waste film when you're shooting Michael Jackson." John didn't want any monitors to show what was being filmed, but Mike and I always used one to see what the cameraman was shooting. Mike and I found it ironic that John then brought friends, agents, and actors to the set and put them in front of Mike's and my one monitor and talked through the takes while we filmed.

Nancy Reagan visited the set. She said to John, "I think we've met before." John said, "I don't think so." Nancy said, "Yes, I think so." John said, "No, I don't think so." Nancy replied, "It was on the Metro set in 1949. Yes. I remember."

"I was born in 1950."

I don't know if it was John's or Mike's idea to create the coda to the short film.

Earlier Mike and I had a rehearsal at Debbie Reynolds Dance Studio. When I walked into the room, Michael was already there in a lime green shirt and black pants. He told me, "I want to show you something. You might think it's dirty." Moving forward in a wide-legged movement, he made the sign of the cross. Then he unzipped his fly and zipped it back up.

"I call this 'Conversations of Lust,'" he said.

"I love it," I said.

"John will hate it."

"Who cares?" I replied. We laughed like naughty schoolboys!

The entire coda would be a choreographed improvisation. Mike would enter a back alley, dance, and transform into a black panther. We discussed not using music, just sounds. We wanted it to be sensual, yet percussive and strong. Mike was electrified by the rawness and the sounds he could create with his own body and voice and intoxicated with the thought of post-scoring the images to make them even more dramatic.

Mike saw this section as an expression of his inner feelings, reaching deep inside to let his pent-up feelings erupt like a volcano. Honest. Animal-like. This was going to be an acting exercise, and he would let himself be really free, the most honest and vulnerable he had ever been on film.

The result was that the film *was* the most real and raw I had ever seen Mike. He thrust himself into a frenzy, smashing car windows, then jumping onto the car roof as choreographed. The crotch grab pretty much came center stage, with Mike unzipping and zipping his pants. And he kept doing it. He got pagan. He got real. I remember John asking Mike and me between takes of the filming, "Are you sure you want to grab your crotch that much?" Mike and I would just look at each other and nod our heads with a smile. He continued doing it on every take.

In one take, Mike dropped to his knees, lost his balance, and fell forward onto his hands. "Vince, I'm sorry, I won't make that mistake next time."

"No, Mike, do it," I said. "Make something out of it, something primal, feline."

The panther bonus dance at the end of "Black or White" was one of the first times Mike had to deal with serious public backlash. He had suffered backlash from his church, the Jehovah's Witnesses, after creating the supernatural "Thriller" video, but that was relatively inconsequential compared to this. "Black or White" premiered on November 14, 1991, in twenty-seven countries with an estimated audience of 500 million people. Adults and children who were in love with Michael Jackson, seeing him as a Peter Pan figure, were deeply unnerved by the violence, no matter how symbolic. The amount of crotch-grabbing brought even more protests.

Mike was devastated. Everything he did was for his fans. And when they turned ugly, became mean, and rejected his work, he was heartbroken. The media critiqued his aggressive video behavior as inciting violence and encouraging anarchy.

"Vince, this is just crazy. I never threw those trash cans to incite race riots. Or smashed those windows to say it was okay to do that. I wanted to show my anger against racism. Why don't they understand?"

They couldn't accept him as an actor portraying the animal inside the body of a man. He was being the world-class performer he always was and expressing that animal nature through dance, purer than anyone else could. MTV deleted the coda because they were flooded with complaints that it was too controversial.

I watched over the years as people all over the world took a pop star and turned him into a saint. Michael Jackson was, and is, a God to many fans, both young and old. But many of these same fans were responsible for dragging him down from the altar they had erected. The negative response of the press and his fans was a crushing blow.

I often witnessed Mike's pain as we talked about personal things on our rests between takes. I remember walking into his trailer during "Black or White" to find him crying over a newspaper. "What's the matter, Mike?" I asked him.

He pointed to an article in which one of his brothers had been quoted by a journalist as verifying a crazy rumor that was spreading about Mike sleeping in a hyperbaric chamber. The media enjoyed preying on Mike, making him appear eccentric and strange. "How can family do this? I don't understand," he said as his eyes overflowed with tears.

We had a long conversation that day about family, love, and the importance of finding friends outside of family. We specifically talked about how friends help you figure out who you really are. We shared our stories of abuse at the hands of our fathers. He told me, "When I was little, I'd wake up in the night 'cause someone was shaking me. 'Wake up, wake up.' I'd open my eyes. My father would be leaning right close to my face with a horrible, rubber monster mask on. I'd start screaming. Why would somebody do something like that to a little child?"

Once, I was leaving Mike's trailer at the end of a shoot day and he asked me where I was going. "To a party. Wanna come, Mike? It's just some friends. Some you already know from other short films we've all done. Why don't you come?"

"Oh, no, I couldn't go to a party," he said. "I've never been to a party like that. If I went to a party like that I would want to stand behind the curtains and just peek out and watch how people acted with one another. To see what people do at a real party."

He didn't come to the party. His loneliness broke my heart. The way he'd make me feel.

MTV 10th Anniversary Television Special

MTV WAS REACHING ABOUT 200 million homes globally and about to celebrate its tenth anniversary on August 1, 1991. They invited only four musical artists to contribute to the televised event: George Michael, R.E.M., Madonna, and Michael Jackson. Sandy Gallin, Mike's manager, called me upon Mike's request to design, choreograph, and direct his segment.

He and I decided to present two diverse songs back-to-back, "Black or White" and "Will You Be There." We'd design a live performance and shoot it in front of an audience in an airplane hangar at the Santa Monica Municipal Airport.

I held rehearsals for "Will You Be There" at Alley Kat Studio in Hollywood. Like most Hollywood productions, we had about four days in a rehearsal room and one day on the stage before the shoot.

Jeremy Railton had designed a set of various leveled platforms that seemed to reach to the heavens. Each of these platforms held a choir of about fifteen to twenty performers. At the highest level stood the elderly performers representing sages, shamans, or spiritual leaders. The graphics on their costumes were symbols representative of those on the robes of priests. On a second platform, the young, virile men represented strength. They wore exotic headpieces nonspecific to any culture but designed to give a sense of worldliness. On another platform stood the women representing purity of spirit, beauty, grace, and love. Finally, the children who represented hope for the future. The choreography for the choirs' hands and arms was designed to feel sacred and ritualistic.

Six dancers would perform with Mike on the stage floor. MJ rehearsed only with the smaller group of dancers. I would teach him the movement alone and then he'd rehearse with the dancers. At one point, he sang the song a cappella for this small group, and we cried at the beauty of this moment.

Jeremy Railton's set design for "Black or White" was simply a junked-up, graffiti-laden car to wink at the panther dance controversy. For the performance, Mike invited Slash, the lead guitarist from Guns N' Roses, to play guitar. Slash is a born entertainer and the sparks flew between them. I had Mike and Slash performing atop floor grates that shot light and air upward, one of Mike's favorite theatrical devices. We used jet-engine fans to blow Slash's hair across his face while Mike's white shirt blustered like a sail in the wind. I had rigged a trash can for Slash to violently kick off the stage to nod to the ridiculousness of the "Black or White" controversy as well. Mike jumped up on the car and grabbed his crotch a few times. The song finished with Slash heaving his guitar through the car windshield, creating a huge explosion of sparks flying everywhere. Rock 'n' roll.

"Will You Be There" followed. Mike moved from platform to platform, singing among the various choir groups and eventually uniting with the dancers on the floor. Throughout their dancing, they handed Michael a globe of the Earth representing the universality of love and the Book of Knowledge representing truth. As an altar boy in the Catholic Church as a child, I remembered handing the Bible to the priest to bless and read to the congregation. Like Madonna when I created the Blond Ambition Tour, MJ was nervous about being lifted by the dancers, but loved the image of reaching even higher for the answers to the questions in his lyrics, so he went for it and thoroughly loved it.

As Michael spoke his final prayer, a beautiful, young deaf boy stood by Michael's side, silently signing the prayer that Michael was speaking:

> *"... Through my fear and my confessions*
> *In my anguish and my pain*
> *Through my joy and my sorrow*
> *In the promise of another tomorrow*
> *I'll never let you part*
> *For you're always in my heart..."*

The exquisite model Angela Ice, suspended above the stage as a modern angel, descended behind Mike and enfolded him in her wings. A real tear ran down Mike's cheek. Moments like these were magical.

The XXVII Super Bowl

DON MISCHER, THE SUCCESSFUL TV director/producer, asked me to meet with him about working with Mike to create the 1993 XXVII Super Bowl halftime show. Mike was hesitant at first about performing for a sporting event. Honestly, I don't believe Mike was much of a football fan and, prior to 1993, the halftime show featured marching bands on the playing field. Don Mischer informed him that the show would be seen in over 127 countries, countries where Mike would probably never have the chance to share his art. Mike liked the idea of bringing his music to a new audience of fans that might not ever get to see him.

Don, Mike, and I collaborated on the concept for the show. For the first time in the decade I had known Mike, he seemed exhausted. Tired of the pressure of being a star, tired of having so many demands made on him, tired of not having any real freedom. I suggested some new choreography, but he wanted to draw on movement from the *BAD* Tour. Mainly, he wanted to promote two issues dear to his heart, world peace and the care of the children of the world. Like in previous performances, he wanted to start off with a bang and touch the audience's hearts by the close of his performance. He also wanted, once again, the effect of smoke coming through the grates on the stage. "And," he said, "let's find a place for a 'magic moment.' Yeah."

The opening of the performance certainly surprised the spectators. We decided to start with "Jam" and "Billie Jean." High in the corners of the Pasadena Rose Bowl stadium were jumbo video screens. Suddenly one of them came to life as Mike's image appeared on it. He executed a spin, then his image got sucked up through the top of the screen. In a puff of smoke, a live Michael Jackson impersonator appeared on the top of the frame of the colossal screen high above the crowds. Then, on the opposite side of the stadium, Mike appeared on another enormous video screen, executing a series of high-speed movements that ended with the crotch grab. His image got sucked up through the top of the screen and, in a puff of smoke, another live Michael Jackson impersonator appeared on the top of that gigantic video frame.

Then all eyes focused on the stage in the center of the Rose Bowl field. Mike's band and his dancers stood at attention waiting for Mike's appearance. In a blast of smoke and light, Mike catapulted from beneath the stage, straight up into the air, then landed on his feet. We began the show with the "magic moment." Mike stood frozen for over ninety seconds, about a minute more than we had discussed...*ninety* seconds at the *Super Bowl*. "I wanted the fans to feeeel it," he told me later.

And then he took off like a rocket. He burst into "Jam" then "Billie Jean" and, I swear, sparks flew from his hands and feet. He gave no mind to the censors, grabbing his crotch often and just being Michael. "Black or White." Then we changed the pace.

With a baton in his hands, Mike led the Rose Bowl audience in a card-flip that encircled the entire stadium, constructing a temporary mural of one-hundred-foot-high drawings of international children holding hands. Voices singing "We Are The World" underscored this piece of magic. After this, a mass of children joined Mike on the field as a globe of the world inflated. The show closed with the entire Rose Bowl audience joining a sing-along of "Heal the World."

Mike was mesmerizing. Pretty much the same dance steps, same moonwalk, same crotch grab, same "hee hee," same poses, same smoke gag. He had the genius to make it seem like the first time every time, like I remember Shirley MacLaine being able to do over a decade before.

This show made history as the birth of the modern-day Super Bowl spectacle. Mike's performance ranks as the top three in almost every survey of Super Bowl halftime shows. And another record was set: the closing segments of Mike's performance were the most viewed moments in the history of television, with over eighty million viewers.

Blood on the Dance Floor

FAST FORWARD TO 1997. I hadn't worked with Mike since the Super Bowl, so I was happily surprised by a phone call from someone in his camp asking me to conceive, choreograph, and direct the short film for his new single "Blood on the Dance Floor."

Though the Super Bowl halftime show was well received, I knew in my heart that it hadn't been as courageous as it might have been. Mike's performance was impeccable, but the material could have been more stupendous if we had rehearsed more. At almost forty years old, Mike was now at a challenging place in his life and career. He had been performing for thirty-three years, had been harassed by the tabloid press as the oddity "Wacko-Jacko" since he had left The Jackson 5, endured child molestation charges, been married to and divorced from a Presley, and he was still winning Grammys, selling out live tours, and was now remarried and about to be a father.

I had some concerns, and it felt necessary to have a heart-to-heart with him before committing. I called him, and we talked.

"Mike, how are you?"

"Fine, thank you. How are you? I would like you to direct this short film for me."

"Well, Mike, I really want to do it, but, you know me, I have to be honest."

"Why? What's it about? I want you to be honest with me."

"I don't want to rehash something we've already done. I want us to do something different. I want to present you in a fresh way, maybe have you not dance so stylized, maybe do a partner dance. There's a Latin feel to this song that I like a lot."

"That sounds good to me."

"Mike, I know you're busy and everyone's pulling on you all the time, but if I do this short film, will you promise me you'll come to rehearsals?"

"I always come to rehearsals," I could hear the smile in his voice.

"Mike…sometimes you're bad." I had a smile in my voice, too. "But, Mike, I'm serious. Will you promise to show up? I'll bring in dancers you know, and we'll have a good time." Mike promised to attend all of the rehearsals.

The budget was diminutive compared to his former short film budgets. Everything with MJ had been big, bigger, and even bigger. I had to think smaller. "Blood on the Dance Floor" didn't have an intricate storyline, so I was less interested in creating a narrative. I wanted to hold Mike back from dancing throughout some of the piece, like a lithe cheetah chained to his animal print chair. I wanted him to be enticed by the irresistible woman "Suzie" (Sybil Azur) dancing on the table in front of him. I envisioned a moment where Mike would grab

Sybil's legs on the table, an homage to a shot in "Jailhouse Rock" where Elvis is seen through the legs of the showgirl Gloria Pall.

Because the sets would be relatively simple, I needed a brilliant cinematographer who would not only paint beautiful pictures but who would excite Mike. I contacted the charming Conrad Hall, who had won three Oscars and had seven Oscar nominations to his credit. "Sir, I'm directing a music video for Michael Jackson, and we were wondering if you might have any inclination to shoot it?"

"For Michael Jackson? I think he's great. Love to do it. I'm on board."

I wanted to explore partner dancing with Mike in "Blood," a decade before *Dancing with the Stars* would bring partner dancing back into primetime. I wanted to showcase Mike as a strong, dominant, sexy man—a Mike I felt had never been captured on film. I taught everyone a dance called the canyengue that I had learned in Argentina.

"Blood on the Dance Floor" had the most phenomenal cast of dancers in any short musical film since "Thriller" or "Smooth." Many would go on to be part of Hollywood dance history. Sybil Azur, Mike's dance partner, became a climate activist, a politician, and a writer. Robin Antin would create the Pussycat Dolls and Carmit Bachar would become a future Pussycat Doll. Jamie King would become a director for Madonna's world tours. Luca Tommassini and Kevin Stea both became huge TV celebrities in Italy. Luca partnered Madonna in *Evita*. Kevin worked with me on the Blond Ambition Tour and the film *The Birdcage*. For anyone who follows dancers in the commercial dance world, watching Mike's short films is a veritable who's who of dancers.

Alley Kat Studio in Hollywood no longer exists, but it rivaled Debbie Reynolds Dance Studio as *the* place to rehearse. Our first day of rehearsal was astounding with so many phenomenal dancing talents in the room. On the second day, we enthusiastically awaited Mike's arrival. He was supposed to arrive at 11:00 a.m. At 2:00 p.m., I received a phone call telling me Mike would be late.

"Umm. He was supposed to be here at eleven. It's two? How late?" I asked. "Oh, he'll be there within the hour." Two and half hours later I called back the number I was given and asked if Mike was planning on coming. No. He was not coming that day. I dismissed the dancers.

If I were Michael Jackson, relentlessly hounded by the world, with everyone in my life needing and wanting things from me, maybe I, too, might want to just say "no" for one day and not show up. In fact, I might want to do that a lot. In fairness to Mike, he always took care of everyone. Dancers were often taken advantage of financially in music videos as there were no unions that covered dancers in this genre; however, Mike always paid the dancers SAG minimum day wages. That could mean a difference of hundreds, if not thousands of dollars. So people might have been inconvenienced, but everyone always got paid. Another day was added to the production schedule.

This waiting game with Mike happened a few more times. One day Mike would be a few hours late, and I'd be concerned he was never going to show up. Suddenly, Mike would arrive and dance as hard as the rest of us. He was timid and giggly around Sybil at first. But he became such a masculine force when he began to sing and move that it dissolved any nervousness between him and "Suzie." The next day after a terrific rehearsal, everyone was warmed up and ready for Mike's arrival, but I was informed, "Michael won't be there today." He finally came on the very last day of rehearsal, worked his ass off, and wanted us to all stay late to rehearse with him. We did, of course. His enthusiasm was contagious, and we were ready to shoot.

We shot the short film at Raleigh Studios across from Paramount. Connie Hall was patient with Mike's tardiness, as Mike often kept everyone waiting for hours before showing up or spent hours in his trailer before coming onto the set.

"Hi, Mike. Everything okay?" I'd ask, walking into his trailer.

"Oh, yeah. Sorry for being late," he said apologetically then cheered up. "We're gonna kick some butt."

"You better. See you when you're ready. And don't take all day!" I laughed.

He seemed sad or distracted when he was sitting in his trailer. And he was shy and quiet between takes, but when the camera rolled, he was his astonishing electric self. Connie and I worked quickly and were happy with what we were shooting. I asked him if he'd mind if I brought in a friend of mine to shoot some extra footage. My friend Ivan Dudynsky was an ex-dancer, turning his talents to editing and cinematography. He brought his Super-8 camera and shot some staggeringly hot footage, totally different from what Conrad shot.

Our final day of shooting was cut short when I was called into Mike's trailer.

"Vince, I've gotta go. I'm gonna be a father." Mike's first born, Michael Joseph Jackson, a.k.a. Prince, was born early the next morning. Thankfully, we had everything we needed to make the short film.

Sony was only interested in using Connie Hall's footage, and we edited our MTV version from the film he had shot. They had no interest in what Ivan shot, so Ivan and I edited our own version. The result was that two complete videos now exist for "Blood on the Dance Floor." The official video sanctioned by Sony is stunning. Connie made the images on 35mm film look hand-painted at times. The "Blood on the Dance Floor—Alt Version and Remix" that I recorded with Ivan shows Mike in a way he has never been seen. Writer David Noh described the video as "grainy, overexposed, and sexy as shit." You can watch both and see which one you like more. Sony saw the second version of the video but Mike never did. I think he would have said, with his sly smile, "Ooooo. That's nasty!"

The Last Time I Saw Michael Jackson

IT WAS LATE AUTUMN 2001. We hadn't worked together in four years, but he had been (and still was) a significant part of my life.

Michael was not only my conduit to building a career in the crazy entertainment business, but because of Michael I became more than just another struggling artist trying to make his way in Hollywood. We shared a workaholic passion for creating first-class, original work and, as Mike always said, "Something the world has never seen before. We have to do it for the fans." We clicked as a team. We both loved experimentation and were passionate about venturing into new territories. His extraordinary talent nourished my imagination. Our rehearsals together were an evolution in creativity, for both of us. Our last major project together ended up being "Blood on the Dance Floor."

When I got a call to meet him at the Universal Sheraton Hotel about a potential project, I headed over with cheerful anticipation. I gave my name at the front desk and was sent up to Mike's floor. I was walking down the hall when two strapping African American men in dark suits came out of a side door flanking a thin man with disheveled hair and clothes. He was hunched over and shuffling behind the bodyguards about fifteen feet ahead of me when I noticed his shoes. They were soft black loafers with a royal crest, Mike's shoes. I realized it was Mike. I was shocked by his appearance. He had always held himself erect, hair always brushed, clothing always clean. He had always moved with energy, even in his quiet moments.

"Mike?" I said. He turned around a little, covering his face, and said in his soft, high-pitched voice, "Oh, Vince, hi. Come on down. Come on. Just follow us." We continued to his hotel room.

"Um, Vince, uh, can you wait here, and I'll be right back?" he said.

I sat in the spacious living room of his hotel suite that looked out over North Hollywood and the San Fernando Valley.

When he came back, he had brushed his hair and his clothes were less messy, but he now had three Band-Aids across the bridge of his nose. It looked like he didn't have nostrils, and I wondered how he could breathe. He seemed very tired. He didn't look good.

"Are you okay, Mike?" I asked, concerned.

"Oh, yeah, I'm fine. I'm fine," he said, though his voice was quiet and somehow broken. I waited for the vibrancy I had known, but his voice and body language became only slightly more spirited. "I want to do another short film. I want you to direct it, and I want to make it as good as 'Smooth Criminal' because 'Smooth Criminal' was my favorite short film of all."

"Really?" I asked, a smile on my face. "'Smooth Criminal' was your favorite? I always thought it was 'Thriller.'"

"No, no, no," he said. "It was 'Smooth Criminal.'" It excited me to hear him say this. 'Criminal' was the first time Mike gave me the reins and put me in charge. The persona and moves Mike kept coming back to throughout his performances—the use of suits, the armband, the Band-Aids on his fingers—all had hints of 1987's "Smooth Criminal."

In that hotel room, the Mike sitting across from me was so different from the Mike I had known, the genius artist with lightning speed and unstoppable energy. I was accustomed to looking him in the eyes, but this time it was different. He looked forlorn as he held his head down. I was grateful to be with him, but I felt crushingly sad.

Mike lifted his head. And his eyes, accentuated with dark, tattooed eyeliner, had a hint of that scintillating spark again. I focused on his beautiful eyes as he shared his new idea with me.

"I don't know what song is best for this, but I want to do something that's as special as 'Smooth Criminal,'" he said. "I was thinking it would be something that would be in the Wild West, like in a saloon."

I didn't know where Mike was going with "Wild West" but I was getting concerned. A year earlier, in the fall of 2000, Madonna had invented her latest persona—a cowgirl—for her album *MUSIC*. Cowgirl Madonna graced the cover of the album and used a Western theme for her successful music video "Don't Tell Me." Mike continued to describe the plot from start to finish in almost every detail, only set in a saloon instead of a gangster speakeasy, with gunslingers and saloon girls instead of mobsters and molls.

"I'll come in through some swinging doors and all of these bad guys will be sitting at the tables playing cards," he continued. "And there'll be a long bar. And I want Elizabeth [Taylor] to play Miss Kitty from *Gunsmoke*, you know, like a Madame in a saloon. And I want to have a gunfight in the street, maybe with the Rock [Dwayne Johnson], with the wind blowing and the dust moving across my face and some of those tumbleweeds rolling down the street. And I want the camera to be from the point of view of a housefly that buzzes around my head."

I had never seen Mike like this, slightly nervous and working hard to convince me this idea was great. I couldn't help but wonder what had happened to him since we'd worked on "Blood on the Dance Floor." He must have felt constantly beaten up by the multitude of tabloid gossip that always surrounded him like a horde of mosquitoes. But it wasn't until that moment that I deeply felt the heaviness of his life. He seemed to have turned a corner into a darker world.

I'm sure he believed that this new project would put him back on top where he was used to living, not pulled down by child-molestation scandals and lurid stories about his addiction to painkillers. The general public and the fans don't always understand that celebrities' lives are never truly their own. It's hard to fully comprehend if you haven't seen it in action, and by now I'd seen it from many perspectives. Celebrity means living in a bizarre alternate universe, a world without privacy, often without trusted friends, and with as many people trying to drag you down as elevate you.

That night, the Mike I loved, the artistically powerful man, seemed shrunken down to a sweet-but-lost, defeated soul. I wanted him to rise above it all. Like so many people, I, too, wanted Michael Jackson to have another fantastic hit because I knew how good it would be and how happy it would make him.

Throughout our years together, I had seen his vulnerability up close. He now looked pale and thin, as if an unkind word might crush him. I couldn't tell him that, other than the camera angle from the housefly's point of view, his other ideas for this new project weren't original. For the first time, I didn't know if I'd even be interested in getting involved. But I loved Mike and I owed him a great deal for the opportunities he had given me.

"Mike, let's both think about this. I'm sure we can create something very special together, and you know we always have fun when we do. Thanks for thinking of me. It means a lot."

He said he had to get the money together, and he'd call me when he did. My heart was pounding when I left the hotel. As a choreographer and a director, one of my primary jobs is to solve problems. My professional work with Mike had crossed over into friendship long ago, and I desperately wanted to fix this. Fix him. Fix the world around him. There's a reason so many people were protective of Mike once they got to know him as closely as I did. He was someone who blessed the world with his kindness and held us all in awe of his talent.

He never called. I'm not sure if the money was ever secured. But we never embarked on another collaboration. And the next thing I knew, he was gone forever. I joined the millions of fans who mourned the death of Michael Jackson.

14.

Gurus and Guiding Lights

I ALWAYS HAVE BEEN and always will be a student. Besides wanting to constantly improve my craft, it takes time to understand the intricacies of the entertainment business—how to identify which opportunities will afford growth, how to ascertain when to say "no" when others and your finances tell you to say "yes." When a choice doesn't have the desired result, you must do some soul-searching to discover its lessons. I work to recognize these things to fulfill my potential as an artist. Just as important is recognizing when gurus enter your life.

Michael Peters

MY KNOWLEDGE IS BROADER, my creativity more accomplished, and my life richer because of my time with Michael Peters. Throughout our creative adventures, we were best friends. He taught me much as we laughed, cried, created, and grew together. Working with Peters made me a strong dancer because working with him you had to be. He drew out your potential; he enticed your body to move with intricate rhythms and unbridled joy.

I became his assistant choreographer. He could spit out choreography at the speed of thought. He moved quickly and had no patience for those who didn't keep up. I always kept up. He emphasized the potent benefit of doing your homework. Peters was always prepared. We worked out every detail before teaching it to the dancers, allowing us to squeeze every drop of precious time out of rehearsals. With many choreographers, dancers sit in rehearsal rooms for hours, watching and waiting, while the choreographer contemplates four bars of music with consternation and lack of inspiration. Not Michael Peters. He never wasted the dancers' time. I took this lesson to heart, and it has been a mainstay of my work process.

Undoubtedly, the most important thing I learned from him was to trust my instincts. Michael never wanted for a movement idea. He taught me that if I executed my instincts with conviction, out of a billion choreographic choices, I would always make the right one. "You just have to pick one, Miss Thing. Tsk, tsk," he'd say as he sucked his teeth. Peters never doubted his work and, if he was ever insecure, it never showed.

His triumphs often fanned the flames of his ego, though, and I learned a bit of what I didn't want to project as a successful artist. Riding the celebrity of choreographing many music videos, he became louder, sometimes even rude, though he also brought a tremendous amount of positive energy and inspiration into the rehearsal room. He sometimes made Michael Jackson uncomfortable with his desire to grab the spotlight and be the center of attention. I learned quickly that there can be only one star in the room.

We never discussed any of my work with Michael Jackson, but we did work together again. We had a ball when he played a wacky scientist in a video I choreographed and codirected with Julie Brown, "Trapped in the Body of a White Girl." Like old times.

Throughout the eighties and nineties, AIDS ran rampant throughout the dance community like the plague. Hearing the daily news of the death toll felt like reports from a war zone. I knew close to one hundred dancers, artists, and friends who died from the unforgiving disease. In 1994, AIDS also cut short Michael's life. During his illness, I was one of many who drove him to his visits to the doctors, helped get prescriptions filled, and took him to the movies on occasion.

On his deathbed in his Hollywood Hills home, Michael passionately told me that he had spoken to Michael Jackson earlier that day, the first time since the infamous Pepsi commercial. He shared that Michael Jackson had been kind and full of love. We both cried happily that it had come full circle for him.

Marine Jahan

MARINE JAHAN WAS THE beauty with the mind-boggling body who was the dance-double for Jennifer Beals in *Flashdance*. Marine almost drowned in the famous silhouette/chair scene because no one had the foresight to think about all of that water falling on her while her head was tilted back. It all went up her nose. But she kept on dancing. Marine moved from the French countryside to Los Angeles to study dance. Marine was one of my five selects of the original ten dancers with whom Michael Peters and I chose to work at Roland Dupree Dance Studio when he was discovering his choreographic voice. It was auspicious that she would be crucial in me discovering mine.

Marine had joined me in a dance studio a few times in LA when I wanted to experiment with choreography. In 1983, when the secrecy of Marine having been Jennifer Beals's dance-double backfired, Marine received well-merited publicity for her electrifying work. Italy's RAI-TV offered Marine a featured guest spot on a popular Variety TV series. They invited her to Milan accompanied by a dance partner and a choreographer of her choosing. She asked if they could be the same person and, upon their consent, asked me. She had no doubts about me, and I jumped in with the taste of adventure on my lips.

Before we left LA, I created seven pieces featuring Marine, including a version of her performance from *Flashdance*—originally choreographed by Jeffrey Hornaday. Once we got to Milan, we added a bevy of beautiful Italian dancers to the mix. Working with an extremely tight schedule, all eight dances were rehearsed and filmed in three weeks.

I've learned over time that there are three dominant elements in my artistic process: following my instincts, doing my homework, and focusing while working at lightning speed. This gig with Marine began to reinforce what I had been learning from Michael Peters. It afforded me the chance to integrate these elements into my process, constantly developing and paying off in spades throughout my career. The time in Milan also gave me my first taste of working in Europe, a predilection that has stayed with me and given me cause to say "yes" to some very right choices.

Roy London

AFTER MOVING TO LOS Angeles from Tucson, I searched for an acting teacher. I was going on a few acting casting calls and I wanted to continue this craft. I had an instinct that I might want to direct again and acting class would brush me up on the language of communicating with actors. I was one of a small group that encouraged a friend, Roy London, to teach a scene-study class. Like a band of "gypsies," we moved weekly from apartment to apartment. What began as a small class developed into an acting industry for Roy. He was publicly thanked by Geena Davis when she accepted her Oscar for best supporting actress for *The Accidental Tourist.*

From Roy I learned, as an actor and even more as a direction *to* an actor, the concept of "getting what you want." Roy encouraged me to observe how we use a myriad of methods to get what we want every time we make any action or utter a single word. He opened my eyes to making the most appropriate choices to "win," whether in matters of love, business, or simply getting what you want from the person at the gas company on the other end of the phone. He brilliantly emphasized that all struggles in life are about only two things: Money, power…or both. His illuminating information has infiltrated my personal and professional lives. Roy London was another irreplaceable artist lost to the tragedy of AIDS.

Glenn Close

ONE DAY I WAS SITTING at my desk in the Hollywood Hills and the phone rang. "Hi, is Vincent there?"

"This is Vincent."

"Vincent, this is Glenn Close."

I about died. Glenn was my acting hero, the consummate actor. The movie camera could frame a close-up of her silent face and I could hear her brain buzzing with ideas. Her photo was on my refrigerator as someone I'd hoped to work with one day.

"I've decided to play the part of Ensign Nellie Forbush in a television version of the musical *South Pacific*. I'm not sure why, because, I have to be honest with you, I can't dance. I've got two left feet. But I feel with you as my guide, I can look like a million bucks. Would you be interested in coming on board as the choreographer? We'll rehearse in New York and shoot in Australia. I think we'll have a good time." And then she laughed.

My heart melted. "Yes!"

The rehearsals were sublime. Glenn was an inspiring collaborator. We worked and goofed around during the creation of the dances. She had nothing to worry about because she picked up all the movement quickly and precisely. There was always happiness in the room. During rehearsals we discussed the subtext behind the choreography, and she asked me if I would spend some time with her going over her script. I pulled from the knowledge I had learned from Mr. B and Roy London and felt confident and honored working through Glenn's scenes with her. I remember she couldn't identify with Nellie about a particular thought process. "She's so unlike me," Glenn said. Roy's words came back, "We are everyone. Everyone is in each of us. Perhaps in only a small aspect, but it is there. Find it." I shared this, we discussed and laughed about it then revisited the scene with new eyes.

While filming in the Australian Daintree Rainforest, we fought venomous snakes hidden in the tall grasses, mosquitos the size of small birds, and crocs on the beaches. It was a unique experience in many ways. When we had the premiere showing of our *South Pacific* in NYC, Glenn invited me to stay at her apartment in Manhattan. She insisted on my taking her bedroom while she took the guest room.

Glenn was a lesson in humility. Having a career history behind her, she approached her work with intelligence, focus, curiosity, and graciousness. Her presence was grounding, her thoughts were wise. She radiated kindness and humanity while working diligently and knowing how to have fun. Glenn's photo is still on my refrigerator in the hopes that I will get to direct her in something one wonderful day.

Jacqui Landrum

THE PERSON WHO MOST instilled my deep passion for dance is Jacqui Landrum. From the moment I took her first class, I knew I was in artistic love. I moved to Hollywood knowing that if I studied with her, I'd fulfill my potential as a dancer. A former Beverly Hills spoiled brat who hung out with Hendricks, the Beatles, and had an affair with David Crosby, Jacqui wore a seductive cloak of arrogance that made everyone desirous of being her friend.

In her earlier years, she danced on TV and in Vegas, but her devotion to dance was profound. Dance motivated practically every aspect of her life. I took class from her and her husband Bill almost every day for years. She introduced me to Martha Graham's technique and her classes were a fascinating mélange of styles: modern, jazz, Vegas, even a bit of Broadway. She was ravenous— learning everything about dance techniques and fervidly sharing every bit of new information with her students. She was also one of the pioneers who introduced Pilates and Gyrotonics to Los Angeles.

Three hip replacements—one was a redo after about seven years—never stopped her. She danced unabashedly and with total abandon until cancer arrested her body and took her life in 2008. Her optimistic and ever-positive outlook constantly inspired me. We shared hilarious highs and years filled with love. She lives on in every dance step I take and make.

Joe Pytka

PYTKA. MORE PEOPLE KNOW Joe Pytka by Pytka than Joe. Pytka's star shines in the world of directing commercials. He is an exclusive member of the "One Club Creative Hall of Fame" that honors incredible innovators who've made remarkable contributions to the fields each was instrumental in molding. It's like the Round Table for the most creative knights of our time.

Joe began as a documentarian and brought his shooting style into commercials. Creating with Joe is always working at the tip-top of the ladder, as he is a visionary with power, knowledge, and blue-chip talent at his disposal.

He'll stop at any moment of the workday to toss a basketball, his method of letting off steam and allowing the muses to flow. When I tell anyone in the business I've often worked with Pytka, I acquire a different level of respect.

I believe our relationship grew because we have more than a few things in common. Like Joe, I consider myself a fortunate Polack from Pennsylvania. He's from Pittsburg; I'm from Philly. Polish males wear their hearts on their sleeves. We prefer presenting art that exposes honesty in a character. With all of the accolades he has garnered, Joe considers his daughters his greatest accomplishment. I consider mine allowing myself to deserve to be loved by my husband, Rene. Joe, in an interview, stated that he had no regrets.

When it was suggested I write a chapter in this book on "my regrets," I realized that I had no regrets. If everything that happened to me hadn't happened, I wouldn't be who I am. I like who I am. I like my life. I believe Joe feels the same.

The thread that cemented our working friendship was dance. Joe loves dance and dancers. He is an athlete, a basketball player, and a skier, so he appreciates the focus of a dancer. His love of music combined with his fondness for dance brings so much affection to all of his dance-infused creations. Pytka can be a lion, a bad boy. Like Madonna, he challenges. If you come back as an equal, he respects you immediately. If not, you may be eaten along with some fava beans and a good Chianti. I make it a point to tell every dancer at the first rehearsal,

"If you let him get you, he will. Be clever. Come back with a response."

It worked superbly well for one chorus dancer in one of our Ray Charles Pepsi "Uh-Huh!" commercials. She passed Joe on her way out of the makeup room. Joe, teasingly, remarked, "When are you going to makeup? You look like a dog." The dancer fell to the floor on all fours and began nipping at Joe's ankles. Joe laughed hard. When we filmed the commercial, Joe filmed several close-up shots of her that wound up in the final edit. It bumped the dancer's salary from a "group of twenty" to a "principal," earning her thousands of dollars more.

Oh, I've seen the angry ogre, the one who demanded that one of the Pepsi clients put his nose against the soundstage wall and stand there for fifteen minutes. The man did it. No joke. I've seen Joe decimate members of his crew. He almost tried it with me once. We had completed what felt to be our one-hundredth *Uh-Huh! Diet Pepsi* Commercial. Joe was exhausted and the crew looked more exhausted than Joe. Usually, the crew was brightly enthusiastic when I came onto the set, "Oh, man, Vince, we're so glad you're here. Music and dancing. Joe will be in a great mood." Some lights were being set, and I walked across the soundstage. Joe was sitting behind the camera and yelled, "What the fuck are those things you have on your feet?"

Well, they happened to be very interesting shoes I had just purchased on my trip to Japan. I looked at Joe, smiled, and very slowly waved my index finger back and forth in an "Uh-Uh!" fashion. Joe smiled. It never happened again.

I've also witnessed Joe's vast generosity. After a Pepsi commercial with Shakira, in which the heartbroken tango dancers were nixed just before filming, Joe held a tango milonga for the dancers and their friends at his home in the Hollywood Hills that had been owned by Madonna and originally by Bugsy Siegel. At his Santa Fe estate, he allows a different artist to live in a home on his property, rent free, for a year, to be able to concentrate on their work.

He did one thing for me that was more generous than anything else anyone had ever done. It was not long after 9/11 that I choreographed a piece for the American Choreography Awards in Los Angeles. I was feeling lost as an American, even as a citizen of the world, after that tragic event. On 9/11, the entire world changed. The amount of grief and pain we all felt was enormous, no matter where we lived.

I was driven by the need to express my grief through my artistic voice. My dear friend Suzi Lonergan convinced me to contact some dancers, go into a studio, and manifest my emotions through movement. Because of 9/11, many pop tours were canceled or put on hold. Some of the prime dancers in LA were available, so Suzi and I put the word out that I needed to create, "If anyone's interested, please show up at Alley Kat Studio."

I had the crème de la crème of LA dancers arrive at rehearsal. I was humbled and thanked them for coming. "As an artist, I need to say something about 9/11," I said. "I thought we could play today and at the end of the day, if we feel we want to come back tomorrow, we can, and if nothing happens today, well, we'll have spent a nice afternoon together."

The day before I had gone into the studio to explore movement using a song called "On Earth as it is in Heaven" by Ennio Morricone from the film *The Mission*. The following day the dancers arrived, and we began to dance. I explored physical answers to questions I had been asking myself since 9/11: What happens immediately after we die? What happens if, as innocents, we die a violent death? What happens to souls in a group-death situation?

When the day concluded, we all felt we wanted to return. That night, I printed the names of those who had died in the tragedy and the next morning, alone in the studio, I hung them on the rehearsal room walls. When the dancers arrived, I asked them to walk around the room until each found a name with whom they somehow connected. I asked them to dedicate their dancing to that person.

"Threnody," which means "a lament," was performed live at the American Choreographer's Awards. At the intermission, Joe Pytka came to my agent, Tony, "Who the fuck did that last piece? Look at my face! I got fucking tears running down my face. Who the fuck did that?"

"Vince did it, Joe."

"Fuck, man, look at me. I can't stop crying."

What I always saw in Joe's commercials was hope. He constantly found innovative ways to express humanity's positive spirit. Maybe that's what he recognized in "Threnody" that night. He turned to me.

"What are you going to do with this? Are you performing it again? Are you putting it on film?"

"Honestly, I hadn't planned on doing anything more with it than tonight."

"Well, we're fucking shooting this. This needs to be on film. You're directing it and I'm shooting it. I'll get a sound stage. This has to be on film."

And we did. Pytka actually was the director of photography on a shoot I directed. I don't think he has ever done that for anyone before or since. He paid for everything as well, from the Universal Studios sound stage to the full crew to catering. How do you say "thank you" for that? The short film won the Golden Jury Award at the Houston Worldfest Film Festival.

Joe, like Mike Nichols, always gave me freedom to express myself as an artist. Oftentimes, Joe would phone and say, "I need you to find fourteen dancers and get them down to the set in two hours." And I would. He'd have a space ready for me to rehearse, let me create, and then usually show it to the clients, seeing it for the first time as well. Total trust and respect.

Commercials are challenging. Joe taught me that there can be no wasted moments in a commercial. Every second of the choreography has to be specific and memorable. Having the opportunity to choreograph so many superior quality commercials for Joe gave me the chance to hone my craft.

Over the years, Joe taught me how to see dance through the camera's eye. He taught me the power and difference between the sizes of shots, something that especially paid off for me during the filming of the dance sequences in *Dancer in the Dark*. Joe taught me to have the courage to artistically go for what I believe to be right. Be flexible but be firm. Challenge yourself to be better than you thought you could be. Learn to create the exact right image for the exact right moment. Trust your instincts, know you have a voice, and use it!

And when you've done all of that, go shoot some hoops.

15.
Entrances and Exits

I'VE NEVER WON A major award for my choreography or direction. I received a minor choreography award for an obscure European commercial. Could this be the reason that even now, after accomplishing so much, I stand on a fulcrum balancing my artistic confidence on one side and my insecurities on the other? For many years, I imagined that sometime during the work process, someone was going to tap me on the shoulder and say, "I'm so sorry. You're going to have to leave. We got the wrong Vince Paterson."

Writing this autobiography has been emotional and revelatory. Having never been psychoanalyzed, I felt like I did just that with every chapter. It's brought rumination about my life and career choices. But reflection can be a path to enlightenment. A new awareness now accompanies me into the future.

In the last several years, my directing career has taken precedence over choreography. As my body ages, it becomes less obedient to what I want it to do. My knees aren't in the best shape; I can't execute floor work, leaps, or turns like I had in the past. I've always created every step I've choreographed, feeling it in my own body as I danced in front of a mirror. The only time I couldn't do this was with acrobats in a Cirque du Soleil show I directed. There are choreographers who hire assistants to create the steps. I could never do that.

While recently directing and choreographing *Evita* at the Ronacher Theater in Vienna, I accepted that my body could execute a modified version of what I wanted. I asked my associate choreographer, Barbara Tartaglia, to dance what my body couldn't. I breathed a sigh of relief that I could allow myself to work this way. It was a huge revelation. Even directing full time, I want dance to be part of my life.

I always hope to create honest work that touches, inspires, even educates, that *something* in the performance will generate a positive ripple in the world. It surprises me that moments in my career and what made me an artist brush up against controversy… from the nuns at school to Tipper Gore to the Pope. Moments of sexual innuendo in my work are always accompanied with a wink of the eye. And while I never go out of my way to offend people, I've learned the moment you worry too much about it…the work suffers. I follow my instincts. Always. Then I listen to anyone who cares to share an opinion.

It's clear to me my preferred artistic expression is about revealing truth. I believe that's a very positive ripple. But there's something about truth that people have always had trouble digesting. The search for truth will never change for me. What will also never change is my process. Being thorough in my preparations, I enter every rehearsal with a wealth of research, a calm focus, and an open heart. And a little fear.

As a director, I use every opportunity to rectify inequities that haunted me throughout my career. Not being recognized for one's creativity is a profound injustice. For example, I informed the heads of the Ronacher Theater that I asked about twenty of those who worked behind the scenes with me to create *Evita* to join me onstage for the opening night curtain call. Theater management objected, declaring it would be uncomfortable for those I asked and the audience wouldn't know who these artists were. I replied, "With all due respect, this is my opening night, I am going to thank whomever I want." And I did. Those artists took several bows to thunderous applause.

When I consider my entire career, undoubtedly, the thread is Michael Jackson. Michael Jackson brought so much goodness my way. My collaborations with him, as well as Madonna and others, bring respect and appreciation for my work, giving me the opportunity to inspire other young artists. With an international presence, doors open, and friendships are made.

There is one final story I want to share...

Mike learned the basics of the moonwalk from some talented Los Angeles street dancers. He took that move, originally called the backslide, honed it, and made it his own in months of rehearsals and gave the world what would become the most famous dance step of all time. I had nothing to do with the moonwalk; however, part of my legacy is—dare I admit it—the crotch grab!

It was during rehearsals for the short film "The Way You Make Me Feel" that the crotch grab was *formally* born. Of course, Mike touched himself lightly at the end of the Victory Tour and in the "BAD" video he touched his crotch three times, though seemingly without recognizing it. But there was a distinct moment when the crotch grab became part of Mike's intentional dance vocabulary, and I was there.

Mike and I were in Debbie Reynolds Dance Studio rehearsing one day in 1987. During one section of the music, I slid my hand down my stomach and grabbed my crotch before moving into a Flamenco stance. Mike jumped all over it.

"OOOooo," he said. "What was that?"

"What?"

"You just grabbed yourself. Ooooo. That was nasty. Show me what you did."

"Well, you sort of did it in the 'BAD' video," I said.

"I did? Well, sometimes I touch myself *near there* when I sing... when I feeeeel it. It comes from deep. But I never grabbed myself. Let's put that in."

"Well, if you want to do it, let's do it," I said. "Why not, man!"

As time went on, the move became a more and more emphatic "Michael-ism" because of his repetition of it. It seemed whenever he did a series of lightning-fast movements followed by a falsetto, "Hee Hee," the crotch grab became the period at the end of the movement sentence.

On July 7, 2009, Michael Jackson's funeral service, Michael's Farewell Tribute, was held at the Staples Center in Los Angeles. I didn't attend. I couldn't. It hurt too much. I felt that if I ignored the truth of Mike's death maybe it wouldn't exist. Maybe he'd come back.

Alone in my living room, at the time Mike died, 2:26 p.m., I grabbed my crotch, pointed my finger to the sky, and gave my best "Hee-hee!" as tears streamed down my face.

I believe Mike saw me.

I believe he smiled.

Timeline

1962	Eurotour with Bobby
1963	Sacred Heart Boy
1968–72	Dickinson College
1972	Society Hill Playhouse (*The Screens*)
1975	Tucson Dance Gallery—"Francesco and Paolo"
1977	*CBS Galaxy*
1978	Olivia Newton-John, "Totally Hot"
1979	Shirley Maclaine tour
1979	*John Denver and the Muppets: A Christmas Together*
1980–81	*Barbara Mandrell and the Mandrell Sisters*
1983	Michael Jackson, "Beat It"
1983	Michael Jackson, "Thriller"
1983	Mel Brooks, "To Be Or Not To Be"
1984	Weird Al Yankovic, "Eat It"
1984	Van Halen, "Hot for Teacher"
1985	David Lee Roth, "California Girls"
1985	Lionel Richie, Pepsi commercial
1986	Paul McCartney, "Stranglehold"
1987	Michael Jackson, "The Way You Make Me Feel"
1987	*Mannequin* (Film)
1987	George Harrison, "Got My Mind Set On You"
1987–89	The *BAD* Tour
1988	Michael Jackson, "Smooth Criminal"
1988	Michael Jackson, Grammys

1989	Madonna, Pepsi commercial
1989	Madonna, "Express Yourself"
1990	*Havana* (Film)
1990	Blond Ambition World Tour
1990	Madonna, MTV Awards
1991	Michael Jackson, "Black or White"
1991	*Hook* (Film)
1991	Madonna, Academy Awards
1991–93	Uh-Huh commercials
1992	*Kiss of the Spiderwoman* (Broadway)
1993	Michael Jackson, Super Bowl XXVII
1993	Michael Jackson, MTV's Tenth Anniversary
1993	Diana Ross, Non-Existent Tour
1996	*The Birdcage* (Film)
1996	*Evita* (Film)
1997	Michael Jackson, "Blood on The Dance Floor"
2000	*Dancer in the Dark* (Film)
2001	*South Pacific* (Film)
2003	*Anna Netrebko: The Woman the Voice* (Film)
2004	*Cabaret* (Theater)
2004	*Closer* (Film)
2006	*Manon* (Opera, LA)
2007	*Manon* (Opera, Berlin)
2010	*Cirque Du Soliel* (Theater)
2016	*Evita* (Ronacher Theater, Vienna)

Acknowledgments

MY FRIENDS, FAMILY, AND collaborators have shown me how to be a better man, friend, husband, and artist by being mirrors reflecting who I am and who I continually strive to be. I know that what I give is what I get. And I know that love is always the answer. Yes, love, and a comfy pair of shoes, an occasional joint or glass of red wine, some music, and lots of laughter.

—Vincent

I WANT TO THANK Vincent for the hard work and bravery it takes to look back on one's life and write about it. It's a gift to artists and those who seek to understand artists. Bringing this story to the page has been a wild ride, but worth every difficulty and every moment I almost peed my pants laughing.

—Amy

THIS BOOK COULD NOT have been completed without the wisdom and insight of so many. We'd like to offer our sincere thanks to all involved here.

Publishing Team and Editors: Tyson Cornell, Hailie Johnson, Alexandra Watts, Guy Intoci, Jennifer Psujek

Other Champions: Rene Lamontagne, Tudor Munteanu, Suzi Lonergan, Maxine Taupin, BJ & Turko Semmes, Richard Lecoq, Ro Lohin, Carl Dias, Kim O'Kelley Leigh, Diane Wolf, Che'Rae Adams, Paula Holt, Willem Metz, Martin and Mary Samuel, Crystal Flores, Kersti Grunditz, Danny Kallis, Julie McDonald, Tony Selznick, Scotty Mullen, Luis Reyes, Elise Capron, Brice Najar, Talitha Linehan, Sandy Reiman, Lucette and Nelson Lamontagne